Educational Leadership:
Culture and Diversity

Clive Dimmock is Professor of Educational Leadership and Director of the Centre for Educational Leadership and Management (CELM) at the University of Leicester, UK. He has previously lectured at Cardiff University, and held professorial positions at The University of Western Australia and The Chinese University of Hong Kong.

Allan Walker is Professor and Chair of the Department of Educational Administration and Policy at the Chinese University of Hong Kong. He has previously worked as a principal and lectured in Australia and at the National Institute of Education, Nanyang Technological University, in Singapore.

Educational Leadership:
Culture and Diversity

Clive Dimmock and Allan Walker

⊗SAGE Publications

London ● Thousand Oaks ● New Delhi

SAGE Publications Ltd
1 Oliver's Yard
55 City Road
London EC1Y 1SP

SAGE Publications Inc.
2455 Teller Road
Thousand Oaks, California 91320

SAGE Publications India Pvt Ltd
B-42, Panchsheel Enclave
Post Box 4109
New Delhi 110 017

British Library Cataloguing in Publication data

A catalogue record for this book is available
from the British Library

ISBN 978-0-7619-7170-2
ISBN 0 7619 7170 X (pbk)

Library of Congress Control Number: 2004116089

Contents

Contents

Foreword

Just a decade ago a book that focused on culture and educational management would have belonged in the domain of social-anthropologists. Cross-cultural analysis was simply outside the field of vision of scholars in educational leadership and management. As Dimmock and Walker explain in this volume, the emergence of culture as a conceptual framework for theory building and the analysis of practice in educational leadership and management is a recent phenomenon.

Paradoxically, its emergence has been fostered largely by the same forces of globalization that some observers view as the 'enemy' of culture. Starting in the early 1990s, globalization began to alter the social, political, economic, and cultural fabric of societies throughout the world. Changes in economic structures, political systems and social lifestyles during the past decade have been far-reaching (Drucker, 1995). Yet, as Ohmae has observed: 'The contents of kitchens and closets may change, but the core mechanisms by which cultures maintain their identity and socialize their young remain largely untouched' (1995, p. 30).

Ohmae's assertion highlights the role that education has always played as a process of *cultural transmission*. Culture resides in the background and represents the assumptions, values and norms that underlie our daily activities. Educational institutions are responsible for passing the values, norms and traditions of the particular society on to future generations. The process of changing a society's values and traditions is, however, slower and more difficult than changing social fashions or economic treaties. Educational change always has and always will lag behind the pace of change in the world outside of schools (Tyack and Hansot, 1982).

In prior eras, the practices of cultural transmission that comprised what we termed 'education' were viewed almost entirely within the frame of our own particular society. Education was a *national* industry. Nations often prided themselves on the uniqueness of their education systems. National education policy-makers saw little need to be informed about never mind emulate the educational policies and practices of other nations.

Today, however, the same change forces that drive globalization – communication, economic scarcity and competition, technology, transportation – are also spurring on the study and practice of education as a social-cultural process. Global competition has raised the importance of education in the eyes of government policy-makers. Education is increasingly viewed as a key lever for national economic competitiveness and development. For example, the Asian economic crisis of 1997 has been cited as a salient example of what happens when social systems fail to adapt to changes in a globally interdependent economy. This was noted at a seminar on social and educational reform in Thailand:

> Mr. Amaret Sila-on and NEC [National Education Commission] secretary-general Rung Kaewdaeng were in complete agreement that Thailand's decline in global competitiveness was mainly due to poor quality of education and graft. The IMD's (International Institute for Management Development) study said Thailand's education system did not live up to global economic challenges ... (*Bangkok Post*, 1998a, p. 3)

Similarly, Professor Kriengsak Charoenwongsak of Thailand's Institute of Future Studies for Development noted: 'increasing the quality of Thai products also involves improving the quality of education. The current emphasis on rote learning does not help students assume positions in the workplace which stress problem-solving and other analytical skills' (*Bangkok Post*, 1998b, p. 2).

Education policy-makers are actively seeking out the optimal mix of policies that will foster the achievement of national goals. Less than a generation ago it would have been rare to see education policy-makers attending and speaking at policy forums and research meetings across the globe. Today it is commonplace.

Moreover, in the age of the Internet, policy-makers find it much easier to find out about the education policies and practices of other nations. Consequently, we find that the *policy du jour* adopted in London or Sydney is quickly taken up in Malaysia, Hong Kong and South Africa. As a case in point, take the development of the National College for School Leadership (NCSL) in the UK during the late 1990s. Before the NCSL had actually delivered its first training programmes, policy-makers in Malaysia were already making arrangements to import and deliver its programmes.

Other policy reforms spawned in the USA, Canada, Australia, New Zealand and elsewhere have sped across the globe in a similar fashion. In under a decade, student-centred learning, school-based management, parental involvement and standards-based education have become the lingua franca of education almost regardless of the national context. The globalization of educational policies and practices, well described in this volume, is a 'done deal'. Education is today a global enterprise.

Yet as my former colleague, Terry Deal, used to observe, cultures function much like 'living organisms'. As such they do not respond well to the introduction of 'foreign bodies'. Whether the intruding element is a virus or an education policy of foreign origin, the instinctive reaction of the organism is first to resist its entry and then attack and kill if it makes it past the initial defences. In the human body the white blood cells are the relevant agents of resistance; in the culture of societies and schools the agents of resistance are people.

Dimmock and Walker highlight the fact that globalization has fostered a 'cultural convergence' of values and norms across societies. In education, we see for example that the introduction of student-centred learning in Asia initially generated a strong negative reaction from teachers, students and parents. This approach to learning conflicted with strongly grounded local norms of what it meant to be a teacher or a learner. The widespread resistance that resulted from this policy change actually sensitized the local Asian societies to their own unique cultural values and norms (Hallinger, 2004).

For the first time in the short history of our field, scholars have become interested in how the practice of leadership and management in schools is influenced by culture. Since 1990, Dimmock and Walker have been among the most active international scholars in educational leadership and management investigating the application of cultural frameworks to our field (see also Bajunid, 1995; 1996; Cheng, 1995; Dimmock and Walker, 1998a; 1998b; Hallinger, 1995; Hallinger and Kantamara, 2000; Hallinger and Leithwood, 1996; Heck, 1996; Walker and Dimmock, 1999). This volume draws together much of their work and focuses it more specifically on the tensions inherent between globalization, cultural identity and the management of educational systems.

The question whether the social processes involved in educational leadership and management are 'culturally constructed' seems to have been answered in the affirmative during the past decade. The manner in which schools are organized and managed is fundamentally related to the cultural values of a society. The terminal values of a nation that guide its educators to focus on holistic development of the child, student achievement on tests, reproduction of knowledge, ability to solve problems or social integration of ethnic groups vary demonstrably across societies. The instrumental values that describe the acceptable and unacceptable means by which people work together to achieve those ends are no less culturally determined.

Initially, interest in cultural processes in educational leadership and management was stimulated by the apparent differences that exist between education in Asia and the West. Debates about 'Asian values' centred on their role in stimulating the economic and social transformation of Asia's dragons and tiger nations. Obvious differences in the practices of education and educational management in these nations were linked back to their cultural values and norms.

Singapore, for example, stood out as a nation that had succeeded on Western terms in the construction of a modern educational system. Yet for many years Singaporean education resisted the value-driven policy associated with heterogeneous grouping of students. Singaporean policy-makers grounded their argument for ability grouping explicitly on a unique combination of Confucian values and meritocratic principles.

Pressures for global convergence have more recently raised interest in cultural differences among nations that are at first glance much more similar than comparisons of the East and West. The integration of Europe has caused Europeans from many nations to reflect more closely on the cultural values and normative practices of their own societies. These differences extend to management and labour practices in the societies.

For example, the inclination for workers to go on strike is clearly related to the national culture of European nations. France, Italy, Germany and the Netherlands – all members of the European Union – have very different traditions with respect to the meaning and use of striking as a form of labour protest.

> A country like France treats a strike as a form of expression, whereas in the Netherlands, it is a last resort ... In Germany, the most effective strike is the one that never gets called ... it's the threat of the strike that produces the result ... [In the Netherlands], we are more interested in ending the discussions in peace ... We hardly strike and we are rather proud of it. (Fuller, 2004, p. C-1)

Explanations for why the Dutch approach strikes in this manner are explicitly framed in the light of the labour union's Protestant roots. Indeed, union leaders even cite a biblical passage from Romans 13 that reads: 'Everyone must submit himself to the governing authorities, for there is no authority except that which God has instituted, and those that do will bring judgment on themselves ... [While the union] no longer officially considers this passage as doctrine ... [it] remains true to its Protestant roots' (Fuller, 2004, C-1).

Explorations of the processes of educational leadership and management demonstrate equally significant differences related to the cultural values of the society (Bajunid, 1995; 1996). The issues involved in understanding management in general or educational management as a cultural process are complex. As Dimmock and Walker delineate in this volume, there are numerous approaches to inquiry drawn from a cultural perspective. Religion, cultural values and norms as well as institutional traditions are all relevant to our understanding of educational leadership and management as a cultural process.

As someone involved in the practice and study of educational leadership and management, I believe that this book makes three distinct contributions to the field. First, for those still unacquainted with the rationale for viewing management as a cultural process, it will provide a firm foundation. Second, the book provides a deeper analysis of this rationale in both theory and practice than has appeared in published journals. The authors critically assess competing perspectives on culture and its utility as a conceptual framework for understanding school leadership and management. Finally, the authors explicitly apply a cultural framework to current perspectives on school leadership and management in practice. In doing so they demonstrate the manner in which cultural values from one culture can be used – unwittingly – to define the discourse around administrative processes. The result, in this era of globalization, can be the untested application of normative practices defined as 'preferred' or 'good' in one culture to education in another culture.

These contributions define the value of this volume. While the authors provide few empirically proven answers to important questions concerning school leadership, their discourse both drives forward the global debate and reframes key questions. In doing so, Dimmock and Walker are pressing scholars to address what Ron Heck and I have termed 'blind spots' in our field. These represent the unseen issues and assumptions that underpin our models and limit the potential of inquiry in educational leadership and management (Heck and Hallinger, 1999; in press). For helping us to see the field more clearly, the authors are due our debt of gratitude.

Professor Philip Hallinger
Mahidol University
Bangkok Thailand

References

Bajunid, I. A. (1995). The educational administrator as a cultural leader, *Journal of the Malaysian Educational Manager,* 1(1), pp. 12–21.

Bajunid, I. A. (1996). Preliminary explorations of indigenous perspectives of educational management: the evolving Malaysian experience, *Journal of Educational Administration,* 34(5), pp. 50–73.

Bangkok Post (1998a). Graft blamed for fall in world ranking: kingdom slides from 29th to 39th place, *Bangkok Post,* 3 November, p. 3.

Bangkok Post (1998b). Higher-value products and better education seen as vital, *Bangkok Post,* 25 November, p. 2.

Cheng, Kai Ming. (1995). The neglected dimension: cultural comparison in educational administration, in K. C. Wong and K. M. Cheng (eds), *Educational Leadership and Change: An International Perspective* (pp. 87–104). Hong Kong: Hong Kong University Press.

Dimmock, C. and Walker, A. (1998a). Comparative educational administration: developing a cross-cultural comparative framework, *Educational Administration Quarterly,* 34(4), pp. 558–595.

Dimmock, C. and Walker, A. (1998b). Transforming Hong Kong's schools: trends and emerging issues, *Journal of Educational Administration,* 36(5), pp. 476–491.

Drucker, P. (1995). *Managing in a Time of Great Change.* New York: Talley House, Dutton.

Fuller, T. (2004). Differences in nations striking, *International Herald Tribune*, 6 October, p. C-1.

Hallinger, P. (1995). Culture and leadership: developing an international perspective in educational administration, *UCEA Review*, 36(1), pp. 3–7.

Hallinger, P. (2004). Making education reform happen: Is there an 'Asian way?' paper presented at the international conference, Making Education Reform Happen: Learning from the Asian Experience and Comparative Perspectives.

Hallinger, P. and Kantamara, P. (2000). Leading educational change in Thailand: opening a window on leadership as a cultural process, *School Leadership and Management*, 20(1), pp. 189–206.

Hallinger, P. and Leithwood, K. (1998). Unseen forces: the impact of social culture on leadership, *Peabody Journal of Education*, 73(2), pp. 126–151.

Heck, R. (1996). Leadership and culture: conceptual and methodological issues in comparing models across cultural settings, *Journal of Educational Administration*, 30(3), pp. 35–48.

Heck, R. and Hallinger, P. (1999). Conceptual models, methodology, and methods for studying school leadership, in J. Murphy and K. Seashore-Louis (eds), *The 2nd Handbook of Research in Educational Administration*. San Francisco, CA: McCutchan.

Heck, R. and Hallinger, P. (in press). Shifting perspectives on studying the role of educational leaders' *Educational Management and Administration*.

Ohmae, K. (1995). *The End of the Nation State: The Rise of Regional Economies*. New York: Free Press.

Tyack, D., and Hansot, E. (1982). *Managers of Virtue*. New York: Teachers College Press.

Walker, A., and Dimmock, C. (1999). A cross-cultural approach to the study of educational leadership: an emerging framework, *Journal of School Leadership*, 9(4), pp. 321–348.

Acknowledgements

We are indebted to a number of people who have helped bring this book to fruition. First, Michael Wilson has made a significant contribution in two ways: he has written Chapter 4 and contributed to Chapter 11, and he has read the manuscript through in its entirety. The authors, however, accept full responsibility for any errors that remain.

We are also grateful for the unceasing diligence and effort of Anthon Chu Yan-kit and his assistant, Veronica Chan Sze-wei, whose technical support and efficiency towards the end of our writing were so admirable.

Finally, we are most appreciative of the opportunity to publish this book afforded us by Sage, and especially Marianne Lagrange and her assistant Emma Grant-Mills, whose patience has been exemplary.

We acknowledge the following publishers for their generous permission to quote from some of our previous publications:

1 Dimmock, C. and Walker, A. (2000). 'Developing comparative and international educational leadership and management: a cross-cultural model'. *School Leadership and Management*, 20(2), 143–160.
2 Dimmock, C. and Walker, A. (2000). 'Globalization and societal culture: redefining schooling and school leadership in the 21st Century'. *COMPARE*, 30(3), 303–312.
3 Dimmock, C. and Walker, A. (2002). 'Connecting school leadership with teaching, learning and parenting in diverse cultural contexts: Western and Asian perspectives'. In K. Leithwood and P. Hallinger (eds), *Second International Handbook of Educational Leadership and Administration* (pp. 326–395). Dordrecht: Kluwer Press.
4 Dimmock, C. and Walker, A. (2004). 'A new approach to strategic leadership: learning-centredness, connectivity and cultural context in school design'. *School Leadership and Management*, 24(1), 39–56.
5 Walker, A. and Dimmock, C. (2000). 'Leadership dilemmas of Hong Kong principals: sources, perceptions and outcomes'. *Australian Journal of Education*, 44(1), 5–25.
6 Walker, A. and Dimmock, C. (2000). 'Mapping the way ahead: Leading educational leadership into the globalized world'. *School Leadership and Management*, 20(2), 227–233.

7 Walker, A. and Dimmock, C. (2000). 'One size fits all? Teacher appraisal in a Chinese culture'. *Journal of Personnel Evaluation in Education*, 14(2), 155–178.
8 Walker, A. (2003). 'Developing cross-cultural perspectives on education and community'. In P. Begley and O. Johansson (eds), *The Ethical Dimensions of School Leadership* (pp. 145–160). Dordrecht: Kluwer Press.

Introduction and Overview

As the title signifies, our aim in writing this book is to explore the relationships between school leadership and culture. Both concepts have proven difficult to define, despite both promulgating a wealth of past and present literature. However, the voluminous writing on both educational leadership and culture has mainly focused on each as separate entities, with relatively little consideration to their interrelationship. It is this interrelationship between leadership and culture that is the focus of this book.

Our aim is to begin to redress this situation. Our research and publications over the past ten years have been focused primarily on studying educational leadership from a cultural and cross-cultural perspective. Our interest in this aspect of leadership emanates from the fact that we were Westerners living and working in a Chinese city (Hong Kong). At first hand we became aware of important and significant differences in people's expectations and in how things were done in society and its organizations. Equally, when it came to improving practice in those organizations, we realized a high dependency in that environment on Anglo-American ideas, policies and practices that often seemed to be misapplied and adopted unquestioningly in settings that were very different from those in which they originated. This concerned us.

Educational leadership is a socially bounded process. It is subject to the cultural traditions and values of the society in which it is exercised. In this it is no different from other social processes. It thus manifests itself in different ways in different settings. In this sense it is remarkable that many current debates in educational leadership continue to be couched in general or universal terms without taking into account the particularities of the local cultural context that influences and shapes. A good example is the current somewhat sterile and overly generalized debate taking place around the concept of 'distributed' leadership, most of which focuses on clarification of the concept and its wholesale advocacy, irrespective of context or culture. Yet, the relevance and the form of the concept should be seriously questioned, especially in those societies whose cultural and power relations assume a totally different configuration from more egalitarian 'Western' countries. Even for schools within the same societal culture, their conditions may be so diverse that factors such as recent problematic history, size, characteristics and functions render statements about the appropriateness of 'distributed' leadership highly questionable.

This book aims to explore and highlight the cultural and contextual basis of leadership. It argues against assumptions underpinning much of the current

1

leadership literature that would have us believe in the universalistic nature of leadership. It holds that leadership studies are needed that identify the particularity and diversity of cultural and contextual conditions within which leadership takes place. While acknowledging the importance of generic and universal leadership characteristics, it argues that previous studies have ignored the particularities and contextual diversity of leadership, and it is this aspect that needs redressing. It challenges the universalistic nature of much that is written about leadership, especially from a 'Western' perspective. It is highly suspicious of Western ideas, theories and frameworks applied to non-Western settings as means of understanding leadership. Rather, it champions the cause of developing authentic leadership studies grounded empirically in the distinct societal and cultural conditions of particular societies and their organizations.

Another way of making the point is that, as we have documented elsewhere (Dimmock and Walker, 1998a; 1998b), far too much of the current educational leadership literature is ethnocentric and written from a monocultural standpoint. This phenomenon not only leads to the overgeneralized nature of claims and applications; it also means that opportunities to learn about leadership, a process that can enhance the understanding of leadership in one's own culture in other societies, are lost.

We freely acknowledge that both of the core concepts of the book – leadership and culture – are contested and difficult to define, in education, as elsewhere. Hence it is a further aim of the book to attempt to bring some further clarification and definition to these hitherto loosely defined terms.

Our research agenda to date has emphasized two thrusts within the nexus of societal culture and leadership. As elaborated below, the first concerns societal cultures per se and their relationship with leadership and schooling; the second relates to the leadership of multi-ethnic schools, and the mix of different societal cultures within the same organization and community.

Connection between societal cultures and multi-ethnic schools

When we discuss societal cultures per se, we tend to look at the interrelationship between particular societal cultures and schooling and educational leadership within their defined geopolitical boundaries. However, when attention shifts to multi-ethnic schools, the focus changes to the interrelationships between a mix of societal cultures within particular schools. These interrelationships refer, on the one hand, to the mix and juxtaposition of different societal cultures forming the school and its community, and on the other, schooling and educational leadership. Furthermore, this interaction and the relationships between the different cultural groups within multi-ethnic school communities are invariably complex and variable. For example, the relationship is often one of coexistence between a prevailing culture and minority cultures. The complexity to which we refer may apply to a predominant culture associated with an indigenous group and one or more minority cultures. Alternatively the situation might be reversed, that is, the so-called minority cultures paradoxically become the predominant influence in a particular school community.

While the previous paragraph clarifies the shift in focus from societal cultures to multi-ethnic school communities, the process by which we link the two remains unexplained. Accordingly, we set out below the steps in our research agenda in moving between and linking up the twin thrusts of, first, leadership and societal cultures, and, secondly, the leadership of multi-ethnic schools.

1 Our agenda to date has been to investigate how particular societal cultures influence schooling and school leadership in their indigenous settings. This work has focused on how particular societal cultures influence schools and leadership in the same geopolitical area. An example would be how the Hong Kong Chinese culture influences understandings and behaviours in Hong Kong schools. Much of our work over the past few years has drawn attention to the relative neglect of such work and to its importance in furthering the knowledge base in educational leadership. In our opinion, this remains a significant avenue of research deserving of further development.

2 Increasing mobility and migration characterizing the world today inevitably results in people from different societal cultures forming communities within the same geopolitical areas. These multi-ethnic communities give rise to multi-ethnic schools.

3 Multi-ethnic schools themselves comprise complex and varied relationships, depending on the composition of, and relative influences among, the different ethnic groups and between them, and what is seen as the indigenous group.

Three main propositions

Threading through the book are three central propositions. These are presented as follows. First, leadership is a culturally and contextually bounded process that means it is inextricably intertwined with its larger environment – at levels ranging from the organizational, to local community through to larger society. Writers and practitioners who continue to ignore this fact fail to appreciate the conceptual and practical complexity of leadership and invariably present a piecemeal picture at best.

Second, the cultural influence on leadership is multidimensional, often difficult to discern, subtle and easy to overlook – to the point that it is underplayed by many, and even dismissed and ignored by some. Yet it is no less important for that. Its true recognition by researchers and practitioners often involves them in 'mining deep' to find it.

Third, we contend that recognizing the nexus between leadership on the one hand, and cultural and contextual influences on the other, can lead to improvement in its practice. For example, we argue that given the multi-ethnic nature of schools around the world, leaders nowadays shoulder responsibility for shaping their organizations in ways that value and integrate heterogeneous groups into successful learning communities for all. The successful leadership of such communities calls for very specific knowledge and skills attuned to ethnicity and multiculturalism. More generally, according to our argument, improving leadership practice and effectiveness involves a more integral and harmonious fit between leadership per se and the particular characteristics and requirements of the context with which it interacts and within which it is exercised. Among a host of considerations that need to be taken into account in this respect, 'distributed' leadership may need to assume a very specific form, and may not even be a priority.

Target readership

The book has been written with a wide audience in mind. To begin with, every society has educational leaders and its own culture(s). We have written the book for broad appeal across a wide and diverse spectrum of cultures – including those grouped and labelled as Western and Asian. We have combined theoretical, conceptual and research-based ideas with very practical material. Hence, the ideas and issues discussed will be of relevance and appeal to professionals in education – practitioners and academics alike. As stated above, one of our aims is to provide a better understanding of why leadership assumes the form it does, and how it is shaped by, and differs according to, context and culture. We intend the book to enable practitioner-leaders to understand their own contexts better, while appreciating the contextual differences with their counterparts elsewhere.

School principals and leaders at all levels – including middle managers and teachers – will find substantial sections of the book helpful to their practice. Many such practitioners may also be studying for postgraduate degrees and/or professional qualifications, such as leadership training programmes aimed at preparing for, or improving, the principalship. If so, then this book contains much that will be of assistance in furthering understanding of leadership and placing it in context. In this regard, because a key aim is the consideration of leadership in its cultural context, the book is of relevance for practitioners wherever they happen to be – whether in Asia, the UK and Europe, the USA and North America or Australia.

Lastly, the book will be of interest to academics engaged in lecturing, course development and researching who are increasingly looking for references and ideas to extend knowledge of leadership beyond their immediate environments.

This book will help them to gain an understanding of their local practice and, moreover, to place it within a wider, international setting.

Structure of the book

In keeping with the book's central theme, each of the 12 chapters addresses a key aspect of school leadership from a specifically cultural viewpoint. Chapter 1 provides a backdrop by juxtaposing the ubiquitous trend of conformity through globalization with the equally compelling influence of diversity represented by societal cultures. The rather contradictory tensions that both of these present to educational leadership are noted. In Chapter 2, we outline a framework within which to map and locate a systematic approach to leadership and culture. We argue the need for such frameworks in attempting to bring clarity, rigour and systematization to culturally based studies of leadership. Some of the present deficiencies in studying leadership from a cultural perspective are acknowledged in Chapter 3. Many of these are caused by the infancy of the area as a field of study, and prompt a sketching of the problems and possibilities of applying research methodologies as the field develops.

Our approach to leadership engages culture at two levels – societal and organizational. Much of the book centres on the former, but in Chapter 4, we address the theme of leadership and organizational culture, mapping and explaining a model by which to gauge and understand the relationship between leadership and culture. We acknowledge that more has been written about organizational culture and educational leadership than about culture in its other manifestations. Yet, despite this, the symbiotic relationship between leadership and organizational culture remains ambivalent and difficult to chart. In Chapter 5 we turn attention to the wider societal context, and major comparisons and contrasts between Asian and North American societies in terms of family, home, socializing and parenting influences. Many of these differences provide a backcloth against which to understand significant diversity in school leadership behaviour and priorities.

Chapters 6 to 9 address key aspects involved in leading and managing schools. Chapter 6 specifically argues for a particular new approach to strategic leadership in schools – one that encompasses culture as part of the organization's future design. Chapter 7 focuses on the important axis between teaching and learning, and leadership, a relationship increasingly accepted as vital in achieving school improvement. However, little credence hitherto has been given to the cultural aspect. For example, learning, teaching and leadership are all activities and processes that are culturally influenced. They will thus reflect differences (and similarities) around the world and, often, differences within schools in the same society. In Chapter 8 we approach the leadership and management of staff from a cross-cultural perspective. Chapter 9 continues the theme of approaching human resource management from a cultural perspective by focusing on appraisal. Both Chapters 8 and 9 argue the danger of overgeneralizing about human resource management when cultural differences come into play. The cultural differences to which we refer may be found between schools in different societies, and even within schools in the same society.

In Chapter 10 we move the discussion forward by considering leader reactions and responses to dilemma situations. It is our belief that we often learn most about cultural influence on leaders when they find themselves in situations of extreme difficulty. At such times there is a tendency to revert to basic cultural values, and these seem to differ cross-culturally. The focus on culture shifts in Chapter 11; here, we discuss cultural difference within multi-ethnic schools and the implications this phenomenon has for their leadership. Besides the fact that such schools are increasing in number, it is somewhat surprising that relatively little attention has been devoted to their leadership. Finally, in Chapter 12 we summarize key points from the book, and point the way to possible future developments in leadership as a field of study and practice that necessarily embraces culture in one guise or another.

1

Leadership, Culture and Globalization

In this opening chapter, we provide a backdrop to our argument in later chapters by juxtaposing globalization, and its accompanying trend towards conformity across societies, with the equally compelling influence of societal culture, and its connotation of diversity and difference between societies. We explore the relationship between these somewhat contradictory tensions and educational leadership, and draw some important implications therefrom.

Our aim is to highlight the importance of the concept of societal culture to developing theory, policy and practice in educational leadership within an increasingly globalizing educational context. A key argument is that tensions between globalization and societal culture make the recognition of societal culture and cross-cultural similarities and differences more, not less, important. Consequently, the inclusion of societal culture as a factor in investigations covering such themes as the curriculum, teaching and learning, leadership and school-based management, is seen as an imperative for the future development of educational leadership as a field of research and practice. Accordingly, the first part of the chapter clarifies a number of key concepts, notably culture, globalization and leadership. In the second part, globalization and societal culture are juxtaposed and the interface between them is explored. The third part provides an illustration of our argument for greater cultural sensitivity by raising some key issues concerning leadership, school reform and improvement in globalized settings. It is also worth stating that we see the relationship between societal culture and globalization as complex and dynamic. While the nature of globalization is fast changing, so, too, are many societal cultures. Both are evolving and interdependent phenomena.

Culture and related concepts

In a book devoted to culture and leadership, it is important to clarify some of the core concepts, the most important of which is culture itself. Sociologists define culture as the values held by members of a given group that distinguish it from other groups. These include the norms they follow, and the material goods they create (Giddens, 1989). Values are abstract ideals, while norms are definite principles or rules that people are expected to observe. Thus 'culture' refers to the whole way of life of the members of a society or group. It includes how they dress, what and how they eat, marriage customs and family life, their patterns of work, religious ceremonies, leisure pursuits and works of art. It is displayed and expressed through language, thought and action. It is also expressed through physical objects, such as works of art, books, icons, monuments and museums, and through social interaction such as how people relate to one another, make decisions and share experiences. It is the last of these – social interaction – that is perhaps of most significance for educational leadership.

The fact that culture is attributed to a group of people raises the question of group size. In this book, we refer principally to two levels of group size – the society and the organization. Making international comparisons between cultures at societal level inevitably involves simplification and reduction. Simple and convenient descriptions of a society's culture are bound to be reductionist for the following reasons. There have always been regional differences in customs, values and norms within a society. In addition, waves of population migration and increased mobility have nowadays left relatively few culturally homogenous societies. Rather, an increasing heterogeneity or hybridity characterizes most societies, especially the more advanced, developed and urban societies of Europe, North America and Australia. Furthermore, while ethnic and migrant groups tend to cluster within multi-ethnic societies, emphasizing internal cultural divides, a process of intermarriage between peoples, especially among second and third generation migrants, has tended to blur and reduce cultural divides within societies. And while ethnic groups may cling to many of their traditional values and religions, they also gradually assimilate to the host culture. Despite the cultural complexity and hybridity within societies, we still feel compelled to recognize distinctive national cultures. Governments, the media – and people in general – foster and perpetuate the notion of nationality, and its expression through predominant cultural values. We still find it useful and relevant to draw comparisons and contrasts between the cultures of different societies based on their predominant features. These may mask finer points of detail and difference, but they enable groups of people to gain identity.

Culture is clearly a difficult and abstruse concept to define. For example, it is distinct from, but very closely linked to, society. Whereas society is simply the system of interrelationships connecting individuals, culture is the 'glue' that binds people together through a shared and common understanding of an accepted way of life that is distinguishable from other groups (Giddens, 1989).

It is also a contested concept. There is, first, debate about whether it incorporates religion, and what its precise relationship is to politics and economics. Close relationships and overlaps exist between all three. Since basic values constitute the essence of culture, and both politics and religion are underpinned by such values, a strong case can be made for claiming that culture underpins them both. Secondly, there is dispute as to whether culture refers exclusively to the traditional and enduring values and norms of a society (often centuries old), or whether it should include more recent and contemporary changes and additions. Thirdly, there are differences between sociological and anthropological definitions of culture (for a full discussion, see Dimmock and Walker, 1998a).

While universals exist across all cultures – for example language, family system, and religious rituals – the remarkable feature of cultures is their diversity. Values and norms of behaviour vary widely across cultures. Such variety may be found in almost every aspect of life, including socializing the young, teaching the young and ways in which the young learn. As Giddens (1989) claims, small, agrarian and less developed societies tend to be culturally uniform and homogeneous, whereas developed and industrialized societies tend to be culturally diverse, embracing many subcultures. Cities in such societies contain many subcultural groups living side by side. In Chicago's west side, for example, in just one neighbourhood, Suttles (1968) found Jews, Greeks, Puerto Ricans, blacks, gypsies, Italians, Mexicans and Southern whites living in close proximity, each with their own 'territories' and ways of life. Societies receptive to past, present and future migrant waves are clearly bound to be culturally diverse.

Every culture contains its own unique patterns of behaviour that often seem alien to people of other cultural backgrounds. We cannot understand specific practices and beliefs unless we take into account the wider cultures of which they are part. A culture has to be studied in terms of its own meanings and values. That means, wherever possible, we need to avoid 'ethnocentrism', that is, the judging of other cultures from our own cultural perspective. If ethnocentrism is to be avoided when studying schools and school leadership, then understandings need to be explored in terms of the particular cultures (plural) represented in a given community, not simply from the standpoint of the indigenous culture alone. Equally, to avoid ethnocentrism when considering educational leadership in other societies, it is just as important to view and interpret them from within their own cultural perspective as it is to do so from another cultural vantage point.

A number of key concepts related to the notion of culture can now be examined in more detail.

Multi-ethnic and multicultural

Clarification of these key terms is essential in the cultural analysis of schools and their leadership in order to minimize disagreement or misunderstanding. For example, the definitions of, and differences between, the terms, 'multi-ethnic', 'ethnic minority' and 'multicultural' schools, is crucial. Such terms are contestable and arouse people's sensitivities. We use the term *multi-ethnic school* to describe a school whose student/staff profile has more than one race represented. The term *ethnic minority school* refers to a situation where at least one ethnic group experiences or perceives discrimination, group closure and solidarity. The term *multicultural school* describes a school that is achieving some measure of success in creating a learning environment that meets the ideals of multiculturalism. This may include a school community structure that accommodates culturally diverse students, a curriculum that adequately addresses issues of cultural diversity, and learning outcomes that indicate success for students of different cultures.

Cross-cultural

This is a useful term to indicate comparison across two or more societal cultures. Elsewhere (see for example, Dimmock and Walker, 1998a; 1998b), we have argued the case for more rigorous and systematic comparisons between the education systems of different societies. Following trends in international business management and in cross-cultural psychology, we believe that culture provides a fruitful basis for undertaking comparative analysis. For example, the leadership of educational institutions in China might be compared with that of British institutions by adopting a cultural perspective of leadership in the two societies.

Western and Asian cultures

Descriptors of groups of cultures are notoriously misleading overgeneralizations. Terms such as 'Western' and 'Asian' are imprecise and potentially misleading labels, the use of which is more convenient than accurate. There is as much variation within 'Asian' and within 'Western' cultures as there is between them. For example, differences between Malay and Chinese cultures, or between English and French cultures, may be as significant as those between, say, Malay and French. The labels do not even equate with geographical regions. For example, 'Western' is often used to include Australia and New Zealand, as well as the USA, Canada and the UK. A more useful terminology we have found is 'Anglo-American' to refer to the USA, UK, Canada and Australia, and 'Confucian heritage cultures' (CHCs) to refer to China, Japan and Korea, all of which have been deeply influenced by the values attributed to Confucius. However, once again there are major differences to be found within these groups. The Japanese and Chinese, like Americans and British, for example, while sharing many values, have some noteworthy differences. It seems that there are no entirely satisfactory group descriptors of regional cultures. If we use such labels, we should do so while mindful of the pitfalls and inaccuracies.

Organizational culture

Earlier, it was stated that our concern in this book was with two levels of group culture – societal and organizational. So far we have discussed the former. In much the same way that societies at large possess distinctive cultures, so do organizations such as schools and businesses. They develop their own sets of values and priorities, their own myths, legends and ways of doing things. Indeed, just as in the larger society, some in the organization may deliberately and consciously cultivate and perpetuate certain cultural features. This serves to unite the members of the organization and to create synergy. It also is a means to distinguish the organization from others, and to give it an identity to which members feel they can belong.

While parallels may exist between the two levels of culture, it is easy to overplay these and to ignore important differences. For example, while societal culture is deeply ingrained in tradition and tends to evolve slowly, organizational culture is more superficial and malleable. While societal culture is taken as a given by individuals (it shapes them rather than they shape it), leaders of organizations often set out to change the existing culture and create a new culture, even in the short term. Organizational cultures are more reflective of practice than deep-seated values (Hofstede, 1991), and practices are more susceptible to change than values.

When the two levels of culture – societal and organizational – are brought together, the resultant fusion is complex and difficult to comprehend. Organizations exist within, and are integral parts of, societies; hence people who live in a society and work in an organization bring their cultural values with them into the organization. However, the organization itself develops a culture, which may be conceived as superimposed on, and interactive with, the societal culture. Organizational practices and values may or may not align with those of the society. Multinational companies and international schools may have values that transcend those associated with the host society in which they happen to be located. Where organizational culture aligns with the values underpinning societal culture there is cultural consistency and reinforcement. Where there is no such alignment, individuals may adopt one set of values at work and another set outside in society.

Leadership

By any standard, leadership has proven to be an elusive concept to define. Reasons for this elusiveness include the sheer ubiquitousness of the concept and its multifaceted nature. Almost every year, another group of scholars argue for recognition of yet another dimension of leadership. The consequence of these difficulties is that for a definition to gain even a modicum of agreement, it needs to be generalized and somewhat bland.

There are almost as many definitions of the term as there are scholars who have written about it. Most, however, recognize it to be the influence process between leaders and followers. Some add that the influence amounts to getting staff to agree to act in ways that they may not otherwise have been inclined to choose. Others see leadership as inspiring performances and achievements

11

among staff that extend beyond what might have been reasonably expected. There seems to be general agreement that leadership involves setting the general and longer-term directions of the organization. Above all, as we elaborate below, leadership is a socially bounded and constructed process. Values, thoughts and behaviours that are the essence of leadership are social and interactive processes; consequently, they are culturally influenced.

An increasing tendency for academics and principals to travel internationally and to exchange ideas through the electronic media have led many to comment on those aspects of leadership and the principalship that are generic, common and global. There are certainly many common expectations of, and policy requirements that impact on, principals in different societies and cultures. For example, the widespread trend towards school-based management has led to more conformity in the principal's role. International comparisons that draw attention to the similarities are in fact often supporting the globalization phenomenon. Rather less conspicuous, however, are the interesting differences that coexist alongside the similarities.

Societal culture is a further element complicating the concept of leadership, one that has gone largely unrecognized until recently. However, from the present sketchy knowledge base, it is becoming clear that the meaning of leadership varies across different societal cultures (Walker and Dimmock, 1999a). It is not just the meaning of the concept that differs cross-culturally. Differences extend to the ways in which its exercise is manifested in different values, thoughts, acts and behaviours across societies and their organizations.

Globalization and internationalization

There are important distinctions to be made between these terms. While 'globalization' represents the tendency for the same or similar trends in ideas, policies and practices to spread across national boundaries and societies, 'internationalization' implies the desire on the part of institutions, such as schools and universities, to seek opportunities to expand their operations, or to seek resources, outside their immediate society or environment. Thus schools in one country may try to recruit students from other countries; or, contrariwise, parents may seek overseas schooling for their children. International schools may draw their student intakes from a range of different nationalities. Universities seek to internationalize by offering their courses and degrees in other countries, or through exchange agreements with overseas universities, or by joint research programmes with them.

Thus one important difference between the terms is that while globalization implies sameness, internationalization – while fostering interaction across societal boundaries – may aim to capitalize on difference and diversity. A university may improve its reputation, status and financial standing, or intend to do so, through the diversity that internationalizing will bring.

In the foregoing discussion it is clear that two sets of forces are acting in contradistinction. One of these is a compelling group of factors making for globalization and thus convergence; the other is a group of factors associated with societal culture and divergence. While these two sets of forces may sometimes align, we argue that they are often in tension. Our discussion in the following section articulates these tensions between globalization and societal culture as forces in understanding leadership. We take 'globalization' to mean the adoption of the same values, beliefs, policies and practices in many societies and states across the world, with an emphasis on convergence.

The development of educational leadership as a field, globalization and societal culture

Our argument pivots on the need for educational leadership and policy at a time of globalization to incorporate societal culture – conceptually, theoretically and practically – in redefining and refining the field. There is no disputing the importance of societal culture to developing theory, policy and practice within an increasingly globalizing educational context. To re-state definitions: by 'globalization' we mean the tendency for similar policies and practices to spread across political, cultural and geographical boundaries. By 'societal culture', we mean those enduring sets of values, beliefs and practices that distinguish one group of people from another. To the extent that globalization tends to override societal culture, the latter tends to act as a mediator or filter to the spread of ideas and practices across the globe, resulting in their adoption, adaptation, or even, rejection. Thus in a globalizing world, recognition of the influence of societal culture and cross-cultural similarities and differences becomes more, rather than less, important. Consequently, the inclusion of societal culture as a factor in comparative or international investigations covering such themes as the curriculum, teaching and learning, leadership and school-based management is seen as imperative for the future development of the field.

In evaluating the development of educational leadership and management as a field, there is an over-reliance placed on prescription and opinion, on the one hand, and the underdevelopment of theory, especially empirically supported theory, on the other. A large part of acknowledged theory is Anglo-American in origin. Given the resources available to, and stage of development reached by, educators in North America, the UK and Australia, this may be understandable. It is of concern, however, that much of the theory generated is ethnocentric and, consequently, tailored to those contexts. Moreover, those generating the theory make little attempt to bound or limit their work geographically or culturally, an aspect which is particularly disconcerting for those who work outside Anglo-American societies. For example, why should the principle of subsidiarity, or the espousing of 'distributed leadership', or the tenets of decentralization and school-based management be as apposite for Asian settings as they are deemed to be for Anglo-American contexts, taking into account important cultural differences of power and authority relations?

Furthermore, a substantial part of theory in educational leadership and management derives from business management. There are at least three justifiable reasons for this: first, organizations have generic functions, such as mission-stating, goal-setting, recruiting, monitoring, and evaluating; second, comparisons between types of organizations and their management may be instructive; and third, governments are keen to make school management more business-like (Bottery, 1999). There are, however, dangers in simply transferring and applying business management to diverse educational contexts in a less than critical fashion. While schools may share increasingly common characteristics with businesses, in shaping and educating young people they go beyond the rudiments of business. Unlike businesses, schools are not primarily in existence to make profit. They need to be equally concerned with processes and outcomes, many of which defy easy measurement or quantification. For these and other reasons, the appropriateness of leadership procedures and styles transferred from business are at least questionable for schools.

That schools provide education and that education is a social service is undeniable. It is arguable, however, whether market models and concepts from the business world should be imported into this social service as principles on which to organize and lead. Markets, choice, performance league tables, competition between schools and public relations – all tend to reconfigure notions of leadership and policy. There is evidence of loss in transposing business management and leadership to education. For example, school principals become more isolated from teachers and students, and from the core curriculum functions of the school, as they become office managers focusing on administrative issues and meeting accountability expectations of central bureaucracies. An administrative rather than educational or instructional emphasis to the principal's leadership role is also more likely to result from the policy of school-based management. Self-implementing policies shift major responsibilities from the central bureaucracy to the individual school without necessarily providing commensurate increases in resources.

The development of educational policy and practice is also dominated by Anglo-American initiatives. Although this domination may already be lessening (for example, consider the rise of Japan, China and other European societies), it is still strong and explicable given the Anglo-American pre-eminence in terms of global economic development, communications and technology. As developed societies, they possess the resources and ideas to innovate and to lead change. Moreover, Anglo-American societies are advantaged by having English – increasingly accepted as the global language – as their mother tongue.

For much of the twentieth century, but particularly the second half, it became apparent that the developing world was taking its cues mostly from

Anglo-American societies. The continuation of this phenomenon – otherwise known as globalization – seems assured as other developing countries follow suit. Generations of comparativists, from Sadler onwards (Jones, 1971), have pointed to the reasons for cultural borrowing. These include colonialism, cultural imperialism, the overseas education of leaders, the desire of less developed societies to emulate the more developed, a belief in education as a vehicle for economic and social advancement, international legitimacy for policy formulation, and closer links forged by international agencies, jet travel and the electronic media. Comparativists have also acknowledged the benefits of studying foreign systems of education, including the resultant improved understanding of one's own system. There are exceptions, however, to the phenomenon of policy-borrowing associated with globalization. For example, the Scots and Irish have developed their own education systems that are appreciably different from the English.

While globalization has been emerging, relatively little credence has been given to the concept of societal culture. Yet, as theory, policy and practice are transported globally, they interface with the cultures of different host societies. The interaction merits consideration for a number of reasons. First, as policies such as decentralization and school-based management spread from Anglo-American systems to become more globalized, what are the implications for 'leadership' and 'management' in the host societies? Leadership and management may not mean the same in different societal cultures. In Western societies, for example, leadership is seen to rest on a set of technical skills, whereas in Chinese societies it is viewed more as a process of influencing relationships and modelling what are deemed to be 'desirable' behaviours. Will meanings and styles of leadership converge in the future, or will they remain culture-specific? And if Anglo-American influences over globalization increase in the future, what are the benefits and drawbacks to such developments? Can we assume that there are some organizational procedures and policies that are generically beneficial regardless of the cultural origins of such ideas? Responses to these questions will determine how school leadership and management develops in the future.

It follows that a key direction for educational leadership and management in the twenty-first century is to embrace an international, cultural and cross-cultural comparative perspective. Elsewhere, we have provided a more detailed justification for such an approach (Dimmock and Walker, 1998a) and have developed a framework for its application (Dimmock and Walker, 1998b). Central to this framework is a consideration of the impact of the process of globalization, both in general terms and with reference to specific examples.

Globalization: some general implications

A complex set of forces and trends is shaping the contemporary world. The nation-state as we have come to know it is under threat – politically and economically. At the macro level, multinational corporations transcend nation-states, affecting organizations and the lives of individuals. Plants can be closed down overnight and jobs relocated to other countries. Ohmae (1995) argues that the world economy is increasingly run by economic regions, such as Silicon Valley, California, and Hong Kong and adjacent parts of southern China, rather than by countries. Some also argue that globalization is rein-forced by the growing influence of international agencies, such as the World Bank, the International Monetary Fund (IMF), and the United Nations. In addition, regional conglomerations of nations, many of them trade blocs, such as the European Community and North Atlantic Free Trade Association have further undermined the autonomy of the nation-state. American ascendancy in the political and economic arenas has also given a boost to globalization. The fortunes of organizations and individuals are just as much directly influenced by these global forces as they are by nation-states.

At the same time, globalization has resulted in a proliferation of units smaller than the nation-state. In other words, the demise of the nation-state is accompanied in some parts of the world by a rise in nationalism, as indicated in the Balkans and the setting up of a Scottish Parliament. As Bottery (1999) asserts, whether the nation-state is superfluous or not, 'there is little doubt that the phenomenon of globalization has an impact upon organizations, individuals and values, which is both greater and smaller than the nation-state' (p. 300). He goes on to conclude that prudent organizations and individuals will take cognizance of global forces in their decision-making. It is also worth noting that societal cultures do not necessarily equate with national boundaries or nation-states as recent turmoil in the Balkans illustrates.

There is little doubt that increased opportunity for travel and communica-tions, including the electronic media, have provided a big impetus to global-ization. Bottery (1999), citing Waters (1995), suggests that to use the term 'globalization' does not necessarily imply planetary-wide acceptance. Rather, the term connotes 'a broad spectrum idea, suggesting that there are issues and trends which transcend any particular nation-state, which have significant potentiality for full global effects, but which may not yet have attained this' (Bottery, 1999, p. 301).

Furthermore, globalization takes a number of forms. Waters (1995), for example, recognizes the political, economic and cultural. To these, Bottery (1999) adds the managerial and environmental. It is not the purpose here to expound on each of these, but it is worth noting some points of relevance for educational leadership and management. Forms of political organization beyond the nation-state threaten concepts of national citizenship – often an important concept and consideration in schooling and curriculum – and national sover-eignty over economic affairs. The economic form of globalization, as manifested in trade blocs and international agreements, has the capacity to influence national economic policy and expenditure on education and social welfare provision, thereby ultimately affecting school budgets.

Managerial and cultural forms of globalization are particularly relevant. While management concepts seem global in nature, the 'actual practice of management is context-bound, mediated by the beliefs, values and aspirations of the managers and the managed' (Bottery, 1999, p. 303). Educational managers in the developed world have over the past two or three decades been exhorted to read management 'gurus' associated with the private sector – such as Handy, Drucker and Peters and Waterman – the consequence of which has been the introduction of a business terminology into educational management. They have also been urged to look at practice overseas – especially the USA, but also latterly Japan, Singapore, Taiwan and other Asian systems – in order to identify 'best practice' on a global scale. Insidious dangers, however, lurk in both directions. The first concerns the different agendas and purposes of business and educational management, and the second, the failure to respect the grounding of practices in their own cultural settings. It is to this latter issue that the following discussion turns.

Globalization in educational leadership implies the export of theory, policy and practice from some systems – chiefly the Anglo-American world – and their import into others, particularly non-Western and developing countries. More recently, signs of a reciprocal movement are apparent as the Anglo-American systems look with interest at, and try to explain, the enviable performance of East and South-East Asian school students in mathematics and science (Dimmock, 2000a; Reynolds and Farrell, 1996). It is apparent nowadays that the notion of globalization itself is becoming more complex as ideas, policies and practices flow not just from the Anglo-American and European peoples to other societies, but from a wider range of exporting societies. Such trends are too early and too little to enable us to claim that Anglo-American dominance in globalization is under threat.

The importation of policy reforms formulated elsewhere under different economic, political and cultural conditions presents challenges for the new host cultures. Many observers not only question the suitability of the policy reforms for those systems importing them, but often question their appropriateness for the exporting systems. Theories, ideas and practices originating in one social setting should not be assumed valid in other social-political-cultural contexts. As previously argued, societal cultures – along with local economic, political and religious conditions – act as mediators and filters to policies and practices imported from overseas. As a consequence, such policies may be rejected, adapted or left unaltered.

The fact that policy is imported may give it international legitimacy, which in turn allows the host government to fulfil its task of policy formulation and adoption. However, where such cultural borrowing is ill conceived, there is a failure to match policy with contextual conditions in the host society. In other words, the policy formulation and adoption stages fail to act as effective filters and mediators for adaptation, with the result that problems arise at the implementation stage.

Our argument is not that globalization is a negative phenomenon, nor that societal culture is unnecessarily obstructive. Rather, it is that the transfer and mobility of theory, policy and practice between systems needs to be more 'culture sensitive'. Neither should our argument for cultural sensitivity assume that cultures are static or passive entities always requiring the adaptation of imported policy and practice. Cultures themselves are dynamic and changing, and schools as centres of knowledge organization and transmission play a vital part in that process. For example, cultural transformation may focus on lessening an authoritarian and male-centred orientation to leadership and management.

Nonetheless, the argument for greater cultural sensitivity in a globalizing educational context is robust. If policy, theory and practice are to be made more culture sensitive, then the process needs to begin at the formulation rather than at the implementation stage. International advisers and consultants as well as policy-makers, especially those in the host societies, bear responsibility for making this happen. A more culture-sensitive approach requires a better understanding of culture and cross-cultural similarity and difference.

Examples of cultural sensitivity and globalization in educational leadership

We argue that the foregoing dimensions of societal culture may help facilitate cultural sensitivity when policy, theory and practice are transported between education systems. An illustration of our argument is presented in some of the following issues based on these cultural dimensions.

In the global push for school-based management and decentralization, a reconfiguration in the pattern of decision-making, responsibility and power in favour of principals, teachers and parents, is foreshadowed. Predictably, societal cultures in which power is distributed more equally – for example, Anglo-American societies – would adjust rather more successfully to school-based management than societal cultures in which power is concentrated – such as Chinese communities like Hong Kong and Singapore. This may partly explain the different forms in which school-based management manifests itself – in some societies, simply reinforcing the power of the principal, while in others leading to more genuine participation of teachers and parents.

In many education systems, a trend towards individualizing curricula, teaching and learning is discernible. While such an approach may be harmonious with cultures emphasizing self-orientation, its suitability for group-oriented cultures may be legitimately questioned. Broadly, Hofstede (1991) identifies Anglo-American cultures as individualist and most Asian cultures as group oriented or collectivist. Conversley, however, collaborative learning is generally acknowledged as an effective teaching method, and it may have more in keeping with students socialized or conditioned in group-oriented, rather than individualist or self-oriented, cultures.

A central tenet of the restructuring of curriculum and pedagogy in many school systems is that students accept more personal responsibility for their learning. Accompanying this phenomenon is the espousal of goal-setting at the individual level and school development planning at the organizational level. Each of these tenets assumes the acceptance of responsibility for shaping the future, a capacity associated with proactivism found in Anglo-American cultures. In cultures displaying strong elements of 'fatalism', where control is seen to be in the hands of others or outside human realms altogether, it is less likely that these tenets and behaviours are as appropriate.

A further characteristic of curricular restructuring is the emphasis placed on creativity, problem-solving and higher-order thinking skills. Recent school curricular reforms in Anglo-American societies have given prominence to these aspects, linking them with skills needed by future workers in an information society. The Asian economic crisis, beginning in October 1997, stopped the phenomenal rate of economic growth achieved by the so-called Asian 'Tiger' economies in its tracks. It became apparent that economies such as Hong Kong needed a technologically skilled workforce capable of sustaining a qualitatively different economic structure in the future. While societies such as the USA have cultures (and to an extent school curricula) conducive to creativity – they are what we call 'generative' – some in East Asia are more renowned for their replication and rote learning. Although these school systems are successful in producing high-achieving students in mathematics and science, they are less likely to cultivate creativity in their young people.

Finally, in the pursuit of quality schools and schooling, the part played by competent and effective teachers is generally acknowledged. In pursuit of this goal, it is an accepted principle in Anglo-American cultures that the appointment and promotion of staff is merit based, that is, dependent on achievement or experience against measurable criteria. Anglo-American societies conform to what we call 'limited relationship' cultures; that is, decisions are taken according to specific issues, criteria or performance. By contrast, in Chinese cultures, where more holistic considerations of relationship hold sway, personnel decisions may be made as much on the basis of connections as on merit. For example, a teacher may be appointed because a trusted friend of the school may speak highly of her loyalty, and loyalty is seen as a desirable quality leading to commitment and eventually performance. This more holistic perspective may make the attainment of openness with respect to transparency of selection or promotion criteria more difficult than in Anglo-American 'limited relationship' cultures.

Conclusion

We do not claim that societal culture is the only mediating influence on globalized trends in education policy, theory and practice. Nor is it without conceptual and empirical difficulties. Indeed, culture itself is being affected by globalization. Thus it is misleading to see culture as simply a reactive and mediating phenomenon when it too is subject to change from globalization. How the tension between the two – globalization and societal culture – is resolved, will predictably vary according to their relative strengths in particular societies. Projecting into the future, perhaps the most optimistic outcome will be that each society will develop its own ways of transforming globalized policies and practices in culturally sensitive ways that respect the integrity of their indigenous cultures, while allowing room for change and development. In these ways and for these reasons, we see societal culture as an important and overlooked factor in the study of schooling and school leadership. Importantly, we believe that the incorporation of societal culture into educational policy, research and practice will significantly enrich, contextualize and refine the field.

2
Conceptualizing Cross-Cultural Leadership

In Chapter 1, we argued that educational leadership lags behind other cognate fields and disciplines in understanding the influence of societal culture. Although this situation has been partly redressed over the last few years (Ah Nee-Benham and Napier, 2002; Dimmock, 1998; Hallinger, 1995; Shields, 2002; Walker, 2004) few would dispute that the field continues to over-rely on values, theories and practices drawn from English-speaking, largely Anglo-American, scholars. Our argument is that culture is a significant influence on school leadership in and within different societies because it helps to shape school leaders' thoughts and subsequent actions about concepts such as leadership, followership, communication and learning and teaching (Dimmock, 2000b; Dimmock and Walker, 2000c). We suggest that the field looks to societal culture for at least partial explanations of school leaders' behaviours and actions. Given the potential of culture to increase understanding, we agree with Shield's (2002, p. 215) assertion that: 'It is perhaps surprising, given the diversity of schools, that there is no coherent body of literature related to cross-cultural leadership in education.' We further submit that cultural, cross-cultural and multicultural understanding may be usefully pursued through a comparative approach – one which allows leadership practices between and within different societies to be seen in relation to each other.

This chapter introduces a framework that we believe is useful for guiding cross-cultural investigation of school leadership and school organization. As outlined in Chapter 1, we hold that internationalism as an educational phenomenon is both desirable and largely inescapable. However, we also hold that understandings of and the meanings associated with leadership across, and indeed within, different societal and cultural contexts, are prone to superficial comparisons as apparently similar policies and practices are widely adopted in different countries. In particular, such comparisons, we claim, can be fatuous and misleading without thorough understanding of the contexts, histories and cultures within which they have developed. Our main purpose in this chapter is to propose a comparative model of educational leadership based on cultural and cross-cultural perspectives. Building on the propositions underpinning the book we explicate a conceptual framework that we believe is useful for drawing valid international comparisons in school leadership and management. In short, our framework is intended to facilitate the comparison of educational leadership across cultures and within different cultural contexts. The framework draws on some established writing in the area.

The most widely cited framework for exploring the influence of culture on management and leadership practice remains that developed by Geert Hofstede (1980; 1991; 1994). His work is generally acknowledged as the most influential in the field of international comparative management over the last 18 years. Despite the enduring profile of Hofstede's work, especially in the international and comparative business literature, it has been criticized on a number of fronts (Child, 1981; Trice and Beyer, 1993). Among the more salient criticisms are those pertaining to the grounding of his studies in the context of each society studied, and concern about the representativeness of the IBM employees sampled. Other questions have focused on the narrow range of four or five values used; the appropriateness of using questionnaires to capture complex values; the changing nature of societies into multicultural communities; and the dated findings after 20 years. Two dimensions in particular are troublesome: 'masculinity–femininity' presents a problem of terminology and there is ambivalence in another dimension termed 'uncertainty avoidance'. Notwithstanding the efficacy of such criticisms his framework and its accompanying ideas have been applied and tested repeatedly over the last 15 years and stand, according to Redding (1994, p. 324), as 'a unifying and dominant' influence in the field.

Hofstede's (1980) original work identified four cultural dimensions which he suggested are universally applicable across all societies or nations. The four were *power/distance, uncertainty avoidance, masculinity/femininity, individualism/collectivism*. A fifth dimension, *Confucian dynamism*, was later added to his work by a group of Chinese scholars (The Chinese Culture Connection, 1987). Hofstede's dimensions are suggested as choices between pairs of empirically verifiable alternatives that allow the identification of patterns within and between cultures to emerge, and facilitate their meaningful ordering (Hofstede, 1980; 1995; Hofstede and Bond, 1984). These allow for comparisons to be made. Perhaps the dimension most discussed and researched is that of individualism/collectivism, discussion of which as a cultural theory far preceded the popularizing effect of Hofstede's work (Triandis and Bhawuk, 1997). Individualism and collectivism can be understood around four defining attributes. These are: the *definition of self*, where collectivists view self as interdependent with others and individualists view self as autonomous from the group; *structure of goals*, where collectivist goals are compatible with in-group goals and individualist goals are not; *emphasis on norms versus attitudes*, where collectivist behaviours are determined by norms, duties and obligations, determinants of social behaviours among individualists attitudes, personal needs rights and contracts; and, emphasis *on relatedness verses rationality*, where individualists emphasize rationality (weighing of costs and benefits of relationships), collectivists emphasize unconditional relatedness to the needs of others regardless of advantage (Triandis and Bhawuk, 1997, p. 15).

Building on the work of Hofstede, Trompenaars and Hampden-Turner (1997) suggest that 'culture is the way in which a group of people solves problems and reconciles dilemmas' (p. 6). These authors suggest that cultures distinguish themselves from others in how they approach and solve problems. They suggest seven fundamental categories which can be used for identifying cultural influences and for making comparisons across cultures. Five of the categories are grouped around how people relate to others. These include *universalism versus particularism, individualism versus communitarianism, neutral versus emotional, specific versus diffuse* and *achievement versus ascription*. The remaining two categories relate to different cultural attitudes towards time and the environment.

As discussed below and throughout the book, the framework is not intended to restrict analysis or to encourage the ranking of countries in terms of best or worst leadership practices, management or other school process factors. Rather, it aims to provide a baseline typology to guide comparison irrespective of the methodology employed. The framework aims to increase understanding of the influence of culture on leadership across and within different societies and, consequently, build understanding of how different groups construct meanings of leadership and associated processes. Equally, the framework intends to provide a vehicle appropriate for building increased understanding of the influence on leadership on schools containing communities, teachers and students drawn from different cultures.

The framework proposed is based on our own work into cross-cultural comparative educational administration and leadership (see Dimmock and Walker, 1998a; 1998b; Walker and Dimmock, 2002a) on established frameworks outside education (such as Hofstede, 1991), and on work beginning to appear in the educational leadership literature (such as Hallinger and Kantamara, 2002; Hallinger and Leithwood, 1996b; Heck, 2002). We suggest the framework holds some promise for increasing understanding of the influence of culture on educational leadership, and for comparing educational leadership across and within different contexts. The primary aim of our framework is to promote understanding of the interface between societal cultures, educational leadership and schools and their broader communities.

A cross-cultural comparative framework for studying educational leadership

This section presents an overview of a cross-cultural comparative model developed for the study of educational leadership. This is provided in Figure 2.1. The

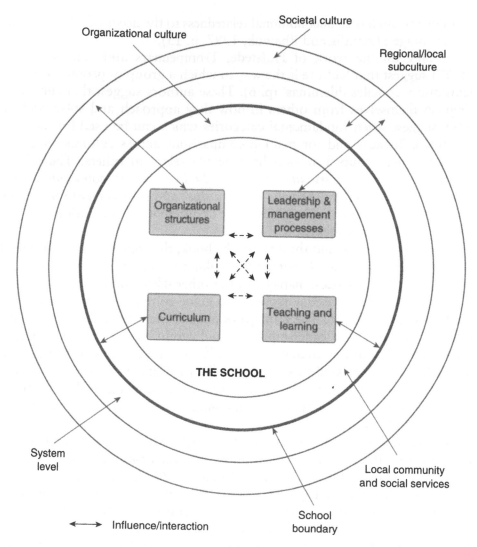

Figure 2.1 *A cross-cultural school-focused framework for comparative educational leadership*

model comprises two interrelated parts. The first part presents a description of the four elements that are taken as constituting schools (see Figure 2.2 for a breakdown). The second part describes a set of six dimensions that apply at the societal cultural level and at the subcultural levels of the region and locality respectively which provide common scales for comparison (see Figure 2.3). It also provides a separate set of dimensions that apply at the organizational cultural level. Our understanding is that the reality of school life results from the complex interplay of cultural elements from society, region and locality, on the one hand, and organizational culture, on the other. The sets of dimensions associated with each of these enable comparison of schools between or within different societies, and even comparisons within particular multi-ethnic school communities.

The framework can be used to guide investigation of societal cultures and their interrelationship with schooling and educational leadership within defined geopolitical boundaries. It can also be used to focus investigation on multi-ethnic schools, or the interrelationships between a mix of societal cultures within particular schools. These interrelationships refer, on the one hand, to the mix and juxtaposition of different societal cultures forming the school and its community and, on the other, schooling and educational leadership. Figure 2.1 illustrates the four elements of schools and the two sets of cultural dimensions – societal/regional/local and organizational. Comparative analysis is aimed at the relationship between the levels of culture and the four elements constituting the school. In Figure 2.1, organizational culture is conceptualized as internal to the school but bounding the four elements, reflecting its capacity as both a dependent and independent variable with regard to the four elements of the school and schooling. Societal/regional and local cultures, however, are depicted as circumscribing the school, but at the same time, spanning the school boundary to interact with organizational culture and to affect the four elements of the school.

We have used the same set of cultural dimensions to describe societal cultural variations, and to capture subcultural (that is, regional and local) differences within entities ranging from societies to individual school communities. The inclusion of the regional and local subcultural levels acknowledges that varying cultural configurations reside within broader societal cultures and that these can exert significant influence on school organization, leadership, curriculum and learning and teaching. Although many societies and communities, by virtue of their history, religion and law, display cultural homogeneity, some are certainly more culturally heterogeneous than others. For example, countries such as Canada, Singapore, France and South Africa have multiple subcultures, each of which influences the nature of communities and their schools, as well as school administration and leadership. Depending on its intended purpose, the framework can be applied to either the societal level or to the regional/local and school subcultural levels.

The model does not claim to explicitly address all variables that influence culture and thus, school communities and their leadership. For example, religion has a significant impact on societal culture and on regional subcultures, as do history, geography and politics, to name but some. In terms of our model, religion is one of the factors that combine to form the values, ideals and assumptions that comprise a society's culture and its subcultures, a point further elucidated in Chapter 3. The influence of religion shifts in terms of emphasis and shape as the culture itself evolves. As an important element of cultural formation, religion helps to differentiate cultures and subcultures to varying degrees. Some societies, such as Thailand, are fairly homogenous in terms of religion, whereas others are heterogeneous. Singapore, for example, has three main religious groups. Religion therefore is recognized as a vital influence on the cultural make-up of groups and societies. It is a powerful, but not the only, determinant of the values and beliefs which form a culture.

The school is taken as the unit of analysis for comparison in our framework and is assumed to comprise four elements: organizational structures; leadership and managerial processes (this is explained in further detail below); the curriculum, a school substructure; and teaching and learning, a subset of school processes (Figure 2.1). Although in this book we focus more specifically on educational leadership, we present the overarching framework because of the context it provides. The four elements comprising the wider frame provide a convenient way of encapsulating the main structures and processes which constitute schooling. Two of the four comprise the managerial and organizational aspects of school life, while the remaining two elements form the core technology of the school concerned with curriculum, teaching and learning. Elsewhere (Dimmock and Walker, 2002), we have explained the four elements in full and the interrelationships between them. Relationships with other parts of the system, such as the district and central office, and with local community and social service agencies, are also considered (see Figure 2.1).

The four elements of schooling

Organizational structures refer to the more or less enduring configurations by which human, physical and financial resources are established and deployed in schools. Structures represent the fabric or framework of the organization and are thus closely associated with resources and their embodiment in organizational forms. They also provide policy contexts within which schools have greater or lesser discretion. For example, schools in strongly centralized systems experience more explicit and rigid policy 'structures' imposed from system levels, with possibly less need for school decisional structures, whereas schools in more decentralized systems, may have more school-based decision-making structures, but fewer policy structures imposed from outside the school. A comparison between the structures of schools is based on the eight aspects outlined in Figure 2.2. For example, how schools select and group students is one element of this category. Students may be selected for entry to schools on the basis of their ability, gender or parents' wealth. Once they become school members, they are grouped into classes for learning. Classes are structures formed on the basis of age, ability, gender or a combination thereof.

Leadership, management and decision processes are at the core of school leadership (Figure 2.2). As with structures, the manifestation and importance of these processes in schools reflect cultural characteristics and the relationship with other

 Influence/interaction

Organizational structures

Degree of centralization–
decentralization influences:

- Physical and technological
  resources
- Financial resources
- Curriculum frameworks
- Time
- Students
- Staff
- Guidance and counselling
- Decision-making structures

**Leadership, management and
decision processes**

Degree of centralization–
decentralization influences

- Position, role and power of the
  principal
- Leadership style and orientation
- Collaboration and participation
- Motivation
- Planning
- Decision-making processes
- Interpersonal communication
- Conflict resolution
- Staff appraisal

Curriculum

- Goals and purposes
- Breadth
- Depth
- Integration
- Differentiation
- Relevance

Teaching and learning

- Nature of knowledge
- Teacher/student relations
- Teacher/home relations
- Generalist vs subject specialist
- Learning outcomes
- Guidance and counselling

Figure 2.2 *The four elements of schooling*

levels of the system, particularly the degree of centralization–decentralization. Consequently, where school-based management has been extended, schools perform more of these processes. However, the processes may vary even in schools in the same system. This may be evidenced, for example, by the nature of the principalship in terms of the position, role and power, which differ between schools and between systems. In some countries, the principal is all-powerful, and is seen as a chief executive of an autonomous unit, while in others, the role carries little more authority than the classroom teacher, and the principal is no more than a line manager or agent acting on behalf of the system. A further example which can serve as a point for comparison is the extent to which there is collaboration and participation of school personnel in the management of the school and the operation of the curriculum. Comparisons between schools are likely to reveal substantial differences in the extent to which staff collaborate and participate in their running and the reasons behind this variation. School comparisons such as these are instructive in terms of the extent to which each of these activities take place and the characteristic forms they take. These are described in more detail later in the chapter.

At the heart of the school's core technology is curriculum, teaching and learning. The curriculum constitutes an organizational structure, since it represents the form in which knowledge, skills and attitudes are configured for delivery to students. However, as a structure concerned with core technology, it deserves separate recognition in its own right as an organizational structure. As previously stated, the culture and configuration of the relationship between system and school (degree of centralization/decentralization) will expectedly determine the discretion and responsibility afforded the school for the curriculum. With that in mind, the curricula of schools can be compared according to the following characteristics outlined in Figure 2.2. The first characteristic concerns the goals and purposes of school curricula. Curriculum goals may vary in line with differences in how curriculum developers conceive the nature of knowledge and with how the purpose of the curriculum is defined. The curriculum may be seen, for example, as having primarily instrumental functions related to future employment, or it may be seen as having more intrinsic cognitive priorities. The relative emphasis placed on knowledge, skill and attitude goals, and on cognitive, affective-expressive-aesthetic and psychomotor goals, may differ, as might the balance between academic and pastoral development.

Teaching and learning activities, as part of the core technology of schools, are processes which warrant separate identification, even though they are related to managerial processes. Differences in the ways in which schools conduct teaching and learning activities can be compared according to the following characteristics, outlined in Figure 2.2. One important characteristic concerns the ways in which teachers and students bring definition to teaching and learning. For example, some East Asian and Western societies tend to adopt different understandings of what it is to teach and learn. This stems from a fundamentally different conception of the nature of knowledge and important differences in the relationship between the teacher and the student. In some East Asian contexts, such as Hong Kong, teachers' knowledge and teachers per se are accorded more respect than in Western societies (see Chapter 7). A further example useful for comparison is the teacher–parent relationship. In some cultures, parental involvement in their children's education is encouraged and seen as essential in promoting learning; in others, parents view teaching and learning exclusively as school activities and thus the responsibility of teachers.

Societal/regional/local cultures	Organizational culture
• Power-distributed/power-concentrated • Group oriented/self-oriented • Consideration/aggression • Proactivism/fatalism • Generative/replicative • Limited relationship/holistic relationship	• Process–outcome oriented • Person–task oriented • Professional–parochial • Open–closed • Control and linkage; formal–informal; tight–loose; direct–indirect • Pragmatic–normative

Figure 2.3 *Dimensions of societal and organizational culture*

Recognition of common characteristics inherent in all cultures is necessary to facilitate cross-cultural comparison. This approach obviates the need to choose a particular culture as a baseline for comparison. Hence the first component of our model is the definition of a set of cultural dimensions commonly present in all cultures but to different degrees.

Six dimensions of societal/regional/local culture

As we discuss in Chapter 3, culture is a difficult phenomenon to measure, gauge or even describe. The identification of cultural dimensions, which we define as core axes around which significant sets of values, beliefs and practices cluster, not only facilitates their description and measurement, but also promotes comparison between cultures. Dimensions provide common benchmarks, against which cultural characteristics at the societal or subcultural level can be described, gauged and compared (Dimmock and Walker, 2002). Despite their usefulness, however, we agree with Hofstede's (1994) cautionary remarks that: 'They are also constructs that should not be reified. They do not "exist"; they are tools for analysis which may or may not clarify a situation' (p. 40). Our research – involving the review of existing frameworks – for the comparative study of educational leadership and management led to our fashioning the six-dimensional model (Walker and Dimmock, 1999a) in Figure 2.3. Our framework acknowledges that the six dimensions may apply at societal cultural and subcultural (regional/local) levels.

Power-distributed/power-concentrated

The first dimension is modelled on Hofstede's (1991) power–distance construct. We relabelled the dimension as power-distributed/power-concentrated because this more accurately captures the essence of power relationships in various cultures. Power is either distributed more equally among the various levels of a culture or is concentrated among relatively few. In societies where power is widely distributed, for example, through decentralization and institutionalized democracy, inequity is treated as undesirable and every effort is made to reduce it where possible. In societies where power is commonly concentrated in the hands of the few, inequities are often accepted and legitimized. People in high *power-concentrated* societies tend to accept unequal distributions of power.

Group-oriented/self-oriented

The second dimension embraces Trompenaars and Hampden-Turner's (1997) individualism/communitarianism category and Hofstede's (1991) individualism/ collectivism dimension. Both of these schemata describe whether people within a given culture tend to focus on *self* or on their place within a *group*, hence our preference for the label 'group/self-oriented'. In *self-oriented* cultures, relations are fairly loose and relational ties tend to be based on self-interest. People in such societies primarily regard themselves as individuals first, and members of a group, second. In *group-oriented* cultures, ties between people are tight, relationships are firmly structured and individual needs are subservient to collective needs. Important collectivist values include harmony, face-saving, filial piety and equality of reward distribution among peers. In *group-oriented* cultures, status is traditionally defined by factors such as age, sex, kinship, educational standing, or formal organizational position. In *self-oriented* cultures, people are judged and status ascribed according to individual performance or what has been accomplished individually.

Consideration/aggression

This dimension is built on Hofstede's masculinity/femininity dimension. We reconceptualized it because of the confusion surrounding Hofstede's label and its discriminatory nature. In what we have called *aggression* cultures, achievement is stressed, competition dominates and conflicts are resolved through the exercise of power and assertiveness. In such cultures the system rewards achievement; in an organizational context, assertiveness is taken as a virtue; selling oneself, decisiveness and emphasis on career are all valued. By contrast, in *consideration* societies, emphasis is on relationship, solidarity and resolution of conflicts by compromise and negotiation.

Proactivism/fatalism

The fourth dimension draws on Trompenaars and Hampden-Turner's 'attitudes to the environment' category, Hofstede's 'uncertainty avoidance' dimension and our own thinking in respect of the concepts of 'opportunistic' and pragmatic/ idealistic. This dimension was relabelled to reflect the proactive or 'we can change things around here' attitude in some cultures, and the willingness to accept things as they are – a fatalistic perspective, in others. The dimension addresses how different societies and cultures react to and manage uncertainty and change in social situations. In proactive societies, people tend to believe that they have at least some control over situations and over change. They are tolerant of different opinions and are not excessively threatened by unpredictability. In fatalistic cultures, on the other hand, people believe 'what is meant to be, will be'. Uncertainty is often viewed as psychologically uncomfortable and disruptive, and people seek to reduce uncertainty and limit risks by hanging on to tradition. This often involves the inflexible retention of rules and dogmas that breed orthodoxy.

Generative/replicative

This dimension, original to our schema, was so labelled to reflect the fact that some cultures appear more predisposed toward innovation, or the generation of new ideas and methods (generative), whereas other cultures appear more inclined to replicate or to adopt ideas and approaches from elsewhere (replicative). In *generative* cultures people tend to value the generation of knowledge, new ideas and ways of working, and they seek to create solutions to problems, to develop policies and ways of operating which are original. In *replicative* cultures, people are more likely to adopt innovations, ideas and inventions developed elsewhere. Whereas these sometimes undergo partial adaptation, they are often replicated *in toto*, with little consideration of alignment to the indigenous cultural context.

Limited relationship/holistic relationship

This dimension builds on Trompenaars and Hampden-Turner's 'specific/ diffuse' and 'performance/connection' categories and on our own work on the importance of relationships in cultures. The dimension reflects an assumption that in some cultures, interpersonal relationships are limited by fixed rules applied to given situations, whereas in other cultures, relationships are more holistic, or underpinned by association and personal considerations. In *limited relationship* cultures, interactions and relationships tend to be determined by rules that are applied equally to everyone. For example, in deciding a promotion, objective criteria are applied in relation to the relative merits of the possible candidates. In *holistic* cultures, on the other hand, greater attention is given to relationship obligations (for example, kinship, patronage and friendship) than to impartially applied rules. Dealings in formal and structured situations in *holistic* cultures are driven more by complex, personal considerations than by the specific situation or by formal rules and regulations.

Six dimensions of organizational culture

Qualitative differences between organizational and societal culture stem from the fact that societal cultures differ mostly at the level of basic values, while organizational cultures differ mostly at the level of more superficial practices, as reflected in the recognition of particular symbols, heroes and rituals (Hofstede, 1991). This allows organizational cultures to be managed and changed, whereas societal cultures are more enduring and change only gradually over long time periods, if at all. Research studies on the organizational cultures of companies found large differences in their practices (symbols, heroes, rituals), but only minor differences in their values (Hofstede, 1995). Six dimensions were found to account for most of the variation in practices, although further validation of these is required. With some modification, we have adapted these six as a useful baseline for organizational culture in our framework. In addition, while Hofstede presents the dimensions as either/or choices along six axes, it is possible that some of them might be multidimensional rather than unidimensional. The six dimensions are introduced below and expanded.

Process and/or outcomes oriented

Some organizational cultures are predisposed towards technical and bureaucratic routines, while others emphasize outcomes. Evidence suggests that in outcomes-oriented organizational cultures people perceive greater homogeneity in practices, whereas people in process-oriented organizational cultures perceive greater differences in their practices. In education, some schools are process oriented, emphasizing the processes and the skills of decision making, teaching and learning, while others are results oriented, stressing learning achievements such as examination results. Many schools and school systems are currently reforming their curricula to reflect specific student learning targets or outcomes expressed in terms of knowledge, skills and attitudes, indicating a trend towards designing curricula on the basis of, and measuring student and school performance by, a learning outcomes approach.

Task and/or person oriented

In task-oriented organizational cultures, emphasis is placed on job performance and maximizing productivity, while human considerations, such as staff welfare, take second place and may even be neglected. Conversely, person-oriented organizational cultures accentuate the care, consideration and welfare of employees. Applied to extremes in schools, a task-oriented culture exacts maximum work effort and performance out of its teachers in a relatively uncaring work environment. A person-oriented culture on the other hand, values, promotes and shows consideration for the welfare of its teachers. It is conceivable that some schools might score high (or low) on both task and person orientations.

Professional and/or parochial

In professional organizational cultures, qualified personnel identify primarily with their profession, whose standards are usually defined at national or international levels. In more parochial organizational cultures, members identify most readily with the organization for which they work. In the school context, some teachers, especially those with an external frame of reference, are primarily committed to the teaching profession as a whole, while others with a strong internal frame of reference are more committed to the particular school in which they work.

Open and/or closed

This dimension refers to the ease with which resources, such as, people, money and ideas are exchanged between the organization and its environment. The greater the transfer and exchange of resources between the environment and the organization, the more open the organizational culture. Schools vary between those which champion outside involvement in their affairs and maximum interchange with their environment, and those which eschew such interaction and communication, preferring a more closed, exclusive approach. Trends in education over the last decade have favoured the opening of school cultures, particularly to parental influence and involvement.

Control and linkage

An important part of organizational culture concerns the way in which authority and control are exerted and communicated between members. In this respect, Hofstede's dimension identifies only one aspect, namely, tightly–loosely controlled organizational cultures. We have added two more aspects, namely, formal–informal and direct–indirect which, taken together, provide a more comprehensive structure to this dimension in schools (Dimmock and Walker, 1998a).

Formal–informal   Organizations vary in the extent to which their practices are guided by rules, regulations and 'correct procedures', on the one hand, and the extent to which they reflect a more relaxed, spontaneous and intuitive approach, on the other. Highly formalized organizations conform to the classic bureaucracies; they emphasize definition of rules and roles; they tend towards inflexibility and are often characterized by austere interpersonal relationships. By contrast, informal organizations have fewer rules dictating procedures, roles are often ill-defined, they display flexibility in their modes of work and interpersonal relationships tend to be more relaxed.

Tight–loose This sub-dimension gauges the degree to which members feel there is strong commitment to the shared beliefs, values and practices of an organization. Such strong commitment might come through hierarchical super-vision and control, or through members' own self-motivation. An organization that has strong homogeneity and commitment in respect of its members' values and practices is tightly controlled (whether control is externally imposed by formal management or self-imposed by workers). Conversely, a loosely con-trolled organizational culture is one with only weak commitment to, or accep-tance of, shared beliefs, values and practices, and little or no control is exerted to achieve homogeneity either by formal management or by workers themselves.

Direct–indirect This aspect captures the linkages and patterns of communi-cation through which power, authority and decisions are communicated. In some organizations, managers either assume direct personal responsibility to perform certain tasks and to communicate directly with their staff, often leapfrogging intermediate levels in the vertical hierarchy or chain of command. In other organizations, managers exert control indirectly by delegating to staff the tasks they would otherwise do themselves.

Pragmatic and/or normative

This dimension defines the way an organization serves its clients, customers or patrons. Some display a flexible, pragmatic policy aimed at meeting the diver-sity of customer needs. Others, however, exhibit more rigid or normative approaches in responding bureaucratically, failing to meet individual needs. This dimension measures the degree to which the organization is client centred. In the educational context, some schools consciously try to meet individual student needs by offering a more diversified curriculum with flexible timetables and alternative teaching strategies. They mould their educational services to meet student needs. Others, particularly the more traditional schools, may be less student focused, expecting them to fit into the agenda determined for them by the school. These schools offer more standardized, normative programmes.

The framework as described is designed to guide investigation of the influ-ence of societal culture on schools and school leadership. The framework can be 'broken up' for the purpose of focusing research on a particular area. The following section attempts to apply part of the framework specifically to the study of the *leadership and management processes* 'box' of the framework (Walker and Dimmock, 1999a). It should be noted that by focusing on soci-etal cultures, and the differences between them, as they impact on principals' leadership, we recognize that we are presenting only a partial picture of reality.

	Collaboration	Motivation	Planning	Decision-making	Communication	Conflict resolution	Appraisal	Staff development
Power distributed/ power concentrated								
Group oriented/self oriented								
Consideration/ aggression								
Proactivism/fatalism								
Generative/ replicative								
Limited relationships/holistic relationships								

Figure 2.4 *Matrix of cultural dimensions and leadership elements (adapted from Hofstede's cultural dimensions)*

A more complete understanding would be gained by including personality and organizational culture. Incorporating all of these in the framework at this time would, however, present an extremely difficult challenge given the limitations of the existing knowledge base.

Leadership and management processes

Using the framework in these particular areas targets principal leadership as expressed through the eight elements and six cultural dimensions (Figure 2.4). It is assumed that leadership practices, as exercised through the eight elements, reflect the societal cultures within which principals live and work. Investigating how principals in different cultures approach their roles is seen as a basis for comparison. Through constructing cultural profiles of principalship behaviours and practices, and using the six dimensions, a basis for comparison is possible. Once formed, the profiles can be used to compare the practices of principals in different cultures. They can help explain, for example, the what, why and how questions underpinning principals' approaches to their jobs in different cultures. In this way, we should be able to increase our understanding of the principalship and, in so doing, help build the knowledge base of school leadership and aid reflection on practice.

School leadership is taken to comprise eight elements. The first group of processes relate to the extent to which teachers and others are involved collaboratively in school management (Pounder, 1998; Telford, 1996). Differences between principals in different cultures may be compared according to the degree of participation they foster among others, achieving the optimal balance between the exercise of 'power over' and 'power through' colleagues (Day et al., 2000). Another set of leadership practices relate to motivation (Brotherton, 1999; Sergiovanni, 1995). It is useful for comparative purposes to explore the extent to which teachers are motivated and whether and how principals enhance teacher motivation, both as individuals (Spear, Gould and Lee, 2000) and as team players (Cacioppe, 1999). The third group of leadership practices relates to school planning, a phenomenon which has become increasingly important in school systems around the world over the last decade, especially in managing both the increased pace and complexity of educational change (Fullan, 2001), calling into question traditional rational approaches to school planning (Fidler, 2002), while considering the need for more flexible and creative strategies (Brooke-Smith, 2003; Wallace and Pocklington, 2002). How principals approach planning, who they involve in the process and what they intend to achieve by it, may be of cultural significance (Quong, Walker and Stott, 1998). How principals approach decision-making may also reveal cultural differences. For example, comparisons may be drawn by identifying the existence and form of decision criteria and the methods by which decisions are made (Everard and Morris, 1996; Fidler, 2002), including leadership concerns not only for the quality of the decisions made but also for the contribution of a shared decision-making process to teacher leadership and professional development (Leithwood, Jantzi and Steinbach, 2003). Another set of leadership practices concerns communication (Goldring and Rallis, 1993). Cultural differences, as well as similarities, may exist in the ways in which principals use written and oral modes of communication, for example, regarding degrees of openness (Ginsberg and Gray Davies, 2003) and the exercise of 'persuasive communication' (Grint, 2003), as well as in the extent to which they rely on different forms of communication inside and outside the school to ensure that institutional objectives are realized in practice (Gilsdorf, 1998; Morrison, 2002).

A further basis for comparison targets the different ways in which conflicts within the school community are approached and resolved (Maurer, 1991). Such comparisons may be useful in highlighting differences and similarities in leadership processes and in developing typologies for the effective management of both *destructive* and *constructive* aspects of internal conflict within schools (DeDreu and Van De Vliert, 1997; DiPaola, 2003). Yet another increasingly important facet of school life for both principals and teachers is how teachers are evaluated or appraised (Cardno and Piggot-Irvine, 1997). The ways principals structure, conduct and view appraisal systems may offer instructive cultural comparisons, building on the comparative approach to the study of teacher appraisal and performance management by Middlewood and Cardno (2001). The eighth and final element relates to comparisons between how principals view the importance and conduct of staff development (Darling-Hammond, 1997), including managing the interface between staff development and both teacher assessment/ appraisal (Jacobson and Battaglia, 2001) and the fostering of teacher leadership development through the promotion of shared decision-making (Leithwood, Jantzi and Steinbach, 2003).

We do not claim that the eight elements present a complete picture; nor do they address all of the complexities in real-life leadership situations. Neither do we claim that all aspects of the elements are operational in all schools, or across all systems. Our contention is that for purposes of analysis, it is valid to recognize these eight elements which together constitute principal leadership in both a formal and informal sense. Moreover, the eight elements, when combined with analysis grounded in the cultural dimensions, provide valid points of comparison between leaders in the same and different cultures.

Operationalizing the framework involves the collection of data using the eight identified elements of leadership (see Figure 2.4). Data collected from principals, teachers and other relevant groups is then analysed in terms of the six dimensions. For each of these dimensions, guiding questions of who, why, what, when, how and where (see below) can be posed. These questions are intended as stimulants to the framework: in other words, the questions are included as a way of operationalizing the framework through providing a basis for data collection. Although placed in cells for ease of understanding, each of the questions can be asked for each of the eight leadership elements. The questions are designed to guide investigation of the dynamic and multidimensional nature of leadership, and to ensure that information for each of the dimensions is cross-checked. The six questions are designed to generate a different perspective of the dimension studied and to confirm, or otherwise, information collected under other dimensions. Examples of these are provided at different points in later chapters. It is helpful to list the type of information each question is designed to generate:

- The 'who' question attempts to identify the major player(s) in each of the processes. Is it the principal, other administrators, teachers or parents, or a mixture of these people who drive the particular function? For example, in relation to participative decision-making, does the principal alone make school decisions, or does he/she share decision-making with other members of staff?
- The 'why' question aims to identify why, or for what purpose, leadership behaviours and practices are conducted in schools. For example, regarding appraisal, is its purpose simply to judge teachers' performance, or is it proposed as a way of developing teachers' potential?
- The 'what' question attempts to describe the form that a particular process takes. For example, in regard to communication, is communication top-down, bottom-up, one, two or multi-channel, written, verbal, or a combination of these?

- The 'when' question aims to discover when particular processes occur and how often they occur. For example, in relation to staff development, when do staff development activities take place? At what time in the school year? Is staff development a one-off event or a continuous, in-built process?
- The 'how' question targets the form and nature of the various processes. For example, in regard to school-level planning, how does the planning process function? Are teachers involved in committees? Do they meet regularly? Or is the process driven by the principal only?
- The 'where' question aims to identify where certain processes take place. For example, under conflict management, are conflicts dealt with in formal group settings or are they dealt with in individual, private encounters? Are they conducted in or out of school? Are conflicts dealt with formally or informally?

Questions within each cell are designed to collect information related to the various leadership elements and to assist in the identification of cultural influence, according to the six cultural dimensions. An example of the type of questions asked is presented in Figure 2.5. Answers to such questions are designed to provide a holistic picture within each of the cultural dimensions rather than information specific to each individual leadership element.

Responses to questions such as those suggested in Figure 2.5 are then juxtaposed with the six cultural dimensions to facilitate cultural comparison. It is worth reiterating that data is collated according to cultural dimensions rather than to the specific leadership elements. A simplified, hypothetical example is presented in Figure 2.6 (Walker and Dimmock, 1999a). A brief example of the type of the information which may be collected using this approach – in this instance on leadership and change – is provided below, and further examples can be found in Walker and Dimmock (2002a).

Leadership and change

The influence of culture on school leadership and management can be seen at all levels of school operation, including policy implementation at departmental and whole-school levels. The following references to two case studies that examined cultural influence on change show how culture can influence implementation.

Morris and Lo (2000) and Hallinger and Kantamara (2000a; 2000b) present case studies of Asian schools attempting to implement curriculum and pedagogic reforms, the origins of which lie in Anglo-American contexts. Each case tells a different story, but both attest to the same conclusion, namely, the crucial role of the principal in transplanting new pedagogy and curricula into indigenous cultures with traditional, deep-seated values. In the Morris and Lo (2000) study, the implementation was generally unsuccessful, for reasons largely to do with

	Planning	Decision-making	Communication	Conflict management
Who	Who does the principal involve in the school-level planning process?	Who makes major school-level decisions?	Who communicates with whom to form the main channels of communication in the school?	Who manages or resolves conflict in the school?
Why	Why, or for what purpose, does the principal and school plan?	Why does the principal involve/not involve others in school-based decision-making?	Why, or for what purpose does such communication take place?	Why does conflict management take place?
What	What emphasis/ form does the planning process and output take?	What criteria does the principal use to make school-level decisions?	What communication methods does the principal encourage and use in the school?	What form does conflict management take?
When	When does school planning take place? When is the school plan referred to and used?	When does participative decision-making take place?	When are these various methods of communication used?	When does conflict management occur?
How	How does the school planning process function?	How does participative decision-making occur?	How does the principal communicate?	How does the principal manage conflict?
Where	Where is school planning undertaken and where is the plan used?	Where does participative decision-making take place?	Where does (in what venues) communication take place?	Where does conflict resolution take place?

Figure 2.5 *Possible questions within each of the leadership elements*

the principal; while Hallinger and Kantamara's (2000b) three cases point to the directors (principals) as primarily responsible for successful implementation.

In Morris and Lo's (2000) analysis of curriculum change in a Hong Kong primary school the principal engineered his school's adoption of the target-oriented curriculum (TOC), a major curriculum reform introducing fundamental changes based on student-centred teaching and learning and new forms of assessment. The new curriculum contradicted traditional Chinese beliefs of student passivity, obedience and examination orientation. Teachers therefore struggled to make the transition. Above all, they had little say in how the scheme was implemented, because the principal maintained his traditional *power-concentrated* Chinese autocratic style of leadership. It was the demands placed on teachers by the new reforms in concert with the principal's unrelenting traditional leadership style that brought matters to a head. The staff

Dimension	Principals in culture A	Principals in culture B
Power-distributed/ power-concentrated	• Relative equality of authority and status between principals and teachers • Delegation/decentralization common • Teamwork and empowerment typical	• Leadership from the top • Respect for seniority • Goals set by top management • Acceptance of wide power and status differentials between principals and teachers
Group-oriented/ self-oriented	• Emphasis on maintenance of harmony and personal dignity • Avoidance of confrontation and conflict • Maintenance of social networks important • Emphasis more on the 'group'	• High levels of trust and openness valued • Emphasizes more the 'self' • Open confrontation of differences • Conflict valued as potentially creative • Support for teachers essential • Drive to secure commitment and high moral
Consideration/aggression	• Conflicts resolved through mediation and negotiation • Student status determined by need (everyone has strengths)	• Teacher and student status based on effort and achievement • Conflicts resolved through edict • Overt competition promoted • Impersonal
Proactivism/fatalism	• Belief in capacity to shape and influence the present and future • High tolerance of ambiguity • Uncertainty accepted as normal • Continuous change viewed as natural and desirable • Sense of urgency • More on care and support and personal interest	• Belief that we can do little but accept life's eventualities • Deep-rooted, shared theologies and philosophies provide relative certainty and security • Long-term view of evolving change • Hierarchy, standardization and conformity stressed • Adherence to mutual duties
Generative/replicative	• Problems solved creatively by groups and individuals • Centralized policy and directives challenged • Experimentation in classroom common and encouraged	• Problems solved mainly through referral to precedent • System policies easily accepted • Traditional approaches to teaching and learning endure
Limited/holistic relationships	• Tasks stressed as much or more than relationships • Advancement based mostly on performance and competence • 'Bottom-line' drives agendas	• Relationships valued as much or more than tasks • Advancement based on relationship as much as competence • Care taken not to alienate people

Figure 2.6 *Hypothetical comparison of principals in two contrasting cultural settings*
Note: Culture A accords with the first construct of each pairing, the culture B accords with the second construct of each pairing.

was transformed from a state of political acquiescence to high political activity, where conflict, bargaining and negotiating became the new established order. In consequence, the school culture dramatically changed. It must also be acknowledged that prior to its implementation in the school, the TOC had already been subjected to much political and professional debate in the national arena, a point not lost on the teachers. The moral is clear: when challenging reforms are imported from other cultures, they demand strong but sympathetic leadership and management from principals to mediate their introduction to the local cultural setting.

This negative Hong Kong experience of implementing a major curriculum reform can be contrasted with the three successful Thai schools reported by Hallinger and Kantamara (2000b). These authors report that the introduction of school-based management, parental involvement and new teaching-learning technologies into selected Thai schools was an attempt by the government to lessen the 'compliance' culture. As Hallinger and Kantamara (2000a) point out, these reforms present stiff challenges in their countries of origin, let alone in the strongly hierarchical cultures of Asia. Successful reform in the three schools was attributed to the three directors who adopted participatory leadership styles, to group orientation and teamwork, and to a combination of pressure and support for change as well as the fusion of spirit and celebration in traditional Thai style. The moral for success here is the subtle combination of traditional Thai leadership with new 'Western' approaches demanded by the nature of the reforms. In other words, the school directors used their hierarchical position to win support for more participatory decision-making. Achieving a delicate and subtle balance between traditional mores and new demands seems to be what matters.

Summary

The literature reviewed during the course of this chapter has shown that until recently there has been very little research on the impact of culture at the societal level on school leadership, and yet this has become an issue of major significance, not least because of the implications of both the forces of globalization and traditional indigenous culture on the effective leadership and management of schools. Clearly, both forces are to a large extent in conflict and give rise to tensions and dilemmas that demand school leadership skills and qualities of the highest order if they are, at least, to be effectively managed and, at best, resolved.

What this chapter has set out to do is to outline a comprehensive model that can be used as a framework for further cross-cultural research into educational leadership, focused on eight key leadership dimensions within both an organizational cultural and a wider societal cultural framework. Its potential value to a deeper understanding of the cultural contexts of school leadership has been illustrated with reference to empirical research studies drawn from Hong Kong and Thailand.

The next chapter builds on the theoretical framework by focusing on two closely related issues: first, a clarification of some of the conceptual problems related to culture and how these might be addressed, and, secondly a consideration of the more practical issue of methodology in conducting cross-cultural leadership research.

3
A Cultural Approach to Leadership: Methodological Issues

To recap the argument set out in the first two chapters – culture at the societal level and its influence on schools and school leadership has received relatively scant attention in the literature base, at least until recently. This is despite the fact that it has received significant attention in other social science literature, and that the concept of organizational culture has been prominent in current discussion within the field of educational leadership. Since culture is reflected in all aspects of school life, and people, organizations, communities and societies share differences and similarities in terms of their cultures, as a concept, 'culture' appears to have universal application – appropriate for exploring influences and practices endemic to educational leadership. Since culture exists at multiple levels (classroom, school and sub-school, local, regional and societal) it provides rich opportunities for exploring key interrelationships, such as those between schools and their micro- and macro-environments. It also helps identify characteristics across organizations that have surface similarity but are quite different in modus operandi. We therefore argue that the concept of culture, and a framework built around it (as described in Chapter 2) offers a dynamic framework by which to study comparatively schools and educational leadership.

Whether utilizing our framework or adopting a less structured approach to investigate issues of culture and leadership, it is important to recognize that the search for improved understanding is fraught with pitfalls which hold the potential to convolute research design, induce deep-seated emotion and misdirect attention. Such caveats are understandable given the breadth and complexity of the concepts spotlighted – culture and leadership – much less their interaction. Given the concomitant breadth and intricacy of the concepts, it is no surprise that increased understanding and scholarly investigation are clouded by imperfections and contestations. This is nowhere more clearly evident than in the definition of the concept of culture itself where ongoing debate has generated multiple definitions and ambiguities. For example, when defined in anthropological terms, as in our framework, the concept of culture does not necessarily have the explanatory power to account for all of the variations between schools in different societies or regions. Clearly, economic, political, religious and demographic factors also play a key explanatory role (Dimmock and Walker, 2000a). In this chapter we discuss this and similar issues which can 'muddy the waters' of understanding about the relationship between culture and leadership. So despite our asserted preference for using culture as the basis of investigation and comparison, and our belief in the framework described in the previous chapter, we recognize that there are a number of issues that cloud its utility and form a basis for ongoing debate. Many of these issues result from the fact that culture is difficult to handle both politically and emotionally. As Harrison (2000, pp. xiii–xxxiv) states, 'It (culture) is also difficult to deal with intellectually because there are problems of definition and measurement and because cause and effect relationships between culture and other variables like policies, institutions … run in both directions'.

The chapter has two main parts – the first deals with a set of conceptual issues relevant to the study of culture, and the second with some more practical methodological issues. In the first part we introduce a number of the more salient problems when studying or seeking increased understanding of leadership and culture. These and other issues will continue to be raised throughout the book. The problems identified are relevant to both researchers and practitioners as they seek more sophisticated understandings to underpin their work and interaction with others (Walker, 2003). The problems identified do not purport to be comprehensive, but we believe they do form a worthwhile starting point to underscore the complexity of the many topics and issues touched upon in this book. The problems addressed in the first section are listed below.

- the difficulties of defining societal culture;
- the explanatory power of societal culture;
- the monolithic and fragmented view of societal culture;
- whose culture to use as the basis for comparison;
- problems of cultural and national stereotyping;
- the relationship between organizational and societal cultures;
- the relationship between individuals and societal culture;
- the shifting and evolutionary nature of culture;
- the contradictory effects attributed to culture; and
- cultural context and differences of meaning.

In the second part of the chapter we discuss briefly a number of issues more pragmatically related to studying culture (Dimmock, 2002). These include partial consideration of paradigms and methodologies, issues of access in different cultural settings, and the advantages of cross-cultural research teams. This is a general discussion only and is supplemented and expanded at various points throughout the book.

The concept of culture

As noted in our introductory chapter, a first and major problem is that of how to define culture. The concept itself is amorphous (Brislin, 1993) and there is only general agreement in the literature on its definition. Although in our research we have adopted the most widely accepted (anthropological) definition of societal culture – namely, that culture consists of the ideals, values and assumptions that are widely shared among people that guide specific behaviour – others endorse more expansive definitions (Pai and Adler, 2000). Lewellen (1992, cited in Heck, 2002) suggests two ways of conceiving culture. The first is in line with the definition provided above – emphasizing more traditional and enduring characteristics – whereas the second conceptualizes culture as an adaptive system where, 'groups adapt to the challenges of their particular environment' (Heck, 2002, p. 88).

In building a comparative cross-cultural base for school leadership we begin with a traditional anthropological definition prevalent in the literature. While our decision to adopt this preference stemmed partly from methodological considerations and receives broad support in the educational administration and general leadership literature (Hallinger, 2000), we are in agreement with Tierney (1996, cited in Heck, 2002) that: 'In reality, however, any cultural system is likely comprised of multiple and competing realities, rather than ordered systems that make intuitive sense to members' (p. 88). The concept of culture in organizations is covered in greater detail in Chapter 4.

Sharp and Gopinathan (2000) adopt a socio-political perspective of societal culture. They argue, for example, that societal culture, 'can be understood as an evolving mix of what we term "traditional" and "modernizing" cultures, which are in turn complexly related to dominant political and economic processes' (p. 88). This perspective embraces what can be labelled as a 'middle' view of culture – one that takes a position between culturalists and modernists (the latter including many economists and 'rational choice' political scientists). In general terms, culturalists (such as Fukuyama) hold that 'contemporary societies are characterized by distinctive cultural traits that have endured over long periods of time' (Inglehart, 2000, p. 81) – and that these traits have an important impact on all aspects of society. Modernists, on the other hand, hold that the world is changing in ways that erode traditional values, and that globalization will inevitably minimize cultural differences. Daniel Patrick Moynihan probably best captured the debate between these two positions (cited in Harrison, 2000, p. xiv) when he stated: 'The central conservative truth is that it is culture, not politics, that determines the success of a society. The central liberal truth is that politics can change a culture and save it from itself.'

While it would be reckless to suggest that culture is the only influence on school leadership, it may be equally hazardous when searching for cultural influence and comparison in school leadership to adopt too broad a definition of culture. For cultural influence to be identified and to be used as a base for comparison, a more focused definition is needed. This point is alluded to by the cultural pluralist, Shweder (2000, p. 164), who describes himself as a confusionist, and elaborates, thus: 'A "confusionist" believes that the knowledge world is incomplete if seen from any one point of view, incoherent if seen from all points of view at once, and empty if seen from "nowhere in particular".' Shweder (2000, p. 164) continues: 'Given the choice between incompleteness, incoherence and emptiness, I opt for incompleteness while staying on the move between different ways of seeing and valuing the world.'

In the field of international and cross-cultural business management, Hofstede (1991) also supports the notion of beginning with a more focused definition of culture when he addresses the concept specifically from a national or societal perspective. Hofstede (1991) defines culture as, 'patterns of thinking, feeling and acting' underpinning 'the collective programming of the mind which distinguishes the members of one group or category of people from another' (pp. 4–5). The 'patterns of thinking, feeling and acting' included in this definition raise the likelihood that culture will simultaneously influence, and be influenced by, organizational structures and processes, since both are subject to people's thoughts and actions (Lau, McMahon and Woodman, 1996). The 'collective programming of the mind' refers to the shared beliefs, values and practices of a group of people, whether that group is a society, nation-state or organization. Building on the work of Hofstede (1991), Trompenaars and Hampden-Turner (1997) suggest that 'culture is the way in which a group of people solves problems and reconciles dilemmas' (p. 6). These authors suggest that cultures distinguish themselves from others in how different groups of people approach and solve problems.

Closely related to mixed definitions of the term 'culture' are the definitions or understandings of associated constructs, dimensions or other categorizations. A review of the literature shows that literally hundreds of these have been used to explain, describe or study societal culture. Whereas some form of description and/or differentiation is useful for comparison, care needs to be taken with application or understanding. One example can be drawn from what is perhaps the most recognizable and commonly used (and debated) dimension for studying societal culture – that of collectivism/individualism. Despite its widespread acceptance and application, the plausibility of the dimension, in terms of meaning and research, has been questioned. This is demonstrated by division of the terms into multiple meanings, that is, the suggestion that there are different types of collectivism. For example, Triandis and Gelfand (1998) refer to horizontal and vertical collectivism. As Walumbwa and Lawler (2003) explain: 'Horizontal collectivism refers to a cultural pattern in which the individual sees the self as an aspect of the group. That is, the self is seen as totally part of the group and interdependent with other members of the group, who are viewed as equal and the same' (p. 1085). Vertical collectivism, on the other hand is a 'cultural pattern' where an individual sees himself or herself as an integral part of the group but that individual differences within the group are acknowledged and valued. Dissension over the definition of concepts appropriate to understand culture, and debate over the definitions of the term itself, present difficulties to researchers and practitioners alike.

Societal culture and schools as organizations

Taken to the level of the school, the debate over how culture should be defined raises the question of whether culture on its own is sufficient to explain differences between school administrators, teachers and schools as organizations in different societies. Stated another way, the question is whether organizations, such as schools, are culture bound or culture free (Trice and Beyer, 1993). The main debate in the literature at the organizational level is between proponents of either convergence or divergence, or what Wilkinson (1996) labels institutionalists and culturalists. Mirroring the wider debate, proponents of convergence (institutionalists) believe that organizations are largely culture free and therefore similar across societal cultures, because the processes of organizing and using technologies make certain universal requirements on organizations, thereby inducing the cultures themselves to become more similar over time. Conversely, the reasons why organizations can be seen as culture bound, and therefore divergent (as espoused by culturalists), are that their internal cultures and formal structures reflect their external environmental cultures. In this event, differences persist because of unique histories, traditions, expectations, resources, demography, stage of development, and cultural inertia (Trice and Beyer, 1993).

'Culturalists', Wilkinson (1996) claims, have a tendency to attribute rather simplistically any residual unexplained phenomena to culture and to ignore 'institutionalist' arguments that it is primarily historical and political conditions that shape organizations. This view is supported by a writer for *The Economist* (1996, p. 30) who states:

> The conclusion must be that while culture will continue to exercise an important influence on both countries and individuals, it has not suddenly become more important than, say, governments or impersonal economic forces. Much of its (culture) influence is secondary, that is, it comes about partly as a reaction to the 'knowledge era'. And within the overall mix of what influences people's behaviour, culture's role may well be declining, rather than rising, squeezed between the greedy expansion of the government on one side, and globalization on the other.

It is important that both perspectives receive acknowledgement, and that culture is seen as interacting with economic, political and sociological factors to shape schools. An exclusive concentration on either perspective may risk constructing an incomplete picture. In fact, the separation and search for any type of causality may, in itself, be too facile given the synchronous relationships between culture and other societal influences. Hofstede (1996, p. 531) makes this very case when challenging the common sociological-institutionalist argument. He states:

> Institutions do differ. But why do they differ? In attempting to understand institutional differences, one needs history, and in understanding history one needs culture. Culture is at the root of institutional arrangements, and even if the sociologist does not dare to venture historical/cultural explanations, cultural differences appear as a consequence of institutional differences ... thinking is affected by the kind of family they grew up in, the kind of school they went to, the kind of authorities and legal system they are accustomed to. The causality between institutions and culture is circular: they cannot be separated.

Hofstede's point is well taken. While we maintain that comparative study in educational leadership, for reasons provided in earlier chapters, should intimately address, and be grounded in, culture, they must also take account of other social, political and geographic and economic environmental factors within which societies and schools exist and operate.

A monolithic or fragmented view of societal culture

The methodological conundrum which emerges from problems with defining culture is how broad to make its definition for framing research. This exposes a tension between taking a fragmented or a monolithic view of culture. The monolithic view assumes culture to be ubiquitous, thereby elevating a particular conception of culture and creating a risk of overgeneralization, making comparisons invidious. As Harrison (2000, p. xv) warns, 'If culture includes everything, it explains nothing'. A fragmented and localized interpretation of culture, on the other hand, through recognizing multiple subcultures and failing to draw any form of generalization, may equally fail to provide valid comparison. The problem here is to seek generalization while at the same time taking into account the specificity of cultural conditions. Research adopting an either/or view, on the one hand, risks conclusions made at too high a level of generality, or, on the other hand, conclusions so micro-specific that they offer no opportunity for generalization.

One response to problems such as this has been to make a distinction between culture-common and culture-specific concepts (Brislin, 1993). Culture-common (etic) concepts can be found among people from different societies and cultures; for example, all societies seek to socialize children, or to build harmonious relationships in an effort to prevent violence. Culture-specific (emic) concepts are additions or variants on culture-common concepts and tend to deal, for example, with *how* different cultures socialize children. As Brislin (1993, p. 71) explains: 'culture specific concepts represent different ways that people deal with culture-general demands'. Cross-cultural researchers in other fields have tended to focus on a combination of culture-common and culture-specific concepts, 'both of which are necessary for an understanding of culture and cultural differences' (ibid., p. 71).

Whose culture?

A further difficulty when using culture as a basis for comparison is to assume that culture has to be interpreted using a baseline culture for comparison. However, the problem then becomes deciding whose culture provides that baseline. For American or British researchers, for example, to automatically assume that their culture should form the baseline for comparison only serves to reinforce, rather than question, the dominance of Western theory and practice. A common error in cross-cultural study is made by researchers believing that their own etic–emic combination is true of all cultures (Brislin, 1993). Moreover, research based on overly simplistic dichotomies can lead to false stereotyping and hidden forms of discrimination. While it is true that some forms of stereotyping may be useful to researchers for purposes of categorization and labelling, the danger is that all individuals and groups within a nationality are assumed to think and behave in the same way – a point we return to below. Equally, without 'deeper' exploration, there exists an even greater danger – that national cultural stereotypes are used as surface generalizations and that the processes operating below the surface are ignored.

Clearly, research into cross-cultural aspects of educational leadership and administration while using some type of baseline must avoid discriminatory stereotyping. Shaw and Welton (1996) argue that this is beginning to happen, as the discipline of cross-cultural research is moving from, 'the direct comparison of nation states with each other, identifying characteristics of the indigenous peoples using complex Western research tools, towards a more sensitive and organizationally-focused approach, using research tools elaborated in mixed-culture teams' (p. 3). The latter point is worth reinforcing. The conceptualization and application of any approach, but particularly one purporting to explore cross-cultural issues, is unavoidably influenced by the researchers' own inherent cultural bias (Ronan, 1986). For English-speaking Western, or other homogeneous groups of researchers, to embark separately on cultural inquiry could be counterproductive and might well restrict the validity of such research. Equally, researchers from within a certain culture may find it difficult to explore their own cultures as, within themselves, cultures tend not to be widely discussed because they simply represent 'the way we do things around here'. In fact Brislin (1993) suggests that in many situations 'outside' researchers can provide insightful analysis because they do not hold the same 'taken for granted' values, norms and behaviours as those who live the culture on a day-to-day basis. In short, a collaborative mix of researchers from within and without particular cultures under investigation may well yield more robust understandings and comparative insights.

Stereotyping and comparing cultures

A further issue that may skew cross-cultural research in educational administration is the tendency by some researchers to assume that cultures are homogeneous within national boundaries, or even with larger groups of countries such as 'Asia' or 'Europe' (Walker and Dimmock, 2000d). For example, within national boundaries one only has to look at the complex cultural composition of societies such as the USA, Australia or Malaysia to see that such perspectives ignore the fact that cultures differ as much within as they do between nations (Redding, 1994). As Tjosvold and Leung (1998) note: 'In Malaysia, Malay, Chinese and Indian managers have their own values systems' (p. 336). Misconceptions also occur through the unwarranted grouping of countries into some homogenized, identical collective. A common example of this inaccuracy is the grouping of Asian countries into an undifferentiated 'Confucian' mass. As Rizvi (1997, p. 21) notes: 'More collectivism modes of social organisation are portrayed as Asian compared to the liberal individualism that is believed to be so dominant in the West.' Tjosvold and Leung (1998) for example, concluded that even though different societies in South and East Asia generally value relationships over a focus on task, they approach conflict management in different ways. A further example is that researchers sometimes assume that schools and school leaders in Taiwan, Hong Kong and Singapore, all predominantly Chinese societies, are subject to identical influences and characteristics when, in fact, they are quite different. As recognized by the framework presented in Figure 2.1, it is important to note that cultural differences are as prevalent across and within national and societal boundaries as they are between them.

The stereotyping of cultures also holds cautions for making comparisons across cultures. As Heck (2002) explains, while anthropologists define culture holistically they recognize that the complexity of culture often calls for the isolation of certain smaller sub-systems (for example, racial or ethnic, occupational, gender, social or organizational). Each of these subcultures may have different economic, political, religious or educational goals which have developed under quite different political conditions (for example, colonization or communism). So if one uses national boundaries or other forms of group identification as a basis for generalization, understanding of values, norms and subsequent influences can become skewed. This obviously makes comparison at any level extremely difficult as it risks decontexualizing values and behaviours, such as those held and displayed by school leaders. However, as Heck explains, 'the notion of generalization (or transfer) of phenomena across settings is at the centre of comparative work'. Researchers, therefore, he adds, 'are faced with a conceptual and methodological dilemma of studying culture and school leadership comparatively' (Heck, 2002, p. 89).

Individuals and societal culture

A further issue confounding the search for the influence of culture on school leadership and organization is the relationship between individual personality and culture. Arguments downplaying the role of culture claim that individuals will behave in ways in line with their own beliefs or mental models, regardless of cultural background. As explained above, in terms of organizations, this may be a circular argument. As Lindsey (2000, p. 284) explains: 'Mental models apply to individuals and groups of individuals – and are identifiable and changeable. Culture reflects the aggregation of individual mental models and in turn influences the types of mental models that individuals have. The two are linked in a perpetually evolving system.'

Culture has the capability to influence and explain the behaviours of individuals and groups of all sizes and complexities. It can be observed as an influence at the macro (societal culture) level, at the organizational (school culture) level and at the individual level, since individual behaviour is the product of the interaction between individual personality and both societal and organizational cultures. Indeed, Hofstede (1991) claims that organizational behaviour results from a complex interplay between the personality and motives of individuals, the cultures of society and organization in which individuals live and work respectively, and generic characteristics of human nature. Hofstede (1991) remarks that every individual is born with, and therefore inherits, universal and generic characteristics of human nature. The individual's personality, however, is formed from both inherited and learned characteristics. Culture, at its different levels, acts as a mediating influence on the learned part of behaviour and personality (Hofstede, 1991). The concept of culture then captures reality by enabling explanations of human and organizational behaviour to be expressed in terms of interactions between individuals (their personalities), the organizations and institutions in which they live and work, and the larger environments which circumscribe both. To reaffirm, the concept of culture is particularly appropriate for studying the relationships between schools and their micro- and macro-environments (Dimmock and Walker, 1998b).

Hybridity of societal cultures

The discussion thus far has related to the shape, definition and influence of societal culture. Such issues are further complicated by the fact that, first, cultures are constantly shifting and, secondly, that cultural values seem to produce different effects at different times. Cultures are not static, moribund entities; rather, they are dynamic and invariably changing (Trice and Beyer, 1993). As Rizvi (1997) notes, with increasing globalization and population mobility, cultures can best be described as hybrids, constantly shifting, growing and developing as they encounter different ideas, new knowledge and changing circumstances. Following this assertion, Rizvi (1997, p. 22) claims: '(We) cannot know cultures in their pristine and authentic form. Instead, our focus must shift to the ways in which culture forms become separated and recombine with new forms in new practices in their local contexts.'

One increasingly important manifestation of the developing hybridity of cultures results from their changing multicultural nature, often caused by migration. Societies such as the USA, the UK and Australia are now truly multicultural, having experienced successive waves of immigrants from diverse cultures. Despite the tendency for particular groups to concentrate in certain communities, especially in large urban areas, the overall cultural impact on societies has been significant. Multicultural communities lead to multicultural schools and, consequently, the problems and challenges associated with providing a relevant and appropriate curriculum to children of diverse cultural backgrounds. While there may be an inclination to focus on the problems presented by such schools for teachers and school leaders – there is also a danger that potential benefits ensuing from culturally diverse schools may be forgotten or ignored. Such benefits include increased understanding of diverse cultures and of interrelationships between students and families of different cultural backgrounds. They also embrace greater awareness of differences in student learning, how values and attitudes vary between cultures and how the diversity of cultures can be harnessed to enrich school life (Walker and Walker, 1998). Hallinger and Leithwood (1996a, p. 6) capture the essence of this perspective: 'This trend toward multi-culturalism has implications for the management of schools and for the knowledge base of schools' leadership. It is crucial to understand better how schools productively can accommodate such diversity and the forms of leadership likely to assist such accommodation.' We address this issue more specifically in Chapter 11.

The constantly shifting composition of cultures makes investigation more troublesome, but does not negate the importance of identifying how it influences organizational behaviour in schools. As has been argued elsewhere, a deeper understanding of the influence of culture is predicated on the need to develop cross-cultural models, frameworks and taxonomies by which to compare schools within the same, and across different, systems (Dimmock and Walker, 1998a; Walker and Dimmock, 1999a; 2002a; see also Hallinger and Leithwood, 1996a). The use of frameworks using broad dimensions and common elements for analysis may, in fact, allow room for cultural forms to shift and develop, even though they unavoidably capture only a snapshot of cultural influences at a certain point in time.

Societal culture and contradictory effects

Researching culture is difficult because at different times the same values seem to produce very different effects. Pye (2000) shows this clearly using the example of 'Asian' values; values which have been used over the last decade to explain both the rapid economic rise of many South-east Asian economies and, conversely, the fragility and vulnerability of these very same economies. Pye uses two hypotheses in an attempt to explain this phenomenon. The first is that the same values operating in different contexts will produce different outcomes: 'That is, the values of the Asian cultures have remained the same but the contexts have changed, and hence what had been positive outcomes become negative ones' (p. 245). His second explanation is that clusters of cultural values can be combined at different times, in different ways, to produce differing effects. Pye concludes that it is impossible to establish any cause-and-effect relationship because of the number and complexity of variables involved and warns that cross-cultural researchers take great care when ascribing weights to specific cultural variables. His parting words signal caution to all cross-cultural researchers, especially in times of rapid change. 'We know that they (cultural variables) are important, but how important at any particular time is hard to judge. We are dealing with clouds, not clocks, with general approximations, not precise cause-and-effect relationships' (p. 254).

Cultural characteristics

The definitional problems associated with culture have the effect of muddying the waters for cross-cultural researchers, but literature in the area does offer some guidelines for consideration when studying culture. A good example of this is provided by Trice and Beyer (1993). Drawing on an extensive literature they list six major characteristics of culture which may be useful for the analysis of organization and management, and suggest that these most accurately capture the essence of culture. The first is that cultures are collective and cannot be produced by individuals acting alone. Rather, they emerge and are sustained through individuals interacting with each other and agreeing on certain values and practices. The second is that cultures are emotionally charged. In other words, cultures are steeped with emotion as well as meaning and, as such, cannot be considered purely rational in terms of either formation or adherence. The third characteristic is that cultures are historically based. Thus, a particular culture will not form overnight but will be based on a 'unique history of a particular group of people coping with a unique set of physical, social, political and economic circumstances' (p. 6). The fourth characteristic suggests that cultures are inherently symbolic, and the fifth that cultures are dynamic, because they are continually changing for various reasons. These include imperfect communication, individuality, unconscious transmission, and the imprecision of symbolism and changing environments. The sixth and final characteristic is that cultures are inherently fuzzy. They are not monolithic entities, but rather typified by 'contradiction, ambiguities, paradoxes, and just plain confusion' (p. 8).

Cultural context and differences of meaning

Since culture permeates all levels of society, it provides rich opportunities for researchers to explore the interrelationships between schools and their micro- and macro-environments (Dimmock, 2002). As promoted through the framework discussed in Chapter 2, studying the influence of societal culture is particularly rewarding at the level of the school, since it is here that the macro and micro levels of culture all interact at the point of policy implementation.

'Culture' is a particularly useful analytical concept in situations where the characteristics of different organizations appear on the surface to possess similarity, but are, in fact, quite different in their actual modus operandi. For example, schools in different societies often appear to have similar, formal leadership hierarchies and organizational structures, while subtle differences in values, relationships and processes are hidden or disguised (Walker and Dimmock, 2000a). Likewise, while different societies may appear to adopt the same policy agenda and framework, the meanings and interpretations each attaches to the core ideas and concepts may vary dramatically. These are important considerations for researchers, as the following illustrations demonstrate.

A policy shift towards school-based management and devolution has been gathering momentum in very different cultures and societies for the past two decades. Associated with these reforms in the management and organization of school systems are new configurations for curriculum, teaching and learning, as well as changes to assessment and evaluation. These are broad sweeping reform packages that are complex in affecting just about every part of an education system – its rules, roles and relationships. They are thus attractive themes for postgraduate research.

In the global push to introduce such measures, a new educational lexicon has been invented based on core concepts such as, 'school-based management', 'accountability', 'collaborative decision-making', 'appraisal', 'national curriculum', 'curriculum frameworks', 'outcomes curriculum', 'student-centred learning', 'school evaluation', 'constructivism', 'league tables', 'performance indicators', 'creativity' and 'quality schools'. Educators across the world – policy-makers, practitioners and researchers alike – increasingly communicate by using this lexicon. The problem is that often, without realization, educators in different cultures attribute different meanings and significance to the same core concepts and ideas. Researchers need to be alert, not only to how globalization spreads the same policy agenda across many societies, but also to how different cultures mediate the meanings and significance of these policies.

This latter point is well illustrated by the current press in many societies for a national curriculum based on student learning outcomes. In Britain, the National Curriculum was introduced in 1988 to replace a situation where each school and local authority exercised considerable discretion as to what was taught and how much time was allocated to each subject. Teaching, especially in primary schools, had come to rely on so-called progressive, student-centred methods. The aim of the British government, therefore, was to establish a clear and detailed prescribed curriculum specifying learning outcomes, where none existed before, and to pare back the progressive methods by advocating direct whole-class teaching and testing. Contrast this with Hong Kong, which already had a prescribed curriculum for many decades, though not one framed in terms of learning outcomes. In contrast to Britain, the problem in Hong Kong – as perceived by the Special Administrative Region (SAR) government – has been too great a reliance on direct whole-class teaching, too much standardization, insufficient attention to individual student differences and too little variation of teaching methods. While the push in both societies is towards a national curriculum based on learning outcomes, the means of achieving the aims is very different. Each is starting from a different position. Each culture attributes different importance and meanings to the same ideas.

Hong Kong, along with other Asian neighbours, aims to introduce more student-centred methods into its otherwise teacher-centred classrooms. Successive British governments, fearing that student-centredness has gone too far, have sought to introduce more basic education and direct teaching. At the policy level, the tendency is for each to move towards the other. In practice, however, culture along with other factors, makes this global tendency difficult to achieve.

If the foregoing analysis is continued, the practicality of student-centred methods is influenced by class size. Despite recent strong argument to reduce the number of students per class, class sizes in Hong Kong are typically 40 or 45, while in mainland China they can be 65 to 70. A question worth asking is – is it possible for Hong Kong or mainland Chinese teachers to practise student-centred learning? In addressing this question, Stevenson and Stigler (1992) show how Chinese teachers manage to combine both direct teaching and student-centredness in a uniquely Chinese style of teaching. They convincingly show that Chinese culture enables teachers to conduct lessons with very large classes and yet still attend to individual needs. Chinese culture is manifested in early childhood socialization in the family, preparing children to conform more readily to school authority and traditional teaching than do Western cultures, presenting few disruptive problems and enabling teachers to focus on learning. Home and school values seem to align more closely in Asian than Western societies, with ramifications for teaching. These issues are discussed further in Chapters 5 and 7.

Elsewhere, Watkins (2000) has argued that there are major cultural differences between Anglo-American and East Asian connotations of rote memorization and learning. The Western view of rote learning and memorization is derogatory, contrasting it with deep learning for understanding. In contrast, Watkins (2000) shows that for the Chinese student, memorization is highly valued as a necessary prior step towards learning for understanding. Chinese students typically learn in a different way from their Western counterparts.

Many other examples are to be found of how culture imparts different meanings and connotations to the same concept. 'Creativity' for example, takes on a different mantra in Singapore, where it is seen as a set of skills to be forged, than in the UK or the USA, where it is viewed as the product of 'free' expression and original thought. Likewise, the notion of appraisal assumes a different connotation in Chinese societies, such as Hong Kong, where the direct face-to-face exchange of views associated with Anglo-American cultures, is considered too threatening (Walker and Dimmock, 2000b).

The foregoing discussion is not exhaustive. Rather, its purpose is to illustrate how researchers, particularly in educational management and leadership need to take cognizance of how identical concepts, policies, ideas and behaviours may hide important differences in meaning and connotation, depending on their cultural context. Other important considerations for postgraduate and academic researchers, however, centre on the conduct of research in different cultural settings. This brings us to a discussion of the second of the two central themes of the chapter – a consideration of key issues in conducting future cross-cultural empirical research in educational settings.

Researching societal culture and school leadership

The issues discussed in the preceding sections reflect some of conceptual problems facing researchers when framing and defining studies addressing culture, debating appropriate methodologies and attempting meaningful comparison. The following issues touch upon some of the more pragmatic methodological concerns.

The minimal comparative research currently being conducted in school leadership and administration tends to be Western-centric, superficial and stereotypical in its approach to understanding school personnel in particular contexts or from particular ethnic backgrounds. Furthermore, such research tends to assume the form of separate country (culture) studies of, for example, school leaders and leadership, rather than more systematic rigorous and authentic analytic comparison. This is not to say that such studies are not useful – they certainly are – but they can tend to paint overly stark distinctions without enough consideration of the values and beliefs underpinning the systems and associated behaviours. Recent international surveys conducted on national differences in student achievement (see Reynolds, 2000) well illustrate these pitfalls.

The focus of these studies has been the extent to which 'effective' practices at school and classroom level are the same or are different in different countries. Cohorts of children at specific ages are used as the database. Studies such as The Third International Mathematics and Science Study (TIMSS), or the numerous studies conducted by the International Association for the Education of Evaluation Achievement (IEA), are achievement tests to provide data on the effectiveness level of schools and national systems. It is clear from these studies that the Pacific-Rim societies such as Taiwan, Korea, Japan and Singapore are superior in their education achievement (according to the criteria set by the research). While such studies provide important comparisons, the cultural and cross-cultural explanations remain highly speculative. For example, reasons postulated for superior performance of Pacific-Rim countries include the high status given to teachers, the value placed on learning and education, and the cultural stress on the role of effort, and high aspirations of parents for their children reflecting 'Confucian' beliefs. However, these remain speculative and much more needs to be considered in connecting these characteristics to school performance.

Indeed, the growing interest in international comparisons of student achievement has given rise to a tendency on the part of some to advocate the adoption of 'effective' practices from particularly the Pacific-Rim countries to English-speaking Western countries. While on the grounds of school improvement this tendency is understandable – and even laudable – it should be approached with great caution. It raises problems with regard to the extent to which these 'effective' practices are culture based. If they are culture sensitive, then recommendations that a particular policy or practice be transposed from one society to another must surely take into account the full cultural and contextual conditions of both societies and their respective educational systems.

A further concern relates to identifying which of the school improvement factors mentioned in the cross-national studies are in fact related to culture. For example, is the fact that Korean and Taiwanese students spend 222 days in school a year (Reynolds, 2000), compared to 192 days for students in England, a cultural or an institutional phenomenon? Furthermore, even if it is an institutional factor, it may ultimately be cultural.

Yet another consideration is the adoption of research methods and tools from other fields, such as cross-cultural psychology and international business management, and the almost complete absence of a methodology for cross-cultural comparison developed within educational administration. There is growing criticism that many of the research tools and concepts used in cross-cultural exploration outside education may not be appropriate to education or to all cultures. Besides the issues of methodological validity, there is also the issue of the appropriateness and respective merits of qualitative and quantitative methods to researching cultural matters.

In the case of qualitative methods, the major issue concerns the almost complete absence of their application to the field of cross-cultural educational administration and leadership. However, we believe that there are promising avenues to be explored within the interpretivist paradigm through the use of narratives, case studies and interviews, and more generally through symbolic interactionist perspectives, emphasizing the perspectives and meanings attributed to school leaders' actions in different cultures. In regard to quantitative approaches, more sophisticated statistical methods developed recently open up the possibility of new insights into cross-cultural study of school leadership. Structural equation modelling, for example, has been advocated by Fidler (2001, pp. 53–54) 'as a way of understanding the connections between intermediate variables', and, as Heck (1998) notes, seems ideally suited to capture data on key interrelationships found between the societal culture, subcultural (regional/local) and organizational levels (Heck, 1996; 1998; 2002). Heck suggests that recent advances in statistical techniques hold the potential to overcome some of the problems associated with pursuing comparison using structural-functionalist models. He explains thus: 'Such techniques allow researchers to investigate models across groups (e.g., schools or cultural settings) or between organisational levels (e.g., classes within schools within districts) and cultural layers (e.g., schools within communities within cultural settings)' (Heck, 2002, p. 81). Some recent empirical studies have applied such techniques to a deeper understanding of school leadership, including the application of structural equation modelling to the study of school leadership and the role of the head of department in Hong Kong secondary schools (Au, Wright and Botton, 2003), and the cross-cultural study of the relative effects of transformational leadership practice on organizational learning outcomes by Lam (2002), through the use of such statistical methods as hierarchical regression analysis.

It is undoubtedly the case, however, that cross-cultural exploration of educational leadership can learn from developments in other fields and disciplines, such as international business, psychology, anthropology, sociology and culture studies (see Brislin, 1993). Researchers in these fields have faced and addressed, to varying degrees, many of the problems now facing cross-cultural researchers in educational leadership and administration. For example, in an expansive review of the field of comparative management theory, Redding (1994) concluded that although the plethora of research in the area remained remarkably confused, there was agreement that research needed to move away from positivism (descriptive) towards ethno-science (interpretative) and from ideographic micro-analytic theory towards more nomothetic theory-building approaches. Our own efforts to address these methodological trends focuses on the development of a mixed methodology, relying on the development and application of a number of data collection techniques. For an excellent discussion of key issues related to methodology it is worth referring to Heck (2002). In his discussion he provides an overview of the different paradigms and methodologies available. When selecting among these, cross-cultural researchers must carefully consider the context within which they are working.

A host of factors related to culture warrant consideration at the early stage of designing a research study. For example, there might be a tradition of using one research paradigm rather than another in certain societies. And even within the same paradigm, some research methods might be more difficult to apply in certain cultures than others. For example, within the interpretivist paradigm, we have encouraged postgraduate students in Hong Kong to adopt the life history approach. These attempts have usually met with only partial success because of a reticence on the part of potential participants to talk openly about themselves, their life histories and the lives of others. Similarly, many subjects and respondents may be reluctant to participate in studies that involve their criticism of authority or government. In addition, cultural differences can account for why certain research paradigms or methodological approaches are particularly inappropriate in some settings. The adoption of a critical perspective or a feminist perspective in Singapore, for example, might be a case in point.

A further consideration is the preference for a particular research methodology or paradigm that researchers in some cultures display. In many developing countries and some developed societies, such as Hong Kong, the preference for quantitative methods over qualitative is quite apparent. Among explanations suggested for this phenomenon in the case of Hong Kong is the alleged aptitude that Chinese students seem to have for mathematics and statistics (a rather tenuous argument often based on the superior performance of East Asian societies on international achievement tests at school). Others have attributed a penchant for mathematics and figures to the Chinese language and its construction of characters based on symbols, while yet others account for it by recognizing that the Chinese prefer to think synthetically and to gain the 'big picture' (hence, to undertake large sampling from which generalizations can be made), whereas Westerners allegedly tend to think analytically and creatively. With the recent expansion of higher education in Hong Kong, however, there is now a growing awareness of, and desire to learn more about, qualitative research methods in educational leadership.

Besides the marked preference for quantitative studies in such cultures, there is also a tendency to focus on policy and descriptive, system-wide studies, a phenomenon recognized by Vulliamy, Lewin and Stephens (1990). Comparative studies of a macro-system level in educational management typify this phenomenon. School-level and classroom-level research, especially of an empirical kind, is less prevalent and case studies of individual principals and teachers are a rarity. There are many promising avenues for future research projects in these latter areas.

A more pragmatic research problem encountered by researchers interested in comparative cross-cultural studies is that of gaining access. In fact, conducting research in some cultural contexts can present significant access problems for even the most experienced academic researcher. In some schools considered 'highly researchable' access might be difficult because so many researchers wish to study them. They become 'over-researched' and access may be denied simply because of disruption to normal school life. There is always the need for researchers to cultivate good relationships with potential participants and, where possible, to offer them some benefit in return for their willingness to participate.

Such problems are relatively minor, however, when compared with the challenges of researching in countries such as Vietnam and mainland China. There, research in school management and leadership is often seen as 'intrusive', the more so if the researcher is from outside the country. School principals, in particular, are extremely sensitive to requests to collect data in their schools for fear of upsetting their superiors; teachers are equally sensitive for much the same reason. Normally, for example, successful access to mainland schools requires the penetration of an elaborate bureaucratic network, highly trusted co-operative relationships with eminent local academics and bureaucrats, and even the payment of fees.

Engaging in research projects in some cultures – even if they are for personal masters or doctoral theses – may require the permission of government authorities. Such is the case in Singapore. Large bureaucracies are not the easiest of organizations to pierce unless key people in prominent positions are known. Even when government bureaucracies do respond positively by granting permission for a research study to proceed, they may insist on changes to the research design that fundamentally weaken it. For example, the authorities may insist that a large sample be reduced in size before it can proceed, with the effect that generalization is rendered impossible. Gaining the willing participation of respondents may also present a problem in cultures where power, influence and status are of great importance. In societies such as Saudi Arabia, Israel and China, participation is more likely if the researcher is perceived by the respondents to have power, standing and status. In such circumstances it is useful if postgraduate students can enlist allies with some influence in the system. Such alliances may best be formed between researchers from differing cultural backgrounds.

In conducting research on educational management and leadership that takes societal culture into account, a key issue concerns the researcher's understanding of the particular culture(s) being studied. This is less of a problem where the culture of the researcher and the education system under investigation are the same. One would expect a native to possess a full appreciation of his or her own culture. Against this, however, is the view that people can be 'blind' to some aspects of their own culture and can take for granted many otherwise interesting characteristics, thus failing to give them due recognition. 'Outsider' researchers also present problems in possibly lacking detailed knowledge and appreciation of the indigenous culture. As Lauder (2000) asserts when describing comparative, cultural research in education: 'There is an experiential component necessary to good comparative research. It involves ... a range of cognitive and emotional understandings that enable individuals to get "beneath the skin" of another culture. In turn, this raises all the problems about the difficulties of translation' (p. 466).

On the other hand, 'outsiders' may bring a 'fresh' perspective, one which may not only highlight key aspects of a particular culture, but recognize salient differences between it and other cultures. A way of capitalizing on the strengths of both 'insider' and 'outsider' researcher is to bring both together in cross-cultural teams. There may be difficulties of language and communication in such teams, especially initially, but these may ease over the course of time.

Summary and conclusion

In this chapter we have attempted to introduce a number of key problems pertinent to using culture as a basis for the study of educational leadership across societies. Although we have not covered the entire range of possible problems, those discussed certainly communicate the need for caution before conducting further research in the area.

The chapter has covered two broad but interconnected themes. The first attempted to unravel no less than ten problematic conceptual issues related to the study of culture, including the difficulties in defining societal culture, its shifting and dynamic nature, and its complex links with socio-political influences, organizational culture and subculture, along with links to individual motivation. It has also been emphasized that although different societal cultures have a shared lexicon of cultural (and related) terms, there are major differences between societies in the underlying meaning and understanding ascribed to such concepts. It is for this reason that the lessons gained from research studies in one cultural setting should not automatically be adopted elsewhere as normative and universally prescribed solutions to the challenges facing educational leadership in all contexts and situations. This point was aptly illustrated with reference to the limitations of recent international research into school effectiveness.

The second theme focused on the practicalities of carrying out cross-cultural research into educational leadership. The respective strengths and limitations of both qualitative and quantitative research paradigms were considered, with a case made in favour of a plurality of approaches, ensuring fitness for purpose. At a more basic level, it was also pointed out that researchers are likely to face formidable ethical barriers and difficulties of access to educational institutions in some countries where there has been less openness or a suspicion that educational research may be construed as critical of current leadership and management practice. It is for this reason that cross-cultural research teams are advocated for the future, not only to assist with the challenges of language and communication, but to avoid potential cultural ambiguities and misunderstandings and facilitate wider access.

The next chapter moves from the broader perspective of societal culture and its various ramifications to a discussion of the concept of organizational culture, with particular reference to schools as organizations and the implications for school leadership from a cross-cultural perspective.

4
Leadership and Organizational Culture

The discussion thus far has focused primarily on the wider perspective of societal culture and its implications for schools as organizations. Two broadly opposing views of the impact of societal culture were explored, namely (a) the *institutionalist perspective*, supporting the view that there is a trend towards a convergence of institutional cultures through leadership and management responses to global forces and universal requirements, (b) the *culturalist perspective*, by contrast, emphasizing divergence as a consequence of the influence of the complex interplay between organizations and their wider social and geopolitical environments. A case was made for not concentrating exclusively on either approach. We also argued the need to explore more fully the issue of cross-cultural leadership, and some of the methodological problems and challenges in achieving this were considered.

The purpose of this chapter is to focus more specifically on culture at the level of the school as an organization and to consider its implications for school leadership from a cross-cultural perspective. First, we selectively review relevant literature on organizational culture. This is followed by an outline of a model based on six dimensions for the framing of organizational culture – a model which we argue has the potential to address some of the cross-cultural and ethnocentric limitations of more traditional approaches. Finally, the more practical implications of applying the model to empirical research in cross-cultural school leadership are considered.

The concept of organizational culture

From the discussion in previous chapters, it is apparent that culture has a major function in binding social groups together. From a sociological perspective, it has been defined in terms of the 'symbolic and learned, non-biological aspects of human society' (Abercrombie et al., 1994), including:

- *customs*: the traditions and shared values and belief systems of society;
- *language*: the medium of transmission of those shared values as the basis of ideology and discourse; and
- *convention*: the norms, rules and social protocols of what is widely regarded as socially acceptable and unacceptable behaviour.

Expressed in these terms, culture is a normative concept, with the underlying assumption that there is a common or dominant culture within society acting as a force for social consensus. This is also reflected in the conceptualization of organizational culture. Mirroring the perceived cohesive social impact of custom, language and convention, Schein (1985) argues that organizational culture has three critical constituents:

- shared learning;
- manifestations of shared learning that are stable; and
- a capacity for integrating disparate elements into a whole.

Organizational culture as an essentially unifying force is also emphasized by other observers. Bush (1998), for example, makes reference to 'shared organizational meanings', characterized by shared values, beliefs and norms, underpinned by rituals and ceremonies and the celebration of institutional heroes and heroines, whose achievements exemplify the values and beliefs of the organization. Ogbonna (1993) goes further in suggesting that organizational culture is 'the interweaving of the individual into the community and the collective programming of the mind' (p. 42). This conception places considerable emphasis on the socialization of individuals, especially those new to the organization, into the norms and values of the organizational community. Such a process reinforces group or institutional identity. In a word, organizational culture is seen as the 'social glue' (Seihl, quoted by Prosser, 1999, p. 10) that binds the community of the organization together. The overt features of organizational culture can therefore be perceived as the shared values and behavioural norms which pervade the organization (Saphier and King, 1985). How this operates varies from organization to organization.

Many typologies of organizational culture have been developed. Handy and Aitken (1986), for example, provide a fourfold classification of organizational culture, which has been applied to schools. The 'club' culture brings about social cohesion through a process likened to a spider's web, with the leader at the centre attracting like-minded individuals into the inner circle of central management and control. This has much in keeping with the small organization directed by the powerful charismatic leader and the leadership of private schools anxious to recruit new staff into the 'club' who have an appropriate social background – in all probability privately and Oxbridge educated. The 'role' culture is seen to predominate in large, complex bureaucratic organizations, including large comprehensive state or public schools, characterized by hierarchical structures and meticulously defined roles and responsibilities. 'Task' cultures, on the other hand, describe those organizations which prioritize collaborative decision-making through the creation of task groups, working parties and cross-sectional teams to address specific organizational challenges. Such cultures are associated with more flexible leadership and management structures and have come to characterize an increasing number of schools during periods of turbulence and rapid educational change. The fourth type of organizational culture – the 'person' culture – describes the cultural norms of those professions where the emphasis is on individual professional autonomy rather than on teamwork (for example in the legal and medical professions). Although teachers have traditionally been associated with individual and autonomous working behind closed classroom doors, the applicability of the 'person' culture to educational organizations is now less convincing as more recent trends towards the sharing of good practice, teamwork and staff appraisal have tended to shift school cultures from individualistic to more collectivist norms.

Studies of organizational culture, as illustrated from the examples cited above, have tended to focus on shared values and organizational structures as forces for uniformity and social cohesion. On closer inspection, organizations are also highly complex and diverse conglomerations made up of individuals and groups divided into subcultures with lines of demarcation frequently reinforced by formal organizational structures, such as student ability grouping and the creation of distinct subject departments or faculties. At the micro level organizations therefore appear to be fragmented into subcultures, which sometimes exist alongside each other in harmony, sometimes in conflict. The distinction between *culture* and *subculture* is a useful one for understanding the social milieu of organizations. On the one hand, the concept of culture can help make sense of such related concepts as organizational consensus, shared values and transformational leadership. On the other, the concept of *subculture* provides the basis for understanding organizational diversity, group identity, conflict and micro-political processes. Such organizational division through subculture can be illustrated with reference to at least three examples drawn from the study of schools as organizations: the relationship between social class and educational opportunity, the division of school staffing structures into academic departments or faculties and the impact of multiculturalism. While exploring each of the three in more detail below, the examples also show how in many cases societal culture and organizational culture (and subcultures) interact.

The relationship between social class and educational opportunity is well known from the various sociological studies of Bourdieu (1977) and Bourdieu and Passeron (1990) on the reproduction and perpetuation of social inequality through the education system. According to Bourdieu, each social class has its own set of meanings and values or cultural framework, which is transmitted to new generations through a process of socialization within the social framework of the family unit. People are thus the product of what is termed *habitus* (the habitual practices, assumptions, values and aspirations of a particular social environment or subculture in which they are raised). Thus for children from relatively affluent and privileged home backgrounds, *habitus* provides 'cultural capital' in the form of supportive, educated parents and a family environment conducive to educational stimulation. The effect is a 'differential take-up of the knowledge that schools formally offer' (Morrison, 2002, p. 26) and continuing divisions in educational achievement between children from middle- and working-class backgrounds, much to the continuing disadvantage of the latter for whom school frequently represents an alien culture. It is against this backdrop that Thrupp (2001) has criticized the preoccupation of school effectiveness research with 'school organization' over 'social composition'. Given the impact of student social composition on so-called school effectiveness, it stands to reason that 'solidly middle class schools have strongly supportive student cultures which allow them to teach an academic, exam-based curriculum and to organise and manage themselves relatively smoothly, while working class schools will, in general, be quite opposite' (Thrupp, 2001, p. 27). Indeed, 'as a school becomes more working class ... it can be predicted that the processes of the school will shift, despite resistance from middle class teachers and students, towards the culture of the increasingly working class groups' (Thrupp, 2001, p. 26).

Turning to the second example, the fragmentation of schools into academic subject departments has been identified as an organizational structure conducive to 'Balkanization' and interdepartmental rivalry, especially in terms of competition for influence, prestige and the preferential acquisition of scarce resources. Ball (1987), for example, has compared the sectional interests of heads of departments with those of 'baronial fiefdoms', motivated more by the needs and priorities of their own departments than the welfare of the school as a whole. Departmental divisions can be explained in part through the identification of distinct organizational subcultures. The work of Siskin (1994; 1997) on subject departments in American high schools is especially illuminating in this respect. Subject departments are described as 'critical sites for teachers' sense of identity, practice and professional community, deeply woven into the social, political and intellectual workings of the profession and of individual schools' (Siskin, 1997, p. 605). Discrete subject cultures are the basis of both perceived 'discipline-based differences' and distinct 'micro-political units'. They not only determine what teachers teach but also how they teach – the very epistemological essence of what they understand teaching and learning to be. In the words of Siskin, 'the subject is not merely an activity ... it is an identity' (p. 611). This cultural identity is reinforced by what she describes as 'microclimates' – the very context in which staff live and work, invariably consolidated around department bases and frequently isolated with the consequence that within-school differences can be as strong as across-school ones. Department leaders as individuals can also exert considerable influence in their styles of leadership and variations in the way they perceive their roles and responsibilities.

The third example draws attention to the major influence of ethnic diversity and multiculturalism on the organizational culture of schools. In the UK context, ethnic diversity and multiculturalism have long been recognized as key challenges for schools, but the issues raised by the Swann Report (DES, 1985) received little if any attention in the Education Reform Act (1988) or the major changes which followed, including the establishment of the National Curriculum and the local management of schools. The MacPherson Report (1999) on the inquiry into the murder of Stephen Lawrence has placed most of these issues back on the agenda, but there are also global trends which have created what Johnson (2003) refers to as the 'diversity imperative', including the impact of globalization and the migration of refugees and asylum seekers from conflict and persecution in the Third World. The inclusion of children from such diverse cultural and ethnic backgrounds into European schools adds greatly to the complexity and diversity of organizational culture already described simply in terms of social class differences and Bourdieu's cultural capital thesis. Children from such diverse backgrounds will be accustomed to different cultural ways of knowing, ranging from individualistic cultures (with an emphasis on independence and the success of the individual) to collectivist cultures (with an emphasis on interdependence and the success of the group). There will also be negative issues to be faced, such as prejudice, racism, discrimination and inter-group conflict, all of which have clear implications for teaching, learning, curriculum development and pupil support. Priorities will need to be focused on team-building, tolerance-building, conflict resolution and awareness-raising, both for staff and for students. Teaching and learning styles will need to be sufficiently flexible to ensure that schools become more interculturally responsive. Close links with parents and community members from culturally diverse backgrounds will also be necessary to foster dialogue and cross-cultural understanding.

Organizational culture, including that of schools, may be conceptualized along a continuum, ranging from relatively unitary and homogeneous to relatively diverse and heterogeneous. Where any particular school is located along the continuum will depend on a number of factors, including the type of school and its location. However, what has been emphasized is that schools generally are likely to become more culturally diverse and highly complex organizations. This assessment has major implications for the nature of school leadership.

The implications for school leadership and management

The twin concepts of organizational culture and subculture pose a dilemma. As we saw in the previous section, organizational culture is more generally conceptualized in terms of its unifying properties, whereas organizational subcultures are more often conceptualized in terms of group diversity with a potential for creating institutional disunity and fragmentation. It is for this reason that Meek (1988, p. 453) rejects the presumption 'that there exists in a real and tangible sense a collective organizational culture that can be created, measured and manipulated in order to enhance organizational effectiveness'.

Nevertheless, there is a growing recognition that school culture holds the key to the effective management of change and school improvement. Rutter et al. (1979, p. 179), for example, identified school ethos as 'more powerful than that of any particular teacher, school policies or indeed behaviour of dominant pupils', while Schein (1985, p. 2) has suggested that 'the only task of a leader is to manage an institution's culture'. In the words of Hopkins (1993, p. 14):

> In many of our successful schools, there is a recognition that the social aspects of change are at least as important as the technical emphasis on prioritisation and strategic planning. It is through such an approach to school development that recognises the social complexity of change that some schools are managing to achieve quality in times of change.

Effective school leadership and management are therefore seen in terms of their capacity to build strong institutional cultures based on shared values conducive to promoting collaboration in enhancing quality, especially in teaching and learning, thus bringing about school improvement. Stoll (1999) argues that school culture can either be a 'black hole' or a 'fertile garden' for school improvement. In the case of the 'black hole', the culture of the organization imposes 'situational constraints' on change and improvement, including: the micro-politics of subcultures and Balkanization; the subversion of whole-school initiatives by groups or individuals; and inter-group competition, conflict and struggle. Based on this framework, Stoll and Fink (1996) provide a cultural classification of schools according to a matrix constructed along two axes: *effective* versus *ineffective*, and *improving* versus *declining*. Schools which are deemed both effective and improving are described as 'moving' (what might be exemplified in the so-called 'beacon' schools), while at the opposite extreme, those which are classified as both ineffective and declining are described as 'sinking', typified by schools with weak leadership and low staff morale which are placed under 'special measures'. Intermediate categories include 'cruising' schools, seen as effective but declining (including some traditional grammar schools basking in former glory but finding difficulty in adapting to change) and 'struggling' schools, which are currently ineffective but nevertheless showing signs of improvement in responding positively to the challenges that they face, often in areas of significant social disadvantage and deprivation. (A fifth category – that of the 'strolling' school – does not seem to fit the matrix in that such schools are neither improving nor declining; nor can they be said to be effective or ineffective.) Such a categorization is undoubtedly crude and controversial, but it does serve as a cultural map of school differences and indicates very strongly that cultural differences will in turn necessitate differential strategies in effecting school improvement.

If schools are to improve, then significant across-the-board transformations need to take place. There is a need to understand the dynamic relationship between school cultures and change management to ensure improvement through a process of 'reculturing', defined as 'the process of developing new values, beliefs and norms ... [involving] building new conceptions about instruction ... and new forms of professionalism for teachers' (Fullan, quoted in Stoll, 1999, p. 46). Stoll (1999, p. 44) outlines the process as follows. First, understanding the school's culture, is 'a prerequisite for any external change agent'. This involves assessing the current culture and then working towards positive cultural norms. Consideration should be given to how the current culture encourages or inhibits pupil progress. Opportunities should then be provided for people to re-examine their values through discussion and a direct confrontation of the perceived problems. Secondly, the leadership role of the principal will be vital in generating the process of change through providing vision, purpose and direction. Thirdly, *reculturing*, or 'normative re-education' strategies will then need to be put in place, including the clarification and reconstruction of values, improving the problem-solving capacity of staff and establishing supportive structures. However, the process of reculturing must encompass the values and attitudes of all stakeholders, not just teaching staff: 'Reculturing ... needs to go beyond redefining teacher cultures; it must include pupil and community cultures as well. Pupils can be a conservative force when teachers attempt to change their practice ... Similarly ... communities are often resistant to change ... Change agents must therefore attend to both' (Stoll, 1999, p. 47).

In discussing the leadership and development of cultural change within schools, David Hargreaves (1999) provides a number of strategic insights which complement Stoll's notion of *reculturing*:

- first changing behaviour as changes in attitude follow suit; for example, by persuading people to adopt, perhaps on a trial basis, some new way of working;
- devising supportive structures: (a) physical (for example the layout of classrooms); (b) social and organizational (for example the distribution of power, authority and status);
- monitoring the effects and penetration of cultural change, ensuring that beneficial effects are taking place at all levels of the organization, including what goes on in the classroom;
- importing assistance, which has the advantages of: (a) legitimizing programmes for change; (b) providing help at the teacher level; (c) diverting some of the blame if some things do not work out; (d) helping to foster a climate of collaboration and experimentation; and
- ensuring that the unique qualities of the school culture are preserved by following the principles of *logical incrementalism*: 'the organization probes

the future, experiments, and learns from a series of partial, incremental commitments rather than global formulations and total strategies' (Quinn, quoted in Hargreaves, 1999, p. 64).

Hargreaves concludes by arguing that success depends on three deep capabilities that lie at the core of the organization: a *monitoring capability*, scanning the school's internal and external environment, 'linking internal self-evaluation to external potentialities' (p. 65); a *proactive capability*, looking ahead positively and relishing a challenge with optimism and confidence; and a *resource deployment capability*, auditing the full range of resources (human, intellectual, material and financial) and directing them effectively to goal achievement.

Bush (1998, p. 42) summarizes the prescriptions of a number of other writers for managing cultural change effectively, including Turner (1990), Limb (1994) and Bridge (1994). Much of what they say confirms the claims of Stoll (1999) and Hargreaves (1999), but a number of additional observations from these sources are worth noting:

- the provision of effective leadership that ensures clarity of purpose and vision, coupled with sustained development through reflection and creative thinking;
- picking out people in key roles for training to act as catalysts in the process of cultural change;
- making a start by working in areas where there is likely to be least resistance;
- confidence-building through staff support and guidance, thus generating the capacity for sustained change and development; and
- striking the optimal balance between *maintenance* and *development*.

In the words of Bridge (quoted in Bush, 1998, p. 42):

> [It is] dangerous ... for managers to move too fast on cultural change. Many of us have observed ... the damaging effect upon college cultures of management initiatives that are fast, too autocratic, or involve changes that are too radical. The resulting damage to colleges is great as they fail to respond and overheat, with resulting entrenchment of existing cultures and staff returning to the values they always held.

Much of what has been written about the links between organizational culture and school improvement is consistent with the principles of the *learning organization*. From various general organizational studies (for example, Garvin, 1993; Marsick and Watkins, 1999; Senge, 1993) and a number focused specifically on schools as organizations (see Aspinwall and Pedlar, 1997; Southworth, 1994), organizational learning has been equated with organizational cultures characterized by transformational and distributed leadership which encourages open dialogue, clear lines of communication and collaborative decision-making; supports initiative, enterprise and risk-taking; invests heavily in continued professional development that is congruent with organizational needs and systems thinking; and promotes 'double-loop', as opposed to 'single-loop', learning that challenges and keeps under constant review those organizational norms and values that are apt to be taken for granted, especially in times of rapid change.

The importance of the leadership and management functions of transforming organizational culture from a 'black hole' to a 'fertile garden' of school effectiveness and school improvement is undeniable. However, translating the rhetoric into reality is unlikely to be as straightforward as some school effectiveness researchers have suggested. Despite more than half a century of comprehensive education, the gap in pupil achievement on the basis of socio-economic status remains, thus adding weight to the notion of cultural capital. In respect to department subcultures, Siskin (1997) draws attention to the continued frustration of American high school principals in promoting whole-school, systemic thinking, despite various efforts ranging from attempts to break departmental boundaries by creating new structures and initiatives to breach barriers, through an emphasis on instructional leadership and awareness-raising, to building bridges, as in promoting cross-departmental projects and creating interdisciplinary task forces. Moreover, if the notion of the school as a learning organization is to be more than an aspirational ideal, then a number of practical difficulties need to be tackled. There are, for instance, a number of key issues of direct relevance to the creation of the learning school which have scarcely been researched. These include:

1 Workplace learning

The literature on workplace and lifelong learning offers a range of theories on how people learn, as individuals, in groups and in a situated or contextual way (see Boud and Garrick, 1999; Lave and Wenger, 1991); but the theories remain controversial and lack sufficient supporting empirical evidence. Furthermore, these theories cannot be easily transferred from a variety of workplace contexts to the learning of teachers in the school or college workplace. As Foskett and Lumby (2003, p. 175) point out, teacher workplace learning requires the development of specific theoretical models. It is only through first deepening our understanding of how teachers learn in the context of the workplace that we can hope to refine our understanding of the processes that are conducive to the development of schools and colleges as learning organizations.

2 Empirical research

Not only is there very little by way of theories on the collective learning of teachers (a central tenet of the concept of the learning organization), but there is also a lack of empirical research studies specifically focused on schools or colleges as learning organizations. More empirical work on the lines carried out by Southworth (1994) on organizational learning in primary schools needs to be conducted in order to fill this gap in our current knowledge of school improvement.

3 Cultural match

In taking an international perspective, it can be said that the concept of the learning organization is a helpful one in certain cultural contexts. In *low power-distance cultures*, such as the USA or New Zealand, or in countries where there has been a substantial shift in power-distance (for example South Africa), the concept appears to have generated more interest, because such cultures are more consistent with the egalitarian principles of the learning organization, such as critical reflection and double-loop learning, collegiality and participation in decision-making. However, this is less likely to be the case in *high power-distance cultures*, with an expectation of authority and decision-making on the part of senior managers and tight control of learners by staff. Reference has been made earlier to the example of Chinese society as a replicative system, in which 'as a consequence of conflict avoidance and of the requirement for harmonic relationships, decisions and policies are seldom challenged or approached creatively by the group' (Dimmock, 2000a, p. 266). However, there is also much conflict avoidance and unquestioned support of senior managers in Western cultures, whether motivated by professional loyalty or by self-interest. The reluctance to question and to challenge underlying norms and values (central to the notion of double-loop learning) is a serious barrier to what Argyris and Schön (1978) describe as *deep* organizational learning and may require a transformation of cultural norms.

There is a further difficulty in respect to the question of leadership for diversity and multicultural schools. It is far from clear to what extent the more traditional and conventional leadership and management theories are appropriate to organizations characterized by the diversity – as opposed to the homogeneity – of their cultures. The assumptions underlying much leadership training for diversity have rarely been questioned with the result that there is little if any consensus on best practice in the field of 'intercultural competence' (Rosenstreich, 2003). Before school leaders are trained in intercultural competence, it is also imperative that answers are found to at least three basic – and yet still unresolved – questions. First, what is meant by multiculturalism? Second, who should have the authority in deciding what it should mean? And, third, how should it be valued and celebrated? (Yuval-Davis, 1999). Answers to such questions are complicated by the fact that cultures and identities are not necessarily fixed, but rather dynamic and syncretic, and by feminist challenges to notions of patriarchal ethnic community leaders as the determinants of 'real' minority group culture.

We are only beginning to fully appreciate the challenges and training implications facing principals entrusted with the leadership of multicultural schools made up of diverse staff and student populations. Empirical studies suggest that effective leadership for diversity can be developed to some extent within a traditional theoretical framework of leadership. The Leading for Diversity Research (LDR) Project in California from 1996 (Henze, 2000; Norte, 1999), which provides case study evidence of effective leadership for diversity in American 21 schools, draws a number of conclusions about effective leadership that are consistent with the principles of transformational leadership and effective human resource management (HRM), including establishing a shared vision of equity and justice through dialogue and negotiation and creating organizational structures to facilitate collaboration between members of the school community. Smith (1997, pp. 8–10) also emphasizes the fact that effective diversity management should be consistent with the basic tenets of good team management, including the total quality management (TQM) principles of involving stakeholders, good planning, building trust and effective communication.

However, there is also growing evidence that effective organizational leadership for cultural diversity requires an 'intercultural communicative competence' that transcends conventional leadership models (Dreachslin, Hunt and Sprainer, 2000). Moreover, DiTomaso and Hooijberg (1996) suggest a need to examine the assumptions underlying current models of leadership on the grounds that they pay insufficient attention to dealing with the emotions or structures and processes whereby visions are transformed into reality. What has become evident from longitudinal studies on the life cycles of diverse teams is the need to place greater initial emphasis on 'emergent interpersonal leadership activities' to build trust and break down barriers as a prerequisite to accomplishing team project tasks (Watson, Johnson and Zgourides, 2002). Chen and Van Velsor (1996) provide a useful composite model for diversity competency and leadership effectiveness, central to which are the development of three key types of interrelated skills: *motivational* (a value orientation towards others and a willingness to work towards building harmonious relationships); *cognitive* (the acquisition of knowledge and an understanding of the cultural values and norms of diverse groups); and *behavioural* (the skills of working with others from diverse backgrounds and value orientations).

In respect to the internal leadership and management of personnel, the behavioural skills are elaborated by Smith (1997) and Dreachslin, Hunt and Sprainer (2000). They include efforts to reduce isolation between diverse groups and a willingness to engage in positive discussion about differences through full and active participation among team members, while discouraging potentially negative behaviours. This requires a willingness to listen, to respect and to validate different perspectives and alternative realities. It is only through bringing such issues into the open (as opposed to ignoring or denying differences of perception) that misunderstandings can be corrected and mutual trust and a unity of purpose established. These principles equally apply in managing diversity within the community of service users. In the words of Shields, Laroque and Oberg (2002, p. 132) 'a community of difference ... begins, not with an assumption of shared norms, beliefs and values, but with a need for respect, dialogue and understanding'. The acquisition of the key motivational, cognitive and behavioural leadership skills provides the foundations for relationship building which in turn holds the key to leadership effectiveness. In short, effective leaders of culturally diverse organizations are 'people developers', both at the individual and the group level, helping subordinates to work more effectively with diverse others. The leaders teach diversity competencies to their associates: as role models, sponsors, mentors and demonstrators of outstanding team leadership qualities (Chen and Van Velsor, 1996).

Significant strides have been made in achieving a better understanding of those school qualities needed for the effective leadership of culturally diverse organizations including multicultural schools. But we are still far from establishing a sound theoretical base on which further empirical research can be systematically carried out. First, the complex interplay between the respective influences of: (a) organizational culture and systemic thinking, (b) group subculture and sectional loyalty, and (c) human agency and individual choice of action, independent of either institutional or group pressures to cultural conformity, have scarcely been researched. Secondly, leadership models developed in Western countries, including transformational leadership and human resource management, are insufficient in themselves to take account of the complexities of: (a) cultural diversity *within* organizations; (b) cultural diversity *across* organizations located in different societies influenced by contrasting traditions and educational values.

In order to address these limitations, an alternative, more comprehensive paradigm is proposed as a starting point for the investigation of school leadership and organizational culture within an international, comparative and cross-cultural framework. Based on the work of Hofstede (1991), this six dimensions model is outlined in the following section.

Six dimensions of organizational culture

Notwithstanding the cultural complexity of many organizations, especially those which are both large and socially diverse, it can be argued that qualitative differences between organizational and societal culture stem from the fact that national cultures differ mostly at the level of basic values, while organizational cultures differ mostly at the level of more superficial practices, as reflected in the recognition of particular symbols, heroes, and rituals (Hofstede, 1991). This allows organizational cultures to be managed and changed, whereas national cultures are more enduring and change only gradually over long time periods, if at all. Research studies on the organizational cultures of companies found large differences in their practices (symbols, heroes, rituals), but only minor differences in their values (Hofstede, 1995). Six dimensions were found to account for most of the variation in practices, although further validation of these is required. With some modification, we have adapted these six as a useful baseline for organizational culture in our framework. In addition, while Hofstede presents the dimensions as either/or choices along six axes, it is possible that some of them might be multidimensional rather than unidimensional. The six dimensions are as follows.

1 Process and/or outcomes oriented

Organizational cultures may be said to be either process oriented or outcomes oriented. Evidence suggests that in outcomes-oriented organizational cultures people perceive greater homogeneity in practices, whereas people in process-oriented organizational cultures perceive greater differences in their practices. The reason for the apparent greater degree of diversity of practice in the latter can be ascribed to the fact that some organizations are predisposed towards technical and bureaucratic routines, while others are more flexible in adapting their organizational practices and structures in response to the pressures of externally generated change. In education, schools which are process oriented emphasize processes and the skills of decision-making, teaching and learning, while those which are results oriented, stress learning achievements such as examination results. Many schools and school systems are currently reforming their curricula to reflect specific student learning targets or outcomes expressed in terms of knowledge, skills and attitudes, indicating a trend towards designing curricula on the basis of, and measuring student and school performance by, a learning outcomes approach.

2 Task and/or person oriented

In task-oriented organizational cultures, emphasis is placed on job performance and maximizing productivity, while human considerations, such as staff welfare, take second place and may even be neglected. Conversely, person-oriented organizational cultures accentuate the care, consideration and welfare of employees. Applied to extremes in schools, a task-oriented culture exacts maximum work effort and performance out of its teachers in a relatively uncaring work environment. A person-oriented culture on the other hand, values, promotes and shows consideration for the welfare of its teachers. It is conceivable that some schools might score high (or low) on both task and person orientations.

3   Professional and/or parochial

In professional organizational cultures, qualified personnel identify primarily with their profession, whose standards are usually defined at national or international levels. In more parochial organizational cultures, members identify most readily with the organization for which they work. In the school context, some teachers, especially those with an external frame of reference, are primarily committed to the teaching profession as a whole, while others with a strong internal frame of reference are more committed to the particular school in which they work.

4   Open and/or closed

This dimension refers to the ease with which resources, such as, people, money, and ideas are exchanged between the organization and its environment. The greater the transfer and exchange of resources between the environment and the organization, the more open the organizational culture. Schools vary between those which champion outside involvement in their affairs and maximum interchange with their environment, and those which eschew such interaction and communication, preferring a more closed, exclusive approach. Trends in education over the last decade have favoured the opening of school cultures, particularly to parental influence and involvement.

5   Control and linkage

An important part of organizational culture concerns the way in which authority and control are exerted and communicated between members. In this respect, Hofstede's dimension identifies only one aspect, namely, tightly–loosely controlled organizational cultures. We have added two more aspects, namely, formal–informal and direct–indirect which, taken together, provide a more comprehensive structure to this dimension in schools (Dimmock and Walker, 1998a).

Formal–informal   Organizations vary in the extent to which their practices are guided by rules, regulations and 'correct procedures', on the one hand, and the extent to which they reflect a more relaxed, spontaneous and intuitive approach, on the other. Highly formalized organizations conform to the classic bureaucracies; they emphasize definition of rules and roles, they tend towards inflexibility and are often characterized by austere interpersonal relationships. By contrast, informal organizations have fewer rules dictating procedures, roles are often ill-defined, they display flexibility in their modes of work and interpersonal relationships tend to be more relaxed.

Tight–loose This sub-dimension gauges the degree to which members feel there is strong commitment to the shared beliefs, values and practices of an organization. Such strong commitment might come through hierarchical supervision and control, or through members' own self-motivation. An organization which has strong homogeneity and commitment in respect of its members' values and practices is tightly controlled (whether control is externally imposed by formal management or self-imposed by workers). Conversely, a loosely controlled organizational culture is one with only weak commitment to, or acceptance of, shared beliefs, values and practices, and little or no control is exerted to achieve homogeneity either by formal management or by workers themselves.

Direct–indirect This aspect captures the linkages and patterns of communication through which power, authority and decisions are communicated. In some organizations, managers either assume direct personal responsibility to perform certain tasks and to communicate directly with their staff, often leapfrogging intermediate levels in the vertical hierarchy or chain of command. In other organizations, managers exert control indirectly by delegating to staff the tasks they would otherwise do themselves.

6 Pragmatic and/or normative

This dimension defines the way an organization serves its clients, customers or patrons. Some display a flexible, pragmatic policy aimed at meeting the diversity of customer needs. Others, however, exhibit more rigid or normative approaches in responding bureaucratically, failing to meet individual needs. This dimension measures the degree to which the organization is client centred. In the educational context, some schools consciously try to meet individual student needs by offering a more diversified curriculum with flexible timetables and alternative teaching strategies. They mould their educational services to meet student needs. Others, particularly the more traditional schools, may be less student focused, expecting them to fit into the agenda determined for them by the school. These schools offer more standardized, normative programmes.

Having identified the key elements of schooling and school-based management, along with cultural dimensions, both societal and organizational, consideration needs to be given to the operationalizing the model. This can be achieved by applying the cultural dimensions to the elements of schooling and school-based management. For example, in researching the leadership styles in schools located in different societal cultures, data would need to be gathered within the framework of our power-concentrated versus power-distributed cultural dimension to leadership. At the organizational culture level, data would need to be generated by applying the relevant organizational culture dimensions to leadership; in this case, the person–task and the control–linkage dimensions.

In the data collection process, a number of instruments are needed to apply the cultural dimensions to the various elements of the school and school-based management, including both instruments to generate quantitative data, such as survey questionnaires, and instruments to provide qualitative data, such as in-depth interviews and case studies. Given the overarching, holistic design of the theoretical framework, its comprehensive application in matching all of the dimensions to all of the elements would be extremely demanding and may indeed be unnecessary. It is envisaged that the model could be applied selectively, combining those dimensions and elements which are directly relevant to the specific research purpose of the research being undertaken.

Summary and conclusion

Much of this chapter has focused on an evaluative review of the literature on organizational culture with particular reference to schools as organizations. Although organizational culture has been seen as an essentially cohesive and unifying force, it has also been pointed out that organizations are highly complex with subcultures at the micro level that have the potential for organizational division and fragmentation. This has been illustrated with reference to three examples: the social class divisions between students, academic department subdivisions and the exceptional diversity of multicultural schools. The implications of organizational culture for school leadership and management were also considered, with the conclusion that, in spite of the complexity of schools as organizations, it is possible for effective leadership to transform schools; for example, through a process of *reculturing* and school improvement towards what have been described as learning organizations.

Attention has also been drawn to the limitations of earlier studies of school culture and school organization, arguing that they fall short of providing a sound theoretical base for the understanding of school culture and leadership from an international, comparative and cross-cultural perspective. Following on from the work of Hofstede (1991), an alternative model of organizational culture, based on six dimensions, has been outlined as a means of providing a more comprehensive and holistic paradigm for further research into comparative studies of school leadership and organizational culture.

This leads in the next chapter to a discussion of school leadership from the broader perspective of the sociocultural context in which schools operate, illustrating, with reference to examples drawn from both Asian and Western societies, how approaches to school leadership have been shaped both by the cultural influences of local communities and by the wider global context of school reform.

5
Leadership and Diverse Sociocultural Contexts

This chapter addresses school leadership from two perspectives, both of which provide a context to the process. The first connects leadership with the core work of schools, namely, teaching and learning, and contextualizes schooling within its sociocultural environment. The second draws international comparisons and contrasts between these networks in selected Western and Asian communities with the purpose of illustrating cross-cultural differences. Two important themes underpin the argument presented. The first is that leadership is best thought of – not as a separate or discrete set of processes – but in relation to the myriad activities that take place in school communities. Leadership, above all, is interactive and interdependent. The second is that much of the existing body of knowledge on school leadership is based on Anglo-American ideas and empiricism (Dimmock and Walker, 1998a; 1998b). Consequently, relatively little is known about school leadership elsewhere in the world. This second theme centres on leadership being an essentially social and cultural process.

The chapter is structured into three interrelated sections, each of which reflects the perspectives and themes outlined above. The first section centres on the more conceptual and theoretical notions of leadership within the larger corpus of school community activities, while the second contextualizes leadership within the global setting of school reform. In the third section, cultural differences between the home–parent–school relationship are highlighted.

A major purpose of the chapter is the portrayal of teaching, learning, parenting and leadership as interdependent and culture-bound activities. As such, they warrant investigation from a cross-cultural perspective. The comparisons included in the chapter are based mainly on Japan, mainland China and the USA. However, reference is also made to other societies, such as Hong Kong, Singapore, the UK and Australia. Wherever reference is made to societies collectively, such as 'East Asian' or 'Asian' and 'Western', we acknowledge that there is substantial cultural diversity within these regions and that the use of such terms is justified only for convenience. In addition, identification of cultural differences between societies inevitably runs the risk of overgeneralization, since no group of people is completely harmonious, and different groups may share commonalities. Yet the definition of culture itself hinges on the recognition of common values and norms that bind groups of people together, but which at the same time distinguish them from other groups.

Conceptualizing, contextualizing and connecting leadership

For many decades, leadership has been portrayed as a contextual rather than a discrete activity. Leadership is exercised, for example, through the leaders' relations with followers and within the context of given situations and environments. Leadership theories developed in previous decades, particularly the situational or contingency theories of the 1970s, acknowledged the interrelationship between the leader, followers and the work situation. Such theories, however, tended to simply 'suggest a set of relationships without exploring the basic dimensions of those relationships' (Watkins, 1989, p. 18) and avoided the broader micro and macro contexts that interact to give leadership meaning. For a more complete understanding of leadership, it is necessary to consider its connections to other key processes and activities that take place within schools and outside in their environments. Within school, these other activities include teaching and learning; while outside of school, they involve parenting, socialization and home–school relationships.

While recognizing that other approaches may be applied, this chapter conceptualizes the context of leadership in two ways. First, it assumes that leadership is exercised inside school in relation to people and activities engaged in teaching and learning, while in the external environment, it is connected to parenting and socialization. Second, it acknowledges that all of these activities – leadership, teaching learning and parenting – are culture sensitive or culture dependent and that, consequently, differences in their form and practice may, at least partially, be attributed to the diversity in societal cultures.

Leadership, educational reform, globalization and societal culture

While societal culture provides an important backdrop to, and influence on, leadership, current educational reform also provides an important part of the context to school leadership, especially that part concerned with its changing nature and form. However, while it is the differences between cultures that tend to be highlighted, when it comes to educational policy reforms adopted by various governments, it is their global similarity and ubiquity that is given prominence. Societal cultures are characterized by divergence, while globalized policy reform reflects convergence. School restructuring policies which reflect this trend generally include school-based management; school development planning; delegated budgeting and human resource management; increased teacher and parent involvement in decision-making; school-based curriculum development;

centralized curriculum planning using a learning outcomes framework; greater accountability of schools to the central bureaucracy; the empowerment of school councils; system-wide testing of students at regular intervals; increased parental choice of school; and greater competition between schools for students. This is not to claim that all of the systems that have restructured have adopted all of these measures.

In every case, such reform policies impact on schools and on school leaders in particular. Under the weight of these multiple changes, the role of the school leader has undergone substantial 'broadening', 'deepening' and 'externalizing' (O'Donoghue and Dimmock, 1998) and it has done so in diverse and contrasting societal cultures (Walker and Dimmock, 1999b; 2000d). The key point to note is that the emergence of globalized policy reform measures has tended to place similar demands on the role of school leaders in diverse cultural contexts. These, in turn, have tended to shape the role in a convergent way, so that, for example, principals in Hong Kong are expected to involve teachers and parents in school decision-making, in the same way as their counterparts in Australia or the USA.

However, while globalization and trends towards convergence are discernible, so are forces towards divergence. As previously mentioned, these latter forces are associated with societal culture. The relationship between global and international policy trends, on the one hand, and societal culture, on the other, is complex. It seems that in one capacity, societal culture may act to preserve long held traditions of leadership, even in a globalizing context that foreshadows change in the role of leader. As Southworth (2000) states in relation to England:

> leadership is a social construction which while always being refined by successive generations, is also held together by deeper structural beliefs, which have an enduring quality to them. As a construct, leadership in England is a mix of change and continuity, but the continuities are pervasive and provide the foundational beliefs for headship to endure as proprietal, pivotal and powerful. (p. 15)

In a second capacity, societal culture acts as a 'filter' or mediator to policies and practices imported from elsewhere (Dimmock, 1998). This may mean that global policy is reshaped and adapted at a system level to suit the particularities of the indigenous culture (Morris and Lo, 2000). Alternatively, global policy may be modified at the school level (formally or informally) by principals, teachers and others engaged in implementation, irrespective of whether it has undergone adaptation at system level. For example, Hallinger and Kantamara (2000b) describe, using a case study, how three Thai principals, faced with introducing Western-style policies of school change mediated by refusing to jettison some of their traditional culture. Societal culture thus acts as a filter or mediator at many different levels, from system to individual. A crucial part in the acquisition of societal culture is played by parents, family and school.

Parenting, the family and school

The effects of parenting and the general influence of the home on children's learning achievements are now well known (Dimmock, O'Donoghue and Robb, 1996). Such factors include key relationships between parents and children, the opportunities that children have for socializing, the values to which they are exposed, the stimulation they receive from their family experiences and the degree of support for learning from their family environment. Little is known, however, about how parenting contributes to student learning in different societies, even though few would argue that cross-cultural differences in terms of parenting and how children are socialized in different societies tend to vary greatly. Such differences are considered so stark that they are sometimes used to help explain variations in student achievement levels between many of the East Asian countries on the one hand – in particular Japan, Korea, Singapore, Hong Kong and Taiwan – and the USA, for example, on the other.

More empirical research is needed as to how the contextual conditions to leadership – in particular, the influences of parenting, the family and the home – vary across societies. Put simply, children growing up in different societies experience very different lives. Their home and out-of-school lives, in turn, clearly affect their lives in school. We owe much to the work of Stevenson and Stigler (1992) for the present knowledge base with regard to these issues. In the remaining part of this chapter, we explore how parenting and the life of children differ cross-culturally.

Stevenson and Stigler (1992) sampled elementary schools and their communities in particular cities in the USA, Japan, China and Taiwan. They justify their comparative assessment of student learning achievements in those countries by using carefully constructed tests and measures that were, in their own words, 'culture fair' after examining the countries' respective curricula. Their mission was primarily to explain why student learning achievements in East Asia are superior to those in the USA. As stated earlier, the use of generalized labels such as 'Asian' and 'Western' to refer to so many diverse societies is, of course, misleading. However, in the following account we use the term 'Asian', as used by Stevenson and Stigler, to refer principally to Japan, China and Taiwan; 'Western' is reserved for the USA.

Home and school

Research evidence tends to show that there is a closer harmony of values between the home and school in Asian countries than there is, for example, in the USA. There are many reasons for this. Asian children spend more time at school than American children, and hence Asian schools have more opportunity to mould and shape children. Stevenson and Stigler (1992) found, for example, that during a typical school week American children spend about six hours a day and Asian children eight hours a day on average at school. Most Asian children also attend school for an additional four hours on Saturday mornings. In addition, they spend more days each year at school. In Japan, for example, the legal minimum school year is 210 days, but most local school officials insist on 240 days. In Taiwan, 220 days is a typical school year. Moreover, their school terms are more evenly spread throughout the year with shorter holidays than is the case for American children. Asian teachers are normally allocated to a class for two years which promotes more stability in the relationship with students. However, the main point is not that this considerable time spent in school translates into more time devoted to academic learning. Rather, a good part of it is taken for extra-curricular activities. This means that the school occupies a central place in the social as well as academic life of the student. Even during holiday periods, Chinese and Japanese children rarely lose contact with their teachers and school friends (Hess and Azuma, 1991). School and home activities tend to merge, since the structure of the school year is punctuated by relatively more, but short, breaks between terms than is the case in America (Watkins and Biggs, 1996).

Schooling seems to occupy a more central place in the lives of Asian than American children. Asian parents demonstrate strong support for their children's learning at school by sparing little expense in providing conditions conducive for learning in the home (Hess and Azuma, 1991). This is despite home conditions that are – at least physically – anything but favourable. Even among first-year elementary school students, very high proportions of Japanese and Taiwanese parents invest in desks and make space available at home for children to focus on their homework (Stevenson and Stigler, 1992). The average living space for the Japanese family is only 900 square feet. In China and Hong Kong, family living space is even less – typically 500 square feet – yet even here, the present author has noticed that parents are keen to make the dinner table available after the family meal if there is insufficient space for a separate desk.

Parental involvement in homework is less in America than either Japan or China. This is partly because American teachers set less homework. In Japan, because the men tend to work long hours, it is the mother who assumes the main role in assisting her children. In contrast, American parents are found to place far less importance on helping their children. Asian teachers assign more homework and children spend more time doing it than their American counterparts. Close communication between teachers and parents in China and Japan is often maintained through the use of notebooks that pass between them and which monitor the students' progress.

Research evidence shows that homework – providing it has certain characteristics – is a key factor in promoting student academic achievement (see Fraser et al., 1987). In respect of the four Asian school systems, the importance attached to homework is so great that it is often excessive (Turay, 1994).

Strong pressure to set homework comes from both parents and teachers (Stevenson and Lee, 1996).

Despite the cramped and overcrowded conditions in Asian homes, teachers assign more homework and children spend more time doing it, than their American counterparts. Interviews that one of the authors conducted with a group of primary school teachers in Hong Kong revealed that it is not atypical for elementary school children aged eight and nine years to spend four and five hours a night on homework. Such is the homework pressure on young children in mainland China, that the central government has passed a decree forbidding all homework during the first year of elementary school. By contrast, in the year 2000, the Chicago Board of Education imposed a requirement of 30 minutes of homework per day for the first three years of elementary school. Taiwanese teachers tend to set more homework than even Japanese teachers – elementary school children being assigned homework during most of the year, including holidays.

Contradictory evidence exists on whether the effects of excessive homework on students in the four Asian societies are harmful. Stevenson and Stigler (1992) found little or no evidence that the stronger work ethic of Asian children translated into greater psychological problems, although their studies were confined to primary aged children. On the other hand, the pressure of homework combined with university entrance examinations at the upper secondary stage often manifest in severe stress and occasional personal tragedy.

In Japan, it is generally the mother who assumes the main role in assisting her children to complete homework, while in Chinese families, this role is shared. In contrast, American parents place less importance on helping their children with homework. Chinese and Japanese parents are likely to be disciplined over their children completing homework, insisting on its completion before they are allowed to watch television (Stevenson and Stigler, 1992).

At the upper secondary stage, there is an equal pressure placed on examination success (Gow et al., 1996). This is partly explained by the limited number of university places available. In Taiwan and China, for example, only one place per 100 applicants may be available. Pressure on Japanese high school students results in about 90 per cent attending 'juku' or cram schools in evenings, weekends and holidays, in addition to their normal school (McAdams, 1993).

The double effect of excessive amounts of homework and overly competitive examination systems may have negative effects on schooling. For example, the main preoccupation becomes passing the examination rather than learning per se. Even in Hong Kong, where the number of university places increased sixfold during the 1990s, there is still considerable pressure on prospective university entrants. Educational policy-makers in Hong Kong have recently advocated a reduction in examination pressure at both primary and secondary school, arguing that children are over-examined throughout their school lives, which, in turn, has a negative effect on quality schooling.

Differences in leisure time activities between the USA and Asian children are surprisingly few. American children tend to spend more time playing and participating in organized sports than their Asian counterparts, who have less time in school to play. There appears to be little difference between hours spent watching television, but Chinese and Japanese parents are more likely to make it conditional on completing homework. Asian children spend more time reading books and comics than their American counterparts, while American children are more likely to help with domestic chores. Asian mothers claim they would rather their children get on with their homework; and living in smaller homes makes chores less onerous. The critical relationship between the home and school is well summarized by Stevenson and Stigler (1992), thus:

> Japanese and Chinese appear to maintain a relatively sharp differentiation between the functions of home and school. Schools are primarily held responsible for developing academic skills, and the social skills required for integration into group life; the home is responsible for supporting the school's role and for providing a healthy emotional environment for the child. Parents and teachers work together, but do not duplicate each other's efforts. (p. 83)

In summary, Japanese and Chinese children spend more time at home working on activities related to school than do American children. Such activities are strongly supported and nurtured by their families.

Parenting, socialization, effort and achievement

Parenting While parents in America and Asia believe that parenting and early childhood experiences are crucial to future achievement, Stevenson and Stigler (1992) found significant and radical differences between American and Asian parents in their beliefs about, and therefore practices of, child-rearing and socialization. Chinese and Japanese parents make clear distinctions between earlier and later childhood. Up to about the age of six, Asian parents impose relatively low academic pressure and few demands or controls on their children. About the time children enter first grade, however, child-rearing practices change markedly. Parents and children begin to work diligently towards getting a good education.

American parents, in contrast, do not noticeably alter their parenting with time, although an important shift does take place. From very early years, American parents work on stimulating their children, and expect kindergarten teachers to do the same. At the kindergarten stage, American parents press for academic learning and stimulation, while Japanese parents emphasize health and interest in school. Chinese parents fall between the American and Japanese parents. However, when children enter the first grade, although the socialization process continues, the agent responsible for academic socialization changes. In

Stevenson and Stigler's (1992) words, 'Just when Asian parents are getting more involved in their children's academic life, American parents are beginning to abdicate many of their responsibilities to their children's teachers' (p. 73). In other words, the Asian parent becomes more demanding once the child enters school, and begins to support more strongly the work of the teacher. Paradoxically, it is American parents who are more likely to start the education process earlier in the home, and it is they who are more likely to abdicate it to the teacher when the child begins school. Asian parents seem more concerned with socializing the child within the family or peer group.

After entry to elementary school, Asian parents become less lenient than hitherto, and more demanding of respect, obedience and adherence to rules. Studying and doing well in school become the child's main aim. Parents see teachers as needing their help in accomplishing this transition. Any disruptive behaviour is seen as better taking place in the privacy of the home, since 'public face' is all-important. Japanese parents are more tolerant of disobedience than are Chinese parents.

Culture explains many of the differences in beliefs about parenting. Japanese and Chinese parents tend to differentiate sharply the functions of home and school. While schools are seen as imparting academic and social skills, the home is seen as a support for school and for emotional development. Parents and teachers work together but do not duplicate their roles. Americans, by contrast, expect that schools will assume more responsibilities, including socialization and peer interaction, and parents less, once children start elementary school. Close home–school partnerships in China and Japan are forged by various means; for example, as noted earlier children take a notebook to and from school each day, with comments written by teachers to parents and vice versa. It is rare for American teachers to feel well supported by parents.

Socialisation Techniques used by societies for socializing children are also culture based. Modelling desirable behaviour is one such technique. Children in mainland China, Taiwan and Japan are socialized in ways that endorse and support school success (Holloway, 1988; Salili, 1996). Stevenson and Stigler argue that while many Japanese and Chinese cult figures exemplify ideals that value education and high academic achievement, the opposite is the case in America, where cult figures are often sports stars and entertainers. For example, role models that represent virtuous individuals, and selfless contributions to the welfare of the group or state, are extolled. In mainland China, Lei Feng – Chairman Mao's good soldier – is immortalised; in Taiwan, Sun Yat-sen and Chiang Kai-shek; and in Japan, Kinjiro, whose efforts to learn two centuries ago are held up to today's youth. A second method of socializing is through group or peer pressure. It is well documented that Chinese and Japanese culture emphasizes group orientation or collectivism, whereas American culture stresses individualism (Hofstede, 1991). Identification with a group – family, peers, school, community – provides a common bond and a powerful impetus and motivator to achieving goals. In China and Japan pre-schools and kindergartens place great emphasis on building socially interactive skills and strengthening group identification. Pressure on young children to conform is strong – coming from teachers, who are usually held in high esteem, and peers, through strong group identification (Salili, 1996). This same group identity means that Japanese and Chinese children are likely to feel that they are letting their parents down if they do not perform at school (Bond, 1994; Watkins, 2000). Therefore, pressure from both peers and teachers combine. Through a propensity for group participation, co-operation comes more easily to Asian children than it does to American children. Asian parents inculcate a feeling in their children that failure brings shame on the family, because it signifies that the family did not do its job properly in rearing and preparing them. The American family will often believe that a child's failure to do his/her best, brings shame on the child alone.

The influence of the group and peers in collectivist societies is reflected in the relative ease with which students undertake collaborative projects. The differences between Hong Kong Chinese students and Western students in the way group problem-solving is undertaken have been noted (Walker, Bridges and Chan, 1996). When set group problem-solving tasks to be completed within a given time constraint, the Chinese students will subordinate individual differences and work closely together to achieve the goal. By contrast, Western students are more likely to argue their individual points of view, often failing to achieve the task within the time period.

A third approach to socialization is the teaching of classroom and school routines that help children learn, adjust and contribute to the smooth organization and running of the classroom. This caring relationship (Gao, 1998; Jin and Cortazzi, 1998) includes imparting skills such as personal management, keeping tidy desks, use of the bathroom, taking notes and performing classroom duties. In so doing, they take more care to induct the children into school expectations, which in turn, tends to ease problems of classroom management.

In summary, although parents – American and Asian – believe family upbringing affects their children's academic success, cultural differences lead to different goals for, and methods of, socialization. Asian parents stress the goal of academic success more strongly than do American parents, who place more concern on their children developing self-esteem and extra-curricular interests. Asian parents pay more attention to when they should intervene, how the home can support the school, the provision of good models for emulation, peer group influence and the adoption of routines for later learning.

Effort ability and achievement   Major differences are also to be found between Japan, China and America as to the importance of effort, ability and achievement. Americans tend to attribute academic success to innate ability, whereas the Asian societies believe that effort and hard work can compensate for ability. These different social philosophies about what accounts for success – in the case of the Chinese, tracing back to the teachings of Confucius – have enormous ramifications for parental expectations, behaviour at home and teaching at school.

As long as Asians believe that effort will lead to achievement, students are motivated to work for long hours and parents will encourage them. American belief in ability and their preoccupation with measuring it through intelligence tests, however, means that children are soon labelled as either high or low achievers and no amount of hard work can compensate for lack of ability. Parental attitudes and expectations adjust accordingly. For example, a much higher percentage of American than either Chinese or Japanese mothers believe that their children's final school performance is predictable from an early age (Stevenson and Stigler, 1992). The Asian 'effort model' offers a more optimistic scenario for learning outcomes than the American 'ability model', a point borne out by the seeming greater willingness of students to persist for longer when problem-solving in mathematics, compared to their American counterparts.

Standards and expectations are strongly affected by cultural beliefs about the nature of learning and potential. The American belief in ability means that if children fail to perform early on, then parents tend to adjust their expectations downwards. Likewise, schools organize lower streams and adjust standards downwards, the main objective being the preservation of student self-esteem.

In attempting cross-culturally to compare parental levels of satisfaction with schooling, Stevenson and Stigler (1992) asked parents in Chicago, Minneapolis, Beijing, Taipei and Sendai how satisfied they were with their children's performance at school. Forty per cent of American mothers said they were 'very satisfied' compared with 5 per cent of the Chinese and Japanese mothers. When asked the same question four years later, the same result was obtained. American mothers were also more likely to think that their children's elementary school was doing a good job.

In explaining these different levels of satisfaction, Stevenson and Stigler (1992) argue that by American parents holding low expectations of what their children can achieve, they form evaluations of their children's abilities and academic performance that are unrealistically high. American parents tend to rate their children positively and both parents and children hold to the belief that they are doing well in school. While American parents and children tend to be confident both privately and publicly, Japanese and Chinese tend to separate their public thoughts (more self-effacing) from their private thoughts (less modest).

It seems that Asian parents are more demanding and more stringent in their evaluations. Japanese and Chinese parents apply higher standards than do their American counterparts when judging their children's academic performance. This attitude of non-complacency among parents, children and teachers establishes conditions conducive to effective schooling in the four Asian societies. The Asian children in turn accept these standards and are motivated to work hard to meet them. In accounting for these differences in parenting, Stevenson and Stigler (1992) point out that by comparison with Japan, America lacks a common national curriculum and standard public examination; it has relatively poor contact between home and school; and it generally accords lower priority to academic achievement. In addition, there is a greater tendency for American families to break up and thus for single parents, and for parents generally, to place less pressure on children as a result.

Above all, children are motivated to work hard and to succeed as a mark of respect for their parents. Success at school reflects well on the parents and family. Children are highly conscious of parental pressure and expectation on them to do their best at school. In summary, Japanese and Chinese children spend considerable time at home working on activities related to school – much more than their American counterparts. Such activities are strongly supported and nurtured by their families, whose values place education at the forefront of their priorities. Effective schooling therefore spreads well beyond the gates of the school into the home.

In summary, American children generally perform below Japanese and Chinese children on academic achievement tests, while their parents think more positively about their performance and their schools than do their Japanese and Chinese counterparts. Where parental and school values align, and where parents actively support the aims of the school, student achievement and behaviour are improved and effective schooling is more likely to result (Biggs, 1994; Hess and Azuma, 1991). In the Asia-Pacific region, it can justly be claimed that the values underlying societal culture and those underpinning school missions and aims seem to be more aligned than is the case in Western countries (Biggs, 1994). The question that may arise for Americans is, 'Why should schools improve and students strive towards higher achievement when parents are, apparently, relatively easily satisfied?'

Conclusion

While this section has revealed significant differences between cultures in socializing and raising children, by way of conclusion the question remains as to the implications these hold for school leaders. The first point in this regard concerns the respective roles of parents and the home vis-à-vis the school. Since the configuration of this relationship differs between societies, the roles of, and expectations placed on, school leaders naturally vary according to the particularities of the cultural context. In societies, for example, where parents exert a stronger influence on discipline at home, the necessary emphasis given to student behaviour management is a less important facet of the lives of school leaders and teachers. Similarly, in societies where parental expectations on children place greater store by academic success and where children spend longer hours on homework, the role of leaders and teachers may be one of easing stress and fatigue. The scenario is somewhat different for school leaders in other societies where the preoccupation is to get children to do homework in the first place.

A second and related point is that any attempt to compare school leadership in different societies is pointless, unless full consideration is given to the wider societal cultural and contextual conditions within which leadership takes place. Critical relationships at school, such as, principal–student; teacher–student; principal–teacher and student–student, are products of a wider set of values in society at large related to socialization and upbringing.

The third point centres on the fact that despite cultural divergence in the role of school leaders across the world, there are compelling forces of convergence operating such as to pull their roles towards a kind of 'global mean'. The most obvious of these is educational reform, in particular, the trend in many societies towards school-based management, and associated curriculum changes, including new pedagogies, outlined in the previous section of this chapter. At the very least the point to be made, as Walker and Walker (1998) recognize, is that almost everywhere, school leadership is experiencing tension between forces of convergence (linked to globalization) and divergence (associated with societies and their distinctive cultures).

In the next chapter, we turn attention to the question of strategic leadership in schools, raising a number of concerns about the direction of educational policy, including: mandatory school development planning frameworks and the need for strategic flexibility; the undue focus on market-driven criteria in defining the purpose of schools; and the need for heads and principals to be sensitive to the opportunities and constraints of their sociocultural contexts (as well as external pressures) in achieving school improvement strategies that are both sustainable and meaningful to the specific communities they serve.

6
Strategic Leadership and Cultural Diversity

The previous chapter focused on the wider sociocultural context of schools, including a discussion of the important differences between societal cultures in the ways that children are raised, socialized and educated. The focus of this chapter switches to the implications of these significant cultural differences for the effective leadership and organization of schools. It is argued that school improvement rests first and foremost on prioritizing improvements in teaching and learning through an iterative and reflective process that combines both strategic intent and flexibility in meeting the needs and expectations of local communities in times of rapid change and long-term uncertainty. From a more general discussion, the chapter concludes with a consideration of a more specific issue by way of illustration – that of the increasing multicultural nature of schools in many societies. In this section we claim that multicultural schools present special challenges to school leaders that deserve greater attention from scholars working in the field of educational leadership. We therefore return to this key issue in Chapter 11, where the implications of recent research findings into multicultural education are assessed in more detail.

Over the last decade it has become widely acknowledged that a preoccupation with the immediate and the urgent, an overdependence on centralized authority planning for schools, and uncertainty about school-level abilities and boundaries has mitigated against school leaders either looking too far or too deeply into the future. Such a recognition has led scholars, policy-makers and practitioners to recognize the importance of strategic leadership and thinking in schools, and as a consequence, a voluminous literature is currently building (see Davies and Ellison, 2003; Quong, Walker and Stott, 1998). While this awakening of interest in strategic leadership is both welcome and necessary, this chapter argues that there are concerns over the direction that it is taking.

Among our concerns, three in particular are worthy of attention. The first centres on the tendency to connect strategic thinking to school development planning. One problem that arises here stems from schools setting longer-term direction, usually through mission, but then leaving these as inert mechanisms which too often diminish strategic flexibility and subsequent action. This presents a limited or restricted conception of the nature and scope of change in schools. A second problem in terms of connection is that strategy tends to be perceived from a piecemeal and incremental, rather than a holistic, school improvement perspective. The second matter of concern relates to the undue attention and focus currently being given to certain indicators and criteria as underpinning drivers of strategy and strategic thinking. These include market-driven indicators, such as student enrolment and financial criteria. While we are not claiming that these are unimportant, we want to challenge whether they should be the only or even major keystones around which strategy is developed. The third concern is the tendency to neglect – in much recent literature on strategy – the relevance of the cultural context of each school. It is worth briefly elaborating on each of these three concerns by way of justifying our argument.

Our first concern holds two, almost paradoxical, elements; that of maintaining shorter-term flexibility while simultaneously ensuring longer-term connectivity. The first of these expresses the danger of associating strategic thinking, planning and leadership too closely with easily constructed strategic mechanisms such as mission that can become slavishly irresponsive to shorter-term conditions and which eschew the all-important notion of strategic flexibility. Although time-defined direction statements are vital and provide blueprints through which coherence and continuity are gained, they are too often seen as 'set in stone'. On the other hand, we agree with the persuasive evidence that major school change needs to be holistic with high connectivity between the elements, and that many of these changes take between five and ten years to embed in the school (Bain, 2000; Fullan, 1991). The generic issue here concerns the nature of schools as organizations – in particular, how they function, and what enables them to change. There is clearly a need for leadership to be responsive, and at the same time consistently focused, systematic and sustaining of pressure for change over the long term. To make this possible, however, school leaders need an organizational design to structure their long-term effort. This aspect of contemporary leadership has failed to gain the recognition it deserves, as commentators have tended to either play up the need for leaders to be responsive and flexible to shorter-term crises or for them to be able accurately to predict and control the future without adjustment to unpredictable contextual conditions.

In the case of the second concern, namely, the focus of schools on market-driven criteria, including student numbers and finance, this response is understandable within the parameters set by government policy and budgetary realities. However, it is also a government imperative that schools achieve academic learning targets set for their students. The need for clarification of the purpose of schools is the crux here. An undue focus on market-driven criteria may distract attention from the vital strategic thinking and leadership needed in the core technology of the academic programme – namely, the need for an inclusive multi-level curriculum, and the best quality teaching and learning for all students. While arguing for this, we acknowledge that schools are inescapably linked to political structures and agendas, among others, and that strategic leadership therefore needs to take full cognizance of these.

Our third concern is inexorably linked to the first two. In this regard – the need for strategic thinking must take cognizance of sociocultural context – we argue that coherent and robust strategic thinking and leadership is predicated on an intimate understanding and reflection of the cultural and contextual conditions of each school. A particular and increasingly important manifestation of this is the nature and profile of many primary and secondary schools in urban areas, especially inner cities, to reflect the multi-ethnic composition of their localities and intakes.

Against the background of the three concerns sketched above, it can be argued that strategic thinking and engagement needs to emphasize the following features:

- the necessity for longer time horizons (beyond three to five years) *and* shorter-term strategic flexibility;
- the need for a whole-school design approach, the holistic nature of which comprises the interconnected elements that form the school as a system;
- an approach to whole-school design that is learning-centred and focuses on the core technology of curriculum, teaching and learning; and
- an approach that is responsive to the demographic, social and cultural composition of multi-ethnic societies.

Consistent with these themes, a view of strategy is portrayed that derives from both the traditional organizational fallibilities of schools and a clear vision for successful schools. Accordingly, the first section identifies key assumptions about the purposes and organizational characteristics of schools, as well as the nature of their environments, both of which are imperatives in any discussion of strategy in regard to schools. Second, a perspective that views strategic leadership as integrated with, and based on, whole-school design for improvement, is outlined. Third, the process underlying strategic leadership for whole-school design, is considered. Finally, the foregoing ideas are applied to the context of multi-ethnic schools with the purpose of highlighting the influence that a multicultural context has on shaping strategy.

Assumptions underpinning thinking about strategy

Schools have traditionally been seen as conservative organizations, 'loosely coupled', under-led and under-managed, and characterized by a core technology of teaching and learning, the practice of which has been largely left to individual discretion (Bain, 2000; Dimmock, 2000a; Weick, 1976). With these organizational characteristics, the necessary synergy for school effectiveness has been hard to attain. In addition, change has often been piecemeal, whether emanating from without, in response to governmental pressure, or from within. In addition, the purposes of schools and schooling have often been seen as diffuse and ambivalent.

In response to these characteristics, we make two assumptions. The first is the need for learning- or learner-centred schools. The second assumption follows from the first, namely, that complex organizations, such as schools, optimize their learning-centredness when they are intentionally designed.

In regard to the first assumption, the 'learning- or learner-centred' school is one whose mission, organization, curriculum and leadership are all singularly focused on providing successful learning experiences and outcomes for all of its students. 'Learning experiences and outcomes' include the knowledge, values, attitudes and skills considered worthwhile and desirable across the spectrum of academic, social, spiritual, moral, aesthetic and physical domains. In reality, it is extremely challenging and rare for schools to engage all of their organizational elements in a singularly focused way; just as it is uncommon for them to provide successful learning experiences for all of their students, regardless of ability, ethnicity, age and gender. Achieving a balance of learning outcomes also presents major challenges.

A response to the second assumption largely follows from that to the first. The sheer magnitude of the challenge – involving many elements, most of which are interdependent – means that incremental or piecemeal change is unlikely to succeed, as is holistic, but haphazard and inconsistent change. Schools are complex systems of interrelated parts; to change the parts is to change the system and vice versa. The process must be holistic and designed with intent.

The challenge is for strategic thinking to design both the elements and the totality of schools around the concept of learning- and learner-centredness. Attention is thus placed on the quality of teaching, learning and curriculum experienced by all students. In previous work, Dimmock (2000a) advanced several reasons in justification for this focus. Among these were government priorities to raise learning standards and achievements of all students, and judgements about school quality based on the extent to which schools add value to their students' learning.

Whole-school design elements of the learning-centred school

If strategic thinking is to engage with the concept of whole-school design aimed at learning-centredness, then it is essential to distinguish the various organizational elements that comprise the whole school. These have been identified in previous work (see Dimmock, 2000a, for a full explanation) and are listed below:

- learning outcomes and the curriculum;
- learning processes and experiences;
- teaching approaches and strategies;

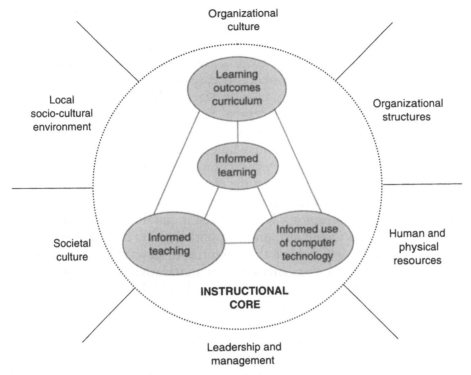

Figure 6.1 *School design model and its learning-centred elements*

- technology, especially computers;
- organizational structures;
- human and financial resources and their management, including appraisal; and
- leadership and organizational culture.

The above list may not be exhaustive, but it includes perhaps the most important elements. While here they are presented separately, in reality, just as in any system, there is functional interdependence. At the heart of the learning-centred school are the interconnected elements forming the core technology (refer to Figure 6.1). They comprise a curriculum based on student learning outcomes, informed learning and informed teaching practices, and computer technology. The school is designed around these core elements in order to optimize learning. Other elements of school design are crucial in supporting, facilitating and furthering the quality of the core technology. These elements include organizational structures, organizational culture, human and financial resources, and their management, including performance evaluation/appraisal, and leadership and culture building. These are interconnected, and each influences the core technology.

Of what significance is a whole-school design approach for strategic thinking and leadership? First, school strategists are expected to be clear on the values, goals and purposes of the school. In the case of the whole-school design model, these centre on being a learning- and learner-centred organization. Second, strategists and leaders need conceptual frameworks and models that map the critical elements that need to figure centrally in their strategic thinking and thus influence their leadership. The whole-school design model with its elements fulfils this function. Third, they must understand the complexity of the relationship and connectivity between the elements, so that the intricacies of strategy and its implementation can be worked out. Fourth, within the values, frameworks and connections, leaders must maintain the cognitive and operational flexibility to distinguish and respond to shifts coming from within and outside the school which have the potential to have an impact upon student learning. This strategic flexibility calls for an iterative relationship between the leader and the knowledge, context and people which comprise the school community. These points are expanded in a later section but now we introduce issues of procedure and process.

Some commentators (see, for example, Davies, 2002) have argued recently that conventional planning is inadequate for complex organizations, such as schools, which need the capacity to evolve and change with time, and which operate in environments aptly described as 'turbulent'. To cater for these conditions, school organizational designs require built-in flexibility for continuous evolution and adaptation to fast-changing environments. Planning and plans, as traditionally conceived and formed, imply too much rigidity.

Consequently, we agree with the approach advocated by Davies (2002), who bases his preference on Boisot's (1995) notion of 'strategic intent' rather than strategic planning. These approaches realistically assume, first, highly turbulent environments, and claim, secondly, 'high understanding' on the part of the organization, namely, the school. There can be little dispute about the turbulence of the education environment. And in regard to 'high understanding', which relates understanding to the environment and their core technology, schools are increasingly well positioned in both respects. First, they are increasingly well informed about, and sensitized to, government policy and the environments within which they function. Second, from a technical-professional angle, there is an increasingly sophisticated body of knowledge, information and understanding about effective teaching and learning, leadership and school improvement on which they can call. This understanding derives from knowledge gained from a host of sources, including research evidence of what works and what is efficacious, theory, values-based prescriptions as well as collective practitioner experience (Quong, Walker and Stott, 1998).

When knowledge is drawn together in this way and applied to areas of professional practice, such as the curriculum, learning, teaching, organizational behaviour and leadership, the result is the formation of 'intuitively formed patterns or gestalt' (Boisot, 1995, p. 36). Strategic leaders have the responsibility of developing such 'intuitively formed patterns' across their school communities for all to share and commit to. Strategic intent gives unity and coherence. It is an amalgam of the rational and the intuitive. It is, however, dependent on a clearly articulated set of values as well as visions of schools and schooling that are enduring over longer-term periods – five to ten years or more – and it assumes that leaders work steadily in a sustained and systematic, yet flexible, way to develop their organizations over this time frame.

Thus the whole-school design strategy that we advocate – based on the notion of the learning – and learner-centred school – conforms to Boisot's (1995) concept of 'strategic intent'. That is, it purports to be a coherent mix of values, vision, research-driven knowledge and intuition that enables schools to take institution-wide initiatives and responses, rather than to rely on the inflexibilities of traditional strategic planning.

In previous work, the concept of 'informed practice' has been used to describe the manifestation of this mix by practitioners (Dimmock, 2000a). We claim that an approach based on 'informed practice' will improve the enterprise of schooling. It will raise it from a plane of individualism, where individuals in organizations act opportunistically and often in isolation, to a higher level, where individuals work collaboratively and, at the same time, experience greater personal satisfaction and success. In these circumstances, the school, as an organization, is more likely to achieve synergy.

Whole-school design and strategic leadership: a backward mapping and iterative process

Applied to schools, the concept of organizational 'design' implies the intentional, deliberate and comprehensive alignment and configuration of structures, processes and cultures in such a way as to optimize school achievement of specified goals and purposes. In the sense in which we use the concept, it brings significantly more specificity to the process of improving schools than either of the terms 'reform' or 'restructuring'. Three key implications are highlighted: first, intentionality is brought to the structures, processes and practices proposed or implemented; secondly, connectivity or linkage between the various elements is considered important; thirdly, reinforcement, synergy and consistency of the different elements and parts are aligned towards the achievement of specified goals and purposes.

We argue that leaders need to engage in strategic thinking using a holistic school design model focused on learning- and learner-centred elements. In following this model, strategic leaders need to conceptualize the design elements

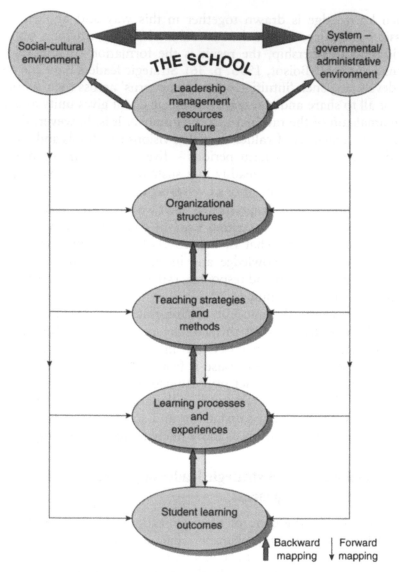

Figure 6.2   *Strategic leadership – a backward-mapping and iterative process*

and their interrelationships. Secondly, they need to construct their holistic school design through the process of backward mapping. Thirdly, they need to exercise strategic flexibility through subsequent implementation – an iterative process of constantly moving backward and forward, multidimensionally, between elements to meet student needs and to respond to other internal and external contextual shifts which may influence these needs and subsequent whole-school responses (refer to Figure 6.2).

Strategic thinking and leadership as a backward-mapping process

In conventional practice, strategic thinking and policy is a top-down process, from system level into school, and then vertically on down through the school. Passage through these many tiers of the organization encourages filtering, interpretation and often distortion of the message. Shared agreement and intended outcomes are less likely if there are more tiers of permeation. Accordingly, Elmore (1979) has suggested a process of backward mapping to reverse the stages of policy-making. In other words, begin with the end in mind and work backwards; clarify the end goals and achievements, and work back from those, drawing out the implications at each stage. Dimmock (1995) has identified the key variables at each stage in advocating the application of backward mapping to five clusters of school-level variables, starting with student learning outcomes, as shown in Figure 6.2. Since the most important stage of the policy process is the delivery of quality teaching and learning to achieve intended learning outcomes, it makes sense to start rather than finish at that point, by first identifying outcomes.

Backward mapping seeks alignment and consistency at each phase and across all stages. It spotlights the most important part of the strategic process, namely, implementation at the point of service delivery. Strategic leaders begin the process at the end point and work back up through the school to the system level in order to derive their own roles in supporting and facilitating the intended outcomes. This model places due importance on the implementation phase of change and on teachers' and students' contributions to the change process.

Through backward mapping, the design process starts with the expression of intended outcomes; in this case, student learning outcomes. The process is underpinned by a purposefully clarified and clearly articulated set of values which are clearly understood and adhered to throughout the school. The beginning goal and the final outcome are then one and the same. Learning is most effective when it is goal directed. The interface between student learning outcomes (goals, skills or competencies expressed in cognitive, affective and behavioural terms) and learning per se, is critical in raising to pre-eminence the strategies by which learning is promoted. Key focus questions are: how do students best learn? What are the individual differences between students in how they best learn? Responses to these questions about learning and individual learning styles are necessary prerequisites for the school's next sequential stage of decisions focusing on teaching and teaching strategies. Key issues here are: how do teachers best teach in order for students to achieve the learning outcomes? What are the individual differences between teachers in how they best teach? Most importantly, at the interface between learning and teaching: how does the school's perspective on student learning shape its teaching? Teaching is therefore driven by learning and responds and reacts to the demands, needs and interests of learners.

The foregoing questions and concerns centring on student outcomes, learning and teaching constitute the core technology of the school. Further sequential stages are important in enabling and supporting the core technology. First, how do school organization and structure (including the use of technology and physical space, and timetable) need to be designed or moulded to provide the framework for delivery of this core technology. Structures are designed to enable the school to optimize the delivery of its core technology and academic programme. Pertinent questions here include: what structures are most enabling for the successful implementation of planned teaching–learning activities? Are present school structures inhibitive or obstructive of the delivery of effective teaching and learning? In this approach, core technology drives the design of organization and structure rather than structure dictate core technology.

In turn, the core technology of effective learning and teaching, with the addition of organizational structures, provides insights into what are the most appropriate leadership, management, resourcing, professional development and culture-building processes. The nature of the school's core technology provides a framework and touchstone for school leadership and management. It provokes the following key questions: how do leadership and management best support effective teaching and learning in the school? Do effective teaching and learning provide the learning-centred purpose and focus of strategic thinking and leadership? Does strategic leadership decide the need for capacity-building and professional development, resource allocation and culture-building on the bases of school needs for effective teaching and learning, and student learning outcomes? Placing the core technology at the forefront of schools raises considerations as to whether existing patterns of resource allocation and utilization enable and support effective teaching and learning. Similarly, a learning focus provokes consideration of the alignment of professional development and school capacity towards the delivery of informed teaching and learning practices and procurement of student learning outcomes. Does school culture reflect the targeted student learning outcomes for all students?

We argue that backward mapping is a powerful analytical tool for strategic thinking and for strategic leadership. It is especially poignant in the initial stages of formulating the strategic intent in regard to the whole-school design and its focus on learning-centredness. It alone, however, is insufficient.

Strategic thinking and strategic leadership as iterative processes

Strategic thinking partly relies on the backward-mapping process, starting with learning outcomes and working back in sequence to determine appropriate strategies for learning experiences, teaching methods, organizational structures, resources, leadership and culture-building. But it also entails a process of checking forwards as well as backwards in an iterative way through the same sequence of elements to ensure the maintenance of harmony, consistency and alignment. For example, a change in student learning outcomes may well necessitate a review of learning experiences and thus teaching methods, and even organizational structures, and so on upward. However, in a reverse direction, it is equally important to ensure that, say, timetabling, an organizational structure, is matching the needs of teaching and learning, which are in turn achieving the desired learning outcomes. The iterative process backwards and forwards is thus imperative at a conceptual level.

It is also crucial at a practical level. Strategic leadership may be conceived as the process of developing a strategic intent, and then constantly trying to secure and maintain alignment, synergy and consistency between all of the interconnected elements of the learning-focused design model, and between these and the external environment. However, few schools are completely independent of central agencies and other formal bodies, such as unions. Government and administration, and the social-cultural context comprise the external environment (see Figure 6.2). Every day, forces may threaten the synergy and alignment of the elements. Organizational politics, for example, may make it difficult for teachers to share agreement on professional practice. Or changes in resource levels from outside the school may have an impact on the implementation of computer-assisted teaching/learning methods, which in turn seriously challenge the attainment of student learning outcomes, and thus the strategic intent. Of course, forces from the aforementioned environments may also present opportunities for adopting or adapting ways which can improve student learning and, as such, leaders would be neglectful not to try to infuse these into the school. For example, as a school enrols more students from specific ethnic minorities, different approaches to teaching and learning may be more efficacious and call for strategic flexibility.

In these and other ways, strategic leadership is constantly balancing, adjusting and compromising the realities of situations against the strategic intent of the learning-focused design. Such leadership then is discerning in the ways which the school meets student needs through continually sifting methodologies and processes which stem from within the school, which Mintzberg (1994) refers to as emergent strategies, from formal external directives, policies and directives, and from the sociocultural identities which the school draws. Such sifting is in essence strategic and relies on the values and purpose which underpin the existence of the school. A learning-centred strategy gives primacy of place to students and by implication their social-cultural background. It is to this that the final part of this chapter shifts. Our intention in this final section is to illustrate the discussion to this point and reinforce that strategic leadership within the framework we have set must be context sensitive. The issue of strategic leadership and multi-ethnicity is therefore considered in outline, with more detailed discussion of the challenges of leading multicultural schools to follow in Chapter 11.

Strategic Leadership and multi-ethnicity

According to the 2001 Census, one in eight students in the UK comes from an ethnic minority background. By 2010, this will have risen to one in five. While students from Chinese and Indian backgrounds achieve academically higher results than the national average, the majority of ethnic minority students, particularly those with a Pakistani, Bangladeshi and Afro-Caribbean background, achieve well below the average. Besides academic standards, there are also issues of problematic behaviour, alienation, disaffection and racial tension to consider. We argue that these and other associated problems are appropriately addressed through strategic thinking and strategic leadership.

The challenges that schools confront in relation to ethnic minority students are multifarious and deep-seated. They not only originate from within the school, but also from the students' social and cultural environment. This implies that adequate responses from schools should be holistic rather than piecemeal. It should be plain by now that this holism does not imply, for example, uniformity in terms of pedagogy, community relations or teacher-related processes within the school (Walker and Quong, 1998). Rather, it means the application of the coherent holistic model so that it makes sense in organizational and learning terms. In short, a strategic intent based on the whole-school learning-centred design concept appears well suited for better meeting the needs of multicultural schools.

Strategic thinking is involved in formulating the strategic intent, and leadership in working through an implementation strategy. The values, mission, and aims of multi-ethnic schools need to be reflected and agreed upon by their school communities, and strategic leadership plays a crucial role in that process.

However, the school's most poignant response to the issues raised is likely to be in the design elements and the backward- and forward-mapping process in which leaders engage. Beginning with the instructional core, the first stage involves a reassessment of the curriculum and associated student outcomes. From changes in the curriculum, the implications for learning processes and experiences can be derived, as can, in turn, the ramifications of these for teaching methods and strategies. Following this, new organizational structures, including timetabling and student grouping, can be decided. Many of these changes will point to the need for targeted teacher professional development, resource allocation, school culture, decision-making, counselling and support, and even the hiring of certain types of teachers (Dimmock and Walker, 2002).

As previously argued, we see this as an iterative process of continuous backward/forward checking for alignment and consistency between the design elements in a learning-centred school environment. Below, we spell out in more detail the implications of this approach for strategic leadership in a multi-ethnic school community. Whereas other themes are obviously important, for convenience, we identify six themes of strategic leadership, and follow as closely as possible the iterative process involved in backward-mapping (see Chapter 11 for a more detailed exposition of these themes).

1   Leadership of the community   If the school's strategic intent is to incorporate concern for multi-ethnicity and cultural sensitivity, then strategic leadership is the process whereby leaders first engage their communities in shaping their standpoint on multi-ethnicity and multiculturalism. All members of the school community should be invited to reflect on the relevance and significance of cultural diversity for their school. This process would form a useful basis on which to formalize their position in terms of a general statement incorporated in the mission and aims of the school. The leadership skills of the head teacher are exercised in bringing together and moulding a diverse multicultural community as a harmonious group, building on cultural divergence and richness.

This is a necessary and desirable preliminary stage to the backward-mapping process that begins at the next stage.

2   Leadership of the educational programme   A major way in which multiculturalism needs to be managed is through redesigning the curriculum. It has already been remarked that redesign focusing on student outcomes, the instructional core and educational programme is fundamental to school improvement in general, and to those schools intending to address multiculturalism, in particular. Too often, present practice fails to offer more than tokenism. Banks (1994) and Sleeter and Grant (1987; 1993) argue that adding increments to the mainstream curriculum, such as special days to celebrate ethnic food or festivals, is likely to offer no more than an interesting distraction from the normal curriculum. If, however, the aim is to go beyond tolerance of cultural difference and towards understanding of, and respect for, other races and cultures, then themes and ideas of a multicultural nature need to be embedded in subjects across the whole curriculum, in an integrated way. Banks (1993) refers to 'content integration' as the process whereby examples, data and information are drawn from a variety of cultures to illustrate the core concepts, principles and generalizations in subject areas. A framework for redesigning the curriculum might be provided by specific learning outcomes for multiculturalism written into various subjects, and evaluation and assessment modified accordingly.

Strategic leadership is not just concerned, however, with curriculum structure and content. In backward-mapping from student outcomes, attention is next given to learning content and processes, before moving to instructional methods. School leaders can promote particular instructional strategies that favour and support multiculturalism. Here, Banks (1993, p. 17) refers to 'knowledge construction' as the process whereby teachers can help students understand how knowledge is created and interpreted through such factors as race, ethnicity, gender and social class. They can also engage in 'prejudice reduction', that is, developing strategies to help students acquire positive cross-cultural and racial attitudes. As Cunningham and Cordeiro (2000) note: 'Teachers who accept cultural pluralism constantly ask themselves how to help students respect and appreciate cultural diversity in the classroom, school and society' (p. 105).

3 School organization and structure reflect multiculturalism School leaders can enhance multiculturalism through the formal and informal structures system in the school. For example, the ways in which students are grouped can either promote or retard social interaction. Streaming and setting by ability, for example, might give way to broader social issues concerned with mixing ethnic and multicultural groups in the same classes. Teachers can exercise the same prerogative by mixing different ethnic and cultural groups to form collaborative groups within classes. Racial and ethnic mixing can also be encouraged through extra-curricular activities, involving sports teams, clubs and societies which themselves respect the values and traditions of various cultures.

4 Human resource management and development Leaders can influence the approach to multiculturalism in their schools through personnel and human resource management. First, staff selection and appointment policies and practices need to reflect a disposition towards, and a commitment to, multicultural schooling. Secondly, the teacher and administrator profile might reflect as near as possible the student cultural mix. A sensitivity to, and knowledge of working and communicating with, teachers, fellow administrators, parents and community members from diverse cultures becomes a key facet of school leadership.

Secondly, teachers will require professional development in understanding different cultures and their values, in designing curricula reflective of multicultural schooling, in adopting a range of new teaching and learning techniques and in creating new forms of assessment, all of which are culture sensitive. Finally, leaders can consolidate and connect curricular and pedagogical practice supportive of multiculturalism through a staff appraisal and evaluation system that reflects the knowledge, skills and attributes necessary for the successful implementation of school policy on multicultural schooling. Where possible, reward systems for teachers involving their promotion and additional responsibility can be grounded in their successful practice and promotion of multicultural education.

5 Culture-building and resource allocation Leadership has no more important function in the multi-ethnic school than building the organizational culture to reflect the values of multiculturalism. Leaders build culture by modelling and demonstrating their own values in interacting with others, making appropriate public pronouncements, establishing supportive reward and discipline systems, and treating and valuing equally students from all races and ethnic backgrounds. A learning environment in which students from diverse racial, ethnic and social groups believe that they are heard and valued, and experience respect, belonging and encouragement, is referred to by Banks (1993, p. 17) as an 'empowering school culture'. How the school raises revenue and allocates resources is also a good indicator of its commitment to multiculturalism.

6 School governance, decision-making and multiculturalism Finally, leaders have a key role in promoting multiculturalism through their involvement of stakeholder groups in school governance and decision-making. Democratic decision-making processes that are inclusive of all members of the school community are vital.

Issues of school governance include those associated with parents and other school stakeholder groups, but also spread directly into the community to greater inter-agency collaboration. Capper (1996) argues that such collaboration provides a powerful means of understanding, interacting and empowering different cultural groups. He suggests that community based inter-agency collaboration can promote the involvement of traditionally disempowered groups across human service processes. Connections between the school, systems, agencies and informal community service organizations that have long been seen as peripheral to schools can be harnessed to promote multiculturalism in schools.

Conclusion

Our main purpose in this chapter has been to present a new perspective on strategic leadership in two respects and at the same time to address a perceived gap in the literature. First, we have connected strategic intent and leadership with school improvement through an approach that we have called learning-centred holistic school design. In developing this approach, we have also suggested a methodology through which it can be operationalized – namely, by adopting an iterative process of backward- and forward-mapping. Secondly, by way of illustration, we have attempted to relate strategic leadership in schools to a cultural context of increasing relevance and concern in many countries, namely, multi-ethnic communities. In these ways, we argue that strategic leadership is most likely to contribute to school improvement and ensure that future schools truly reflect the cultural diversity of their communities.

In the next chapter, we move from the more holistic and multicultural framework of effective organizational leadership and strategic thinking for schools to a more specific focus on its implications for effective teaching and learning strategies within schools.

7
Leadership, Learning and Teaching in Diverse Cultures

Successful learning on the part of students, quality teaching, and school organization conducive to successful learning and teaching are all intrinsic elements of effective schooling. This chapter claims that a key aspect contributing towards effectiveness is the extent to which conditions reflect particular cultural characteristics that distinguish them from practices elsewhere in the world.

A major purpose of the chapter is the portrayal of teaching, learning and leadership as interdependent and culture-bound activities. As such, they warrant investigation from a cross-cultural perspective. As noted in Chapter 1, the comparisons included are based mainly on Japan, mainland China and the USA, with some reference to other societies, including Hong Kong, Singapore, the UK and Australia. Wherever reference is made to societies collectively, such as 'East Asian' or 'Asian' and 'Western', we acknowledge that there is substantial cultural diversity within these regions and that the use of such terms is justified only for convenience. In addition, identification of cultural differences between societies inevitably runs the risk of overgeneralization, since no group of people is completely harmonious and different groups may share commonalities. Yet the definition of culture itself hinges on the recognition of common values and norms that bind groups of people together, but which at the same time distinguish them from other groups.

For a more complete understanding of leadership, it is necessary to consider its connections to other key processes and activities that take place within schools and outside in their environments. Outside school, these activities, involving parenting, socialization and home–school relationships, have already been discussed in detail within a conceptual framework based on the five dimensions defined by Hofstede (1991) (see Chapter 5 for a full discussion). This chapter focuses on activities *within* the school, with particular reference to teaching and learning. The chapter is therefore divided into two main sections. The first investigates the cultural context to learning as the key activity of schools, while the second focuses on the cultural context to teaching and learning.

While recognizing that other approaches may be applied, this chapter mirrors that of the earlier chapters on societal culture, family and socialization by conceptualizing the context of leadership within schools in similar ways. First, it assumes that leadership is exercised inside school in relation to people and activities engaged in teaching and learning. Second, it acknowledges that all these activities – leadership, teaching and learning – are culture sensitive or culture dependent and that, consequently, differences in their form and practice may, at least partially, be attributed to the diversity in societal cultures.

Learning

Learning is the central purpose and mission of schools. Government policy pronouncements across the globe recognize that the main objective of schools centres on enabling all students in their care to experience successful learning experiences and outcomes (Dimmock, 2000a). Consistent with this mission, the task of school leaders is to establish a school ethos whereby both administrators and teachers continuously address the following central questions:

- How do students in this school best learn?
- Are we currently providing these best learning conditions for them?
- If not, how can we improve?

While conditions conducive to learning are partly generic – for example, students are more likely to learn when material is structured – we also know that students differ appreciably in their learning styles. Thus, catering to individual student differences has become a recent priority – especially in Anglo-American societies – as indicated by the press for individualized curricula and student-centred learning. The growing trend of adopting curriculum frameworks expressed in terms of student-learning outcomes recognizes that different students are capable of achieving different levels of outcome. Equally important, recent research reveals important student learning differences related to societal culture.

This section is devoted, first, to outlining the connections between learning and school leadership; secondly, it is geared to explaining how learning and learners differ cross-culturally and the implications this has for school leadership. In regard to the general linkage between learning and leadership, four important connections warrant attention: leaders–

- build a school culture that values learning and believes that all students can be successful learners;
- play an advisory, co-ordinating, overseeing role that is grounded in esoteric and evidence-informed knowledge about how learning takes place in and out of school – this helps leaders to communicate with, and motivate, staff, students and parents;

- establish a personnel and human resources policy embracing the hiring, appraising and developing of staff – all with a learning orientation; and
- implement a school financial resources policy that reflects the primacy of learning across the whole student body.

In regard to leadership and cross-cultural learning, recent research is discovering important insights into cultural differences in student learning. If leadership is connected to learning in the way suggested, then there are important cross-cultural implications for school leaders in different societies.

Adopting a cultural perspective, Stevenson and Stigler (1992) have uncovered a major difference between Chinese and Anglo-American models of learning. Asian societies believe that effort and hard work are the keys to learning and that these attributes can compensate for lack of ability. By contrast, Americans tend to attribute academic success more to innate ability. These different social philosophies about what accounts for success – in the case of the Chinese, tracing back to the teachings of Confucius – have ramifications for parental expectations, behaviour at home and teaching at school (Biggs, 1994; Hess and Azuma, 1991; Holloway, 1988). Each model has consequences for learning. For example, the American view means that children are inclined either to understand at once or not at all. The Asian model posits a long, step-by-step incremental and gradual process, where errors are seen as normal. This may explain why grades and student answers are made public in Asian classrooms while they are more likely to be considered a private matter in American classrooms. It also explains why Japanese teachers, in particular, often use student errors as a way of teaching so that the whole class can learn. An individual student's work may be held up to the class for the benefit of all – an act that would be taken as a grave embarrassment by American students. The Asian step-by-step, incremental, teaching-learning model may also explain why Asian teachers emphasize the acquisition of basic knowledge and skills in subjects such as art, before the children are allowed to progress to the development of creative skills. Children are encouraged to progress to creative pursuits more quickly in American and Western classrooms.

These important culturally related differences of approach to, and assumptions underlying, learning constitute key differences between the learning milieu of schools in the East and West. Learning styles and how learning takes place are influenced by culture. Chinese students in Hong Kong, and it is claimed Japanese and Chinese generally, learn differently from Western students (Watkins and Biggs, 1996). If the appropriate learning environments differ cross-culturally, so presumably will the particular leadership strategies used in their cultivation. There are clearly dangers in making cross-cultural generalizations and assumptions in respect of learning, as revealed by recent research findings on cultural-cognitive differences between Asian and Western learners (Watkins and Biggs, 1996). Basing their work on Hong Kong students, these authors claim that many of the views typically held in relation to Chinese (and other Asian) learners, are in fact, myths. Hong Kong students, it is argued, are representative of students in other Confucian-heritage cultures, such as Korea, Japan, China, Taiwan and Singapore.

The first misconception centres on the contribution that repetition and rote learning make to memorization and understanding. While there is agreement that Chinese and Asian students in general, have a tendency to rote learn, many Westerners tend to attach a derogatory meaning to rote learning, implying that little understanding, reflection or deep learning, takes place. Asian students use repetition more than Westerners, but quite why is difficult to ascertain. However, Watkins and Biggs (1996) argue that for Chinese students, memorization leads to understanding, although whether it deepens understanding or is a precondition for it is not clear. For many Asian students, the relationship between memorization and understanding is a two-way cause–effect phenomenon. In the case of Hong Kong students, studies show that their rote learning is a necessary part of memorization, which in turn is linked to deeper understanding (Kember and Gow, 1990; Marton, Dall'Alba and Tse, 1996; Watkins and Biggs, 1996). While memorization is used to deepen understanding, it can also be used for something as practical as passing examinations. Asian students seem to be sufficiently sophisticated to vary the process to suit the objective. In other words, Hong Kong students memorize in order to understand; the two processes are functionally connected, the one a prerequisite for the other. For Western students it is assumed that no such link exists; rote learning and deep learning are seen as two separate entities. Westerners generally fail to see the advantages of rote learning, instead regarding it as a lower-order form of learning and contrasting it with higher-order learning skills associated with deep learning and learning for understanding. For them, rote learning is to be discouraged in schools as it signifies that the student has achieved no more than surface learning. In the Western mindset, rote learning is regarded as lower-order learning and is contrasted with higher-order learning skills associated with deep learning and learning for understanding. Rote learning leading to memorization, deep understanding and examination passing is a central characteristic of effective schooling in the four Asian systems.

A second myth relates to motivation to learn. On this matter, Watkins and Biggs (1996) assert, 'Western ways of categorizing motivation do not travel well, at least not to the Orient' (p. 273). Westerners tend to see intrinsic motivation as the precursor to meaningful deep understanding. The Chinese student, however, taking a more pragmatic view, may be motivated by a mixed set of forces, including 'personal ambition, family face, peer support, material reward, and yes, possibly even interest' (p. 273). In addition, Confucian characteristics of diligence and receptiveness help in this process. In short, according to Watkins and Biggs, 'the familiar extrinsic/intrinsic polarity collapses' (p. 273). Whereas people in individualistic societies tend to be driven by achievement motivation and the ego-enhancing feeling of success in education defined in competitive terms, the Chinese have a more holistic sense of achievement, one less driven by their own ego alone, but more cognizant of the way significant others, such as family members and even society as a whole, define success.

Collectivist notions also affect the teacher–student relationship, which although hierarchical, can also be warm, caring and supportive (Chan, 1993). In addition, Tang (1996) has found that Chinese students collaborate spontaneously outside the classroom, helping each other to obtain material useful for the completion of, and entering discussion on, assignments. This amount of collaboration appears to be more extensive than Western students engage in. Somewhat ironically, Watkins and Biggs (1996, p. 275) conclude: 'Hong Kong secondary school students would in fact prefer a more collaborative learning environment which they consider would promote the deeper, more achievement-oriented approach to learning.'

Cross-cultural differences in learning and the implications for school leadership

Different cognitive strategies used by students in learning have implications for teachers in their choice of teaching strategies and for leaders in promoting 'good' learning cultures and practices in schools. The nurturing of learning is part of instructional leadership. Since the cognitive processes and technical skills involved in learning vary cross-culturally, one would expect to find these reflected in different interpretations of instructional leadership. Moreover, conceptions of the 'good student' and the 'good teacher' also vary cross-culturally. According to Watkins (2000), the 'good student' in the UK is seen as one who pays attention to the teacher and does what he or she is told. In China, however, this is the expectation of all students, with the result that teachers can focus more on academic and social matters. Likewise, students see the 'good teacher' in the UK as one who raises students' interest and uses an array of effective teaching methods. In contrast, the perception of an effective teacher held by Chinese students centres on warm, caring, friendly relations combined with deep subject knowledge and an ability to model a strong set of morals – all within a hierarchical structure. Notions of what constitutes effective group work and questioning also differ as between British and Chinese teachers.

Teaching

Recent research has indicated important cross-cultural differences in teaching as well as learning. Not only do the findings improve our understanding of instructional leadership across different cultures, they also challenge some of the stereotypical images held about Asian teachers and students. In analysing major differences between teachers in America and China, Taiwan and Japan, Stevenson and Stigler (1992) conducted research in scores of elementary classrooms in these countries from 1980 onwards. It is necessary to point out that their research applies only to primary schools; and that there are major differences within and between Asian and Western countries. Below is a summary of their conclusions:

1 Asian teachers have significantly fewer class contact hours (Cheng and Wong, 1996; Reynolds and Farrell, 1996) than their Western counterparts. In Japan and Taiwan, teachers teach about 60 per cent of the lesson time. In China, a teacher might only teach three or four hours each day (Cheng and Wong, 1996; Stevenson and Lee, 1996). This allows them to plan lessons more carefully, spend more time seeing students who need help, and to discuss teaching techniques with their colleagues. This is not the practice, however, throughout Asia; Hong Kong teachers have class contact hours similar to American teachers – often amounting to 90 per cent of the lesson time.

2 Japanese and Chinese teachers generally spend more time working together and helping each other design lessons. This is facilitated by, first, the existence of a national curriculum, which means that they are often teaching the same material at about the same time; secondly, by the provision of more non-contact time; and thirdly, by close proximity in the same workroom. American teachers, by contrast, lack the time and incentive to engage in such collaboration – they are often following different curricula, they lack the preparation time, and their workrooms are often spread across the school.

3 Primary school teachers in Asia are not expected to be expert in a number of subjects. Whereas elementary teachers in countries like the USA and Australia are expected to teach across subjects (specialist teaching normally starts at the secondary level), this is not so in Asian primary schools. Asian teachers can prepare their lessons during their free periods, rather than in the evenings when they are tired, as their Western counterparts have to do.

4 Asian teachers come closer to practising the principles of 'informed teaching' than their American counterparts (Dimmock, 2000b). In general, they are well informed and well prepared, guiding their students through the material. Lessons are clearly structured: each lesson starts with a purpose and finishes with a summary. During the lesson, there is interaction and discussion, and students are active participants in problem-solving.

5 Asian teachers display technical proficiency, which is one factor in explaining why students concentrate and pay attention in class more than their Western counterparts. A further reason is that the school day in Asia tends to be punctuated by shorter, but more frequent, rest and recreation periods, thus students do not have to study for such long continuous periods.

6   Asian children have more opportunity to interact with their teachers than do American students. American teachers structure their lessons so that they teach concepts during the first part, and then require students to undertake seatwork, that is, work at their desks, in the second part. Asian teachers, however, intersperse seatwork in brief periods throughout the lesson. Seatwork is used as a practice for the skill or knowledge just learned, and affords diagnosis and early corrective feedback if the student demonstrates a lack of understanding.

7   Asian teachers are observed to give more corrective feedback than their American counterparts and this serves to motivate the students. For example, a Japanese lesson might be based on a poor piece of work completed by a particular student, with the teacher exposing all the weaknesses to the whole class so that all can learn from the individual's mistakes. The individual student whose work is exhibited withstands attention and personal embarrassment for the benefit of the whole group. Such a practice in a Chinese classroom would lead to loss of face (Biggs, 1994; Gow et al., 1996). In addition, Asian teachers are more inclined to make use of concrete objects and other devices that children find enhance their learning.

8   Asian teachers are more likely to make subjects more relevant and interesting by relating material to be learned to the children's everyday lives. In mathematics, word problems often serve this function, turning the lesson into an active problem-solving exercise.

9   When Beijing teachers were asked to rank the most important attributes of good teaching, they ranked 'clarity' first, whereas Chicago teachers ranked in first place 'sensitivity to the needs of individuals'. Beijing teachers ranked 'enthusiasm' second, while Chicago teachers chose 'patience'. These results suggest that American teachers see their main role as catering to the needs of individual children – possibly at the expense of whole-class teaching, while Asian teachers devote their attention to the principles and processes of whole class teaching, while still acknowledging the needs of individual children. Despite class sizes of 60 or more, teachers still manage high levels of individual interaction with students (Jin and Cortazzi, 1998).

10   Asian teachers tend to stick to the basic principles of teaching, and have more time and energy to apply them (Biggs, 1994; Hess and Azuma, 1991). They incorporate a variety of teaching techniques into a lesson, rely more frequently on discussions rather than lectures, achieve smooth transitions from one activity to another and spend more time on task (Reynolds and Farrell, 1996).

Stevenson and Stigler (1992) and Biggs (1994) both conclude that certain teaching stereotypes in regard to Confucian-heritage societies are valid. For example, children's experiences at school are highly structured. The school day, as well as the content and sequence of lessons, are tightly planned (Jin and Cortazzi, 1998; Reynolds, 1996). There are also large class sizes, some authoritarianism, and high examination pressures. However, in other respects, the stereotypes fail to capture reality because they ignore cultural factors. The teacher in Confucian-heritage societies has developed culturally adaptable ways of teaching to circumvent what is regarded in the West as unfavourable conditions (especially in terms of class size) for effective teaching. Teachers give thought to the grouping of students, such that they can learn from one another. Children tend to do a lot more group work than individual work. In Japan, this group emphasis is known as the *han*. Membership of each *han* is carefully planned by the teacher to ensure that each student plays a team role and performs to achieve an expected outcome. Thus, in their own way, they integrate hierarchy with warmth and care; they blend whole-class teaching with student-centred approaches and group work; they develop a functional mentor–mentee joint responsibility for learning; they push for high cognitive level outcomes; they plan and co-operate with their colleagues as part of a professional community; and despite the tight structure, schools promote high levels of social interaction (Watkins, 2000). Therefore, students in these Asian societies display a liking for school rather more than do their American counterparts (Stevenson and Stigler, 1992). Asian elementary school classrooms not only manage to promote children's learning, but do so while instilling structure, order and discipline and at the same time, a liking for school.

Other favourable factors are supportive of teachers in Confucian-heritage societies in relation to their Western counterparts. Generally, they enjoy higher social and professional status (Hofstede, 1991). Good quality teaching lies at the heart of effective schooling (Cheng, 1995). The quality of teaching relies on the calibre of entrants attracted to the profession, the pre-service and in-service training provided, and the working conditions under which teachers perform. In what ways do these conditions support effective schooling in the four Asian systems being reviewed? Teacher training methods in the four Asian systems vary considerably. In Japan, teacher training is like an apprenticeship. There is a systematic effort to pass on the accumulated wisdom of past generations of teachers to new entrants and to keep perfecting that practice by providing for continued professional interaction. Beginning teachers, by law, must receive a minimum of 20 days of in-service training, supervised by master teachers, during their first year on the job. Many teachers in mainland China have only rudimentary training. However, conditions vary widely between the more prosperous cities and the poor rural areas. In Hong Kong, teachers receive a preponderance of upfront training in college, supplemented by brief spells of teaching practice in schools, before starting teaching. Thereafter, they receive limited opportunities for in-service training by comparison with Japanese and mainland Chinese teachers, and they certainly lack the school-based professional development practices engaged in by Japanese teachers. It is worth describing these practices in more detail.

Japanese teachers – both beginners and experienced – are expected to hone their skills through interaction with other teachers. Meetings are organized to discuss specific teaching techniques and skills, and to devise lesson plans and handouts. *Kouaikenshuu* is the term used for the continuous process of school-based professional development engaged in by groups of Japanese teachers throughout their careers. According to Stigler and Hiebert (1999), 'These groups play a dual role: not only do they provide a context in which teachers are mentored and trained, they also provide a laboratory for the development and testing of new teaching techniques' (p. 110).

Run by teachers who work together in grade-level, subject or special purpose groups, such as the school technology committee, a range of diverse activities is undertaken all within the auspices of the school improvement plan that sets the goals and focus for each year's efforts. At the heart of the *kouaikenshuu* is the lesson study, or *jugyou kenkyuu*, the principle behind which is that the classroom is the best place to improve teaching. Grounding pedagogic research and experiment in classroom practice mitigates the problems encountered later when transferring ideas developed out of the classroom. Groups of teachers meet regularly over long periods of time (up to a year) to work on the design, implementation, testing and improvement of one or several 'research lessons'. Practices similar to these also occur among mainland Chinese teachers whose teaching conditions and patterns of school organization are conducive to collaborative peer professional development based on effective pedagogy.

How teachers approach their work is partly dependent on their social status and the degree to which, as stated earlier, home and school values align (Stigler and Hiebert, 1999). Japanese teachers, for example, enjoy relatively high salaries and social status when compared with other public sector workers. The supply of applicants generally exceeds demand for teachers, resulting in a higher calibre of entrant to the profession. In contrast, teachers in mainland China are poorly paid but, like teachers in the other three systems, generally exhibit strong levels of commitment. High expectations are placed on them by principals and others, exemplified by many teachers spending long hours in school between 7.30 a.m. and 6 p.m.

Teachers are accorded more respect by students and parents, and they are more supported by the home and family in their efforts to encourage children to learn. Students are more self-disciplined in the classroom and more willing to be attentive, collaborative, more adept at cue-seeking – especially in regard to assessment – and more task oriented in their class work and homework.

The moral is that cultures are systems (Biggs, 1994). This means that it is of little use looking at specific practices or features and trying to identify their presence or effectiveness in another culture. If certain Western features do not seem to be present in Asian settings, it might be that they exist in a disguised or different form, or that they are compensated for by another set of factors. The dynamic interplay between all the parts, not the presence of any one part, is what makes it all work. In short, culture provides the context within which the parts interact.

There is little doubt that many Asian cultures achieve harmony between the school and home environments to a degree that is rare in Western school systems. Some of the so-called Confucian heritage cultures (CHCs), for example, Japan and China, have achieved other commendable features, including decreased teaching loads allowing for better quality preparation; informed teaching practices, such as more wait time and more individual attention within whole-class teaching; more peer interaction and a belief in greater effort when faced with failure. None of these alone makes a significant difference. Rather, it is the harmony achieved between teaching and learning in the CHC cultures and between the school and society, which matters. There is much about the methods of teaching and learning in CHC schools which would be unworkable in Western schools. In Japan, for example, the student – not the school – is seen as the 'twig to be bent'. Western cultures, receptive to the notion that the school accommodates the child, continue to grapple with the problem of putting this ideal into practice.

Cross-cultural differences in teaching and the implications for school leadership

Viewed from a cross-cultural context, the relationship between leadership and teaching is influenced by different practices, organizational traditions and relations with the broader social environment, as indicated below.

Both teaching and instructional leadership are culturally related phenomena. The nurturing of informed and culturally appropriate teaching is part of instructional leadership. Conceptions of the 'good teacher' and therefore the leadership necessary in the promotion of good teaching will vary cross-culturally. As discussed in earlier sections, the concept of a 'good teacher', and what constitutes effective group work and questioning differ between cultures and societies. School leaders in different societies can be expected to resource, nurture and promote the teaching practices regarded as culturally acceptable and appropriate.

Leaders' expectations of teachers and the way in which they approach their work are also culture dependent. Differences in the organizational and structural arrangements for teaching mean that teachers' work roles differ markedly between cultures. Whereas teachers in Anglo-American schools typically teach 80 per cent of total lessons each week, their Chinese counterparts teach about half of the total lessons. Consequently, Chinese teachers have more time to plan and prepare high-quality lessons and more opportunity to collaborate with peers and to engage in professional development. School leaders in East Asia may also expect their teachers to spend longer hours in school – it is commonplace for teachers to arrive between 7.30 a.m. and 8 a.m. and not leave before 6 p.m. Leaders' relationship with, and expectations of, teachers and the way they approach their work is also dependent on the social status of teachers and the degree to which home and school values align. Teachers in East Asian schools tend to enjoy higher social status and closer alignment with family values than do their counterparts in the West.

Conclusion

This chapter has adopted a cross-cultural perspective to understand the context to school leadership. In particular, it has advanced a case for a perspective to leadership that connects with teaching and learning, as well as with parenting, and the broader socializing experiences of children growing up in their unique sociocultural environments. It is argued that leadership, like teaching, learning, parenting and child-rearing are strongly influenced by societal culture.

It is apparent that leadership cannot be fully understood without considering its cultural context. Differences between societal cultures tend to exert divergent forces on leadership. At the same time, leaders are increasingly working within globalizing policy environments that exert convergent forces on their leadership. Consequently, the work context for contemporary school leaders is characterized by tension between powerful forces of convergence and divergence.

It is clear that in developing the field of educational leadership, especially that part concerned with international comparisons, care must be taken to avoid drawing over-simplistic generalizations based on narrow ethnocentric understandings. There is a robust case for more cross-cultural leadership studies to appreciate the full complexity of cultural influences on leadership. These will lead scholars, practitioners and policy-makers not only to a better understanding of school leadership in other contexts, but also their own. The emergence of greater cultural understanding of schools and school leadership is long overdue, especially given the phenomenal rise of multiculturalism and globalization.

In the next chapter, we turn to the question of the leadership and management of staff development in diverse cultural contexts, with particular reference to leadership style, teacher involvement and leader–teacher relationships.

8
Leadership and Staff Management in Diverse Cultures

A greater understanding of the subtleties of cultural influence on leadership can be achieved through comparing school leaders in different societies. In this chapter, we present our recent research conducted with principals in three societies, namely Singapore, Hong Kong and Perth in Western Australia (see Walker and Dimmock, 2002b).[1] Principals' perceptions cannot be attributed to societal culture alone – personal values, the impact of modernization and globalization, and organizational culture are also significant influences – but its influence at various levels seems convincing.

The main purpose of this chapter is to elucidate three themes – namely, leadership style, teacher involvement and leader–teacher relationships – which emerged from a more extensive study into culture and leadership across the three societies. They serve to illustrate the effect of culture on in-school leadership processes. Each of the themes comprises three society-specific sub-themes – one each for Hong Kong, Singapore and Australia – and one 'comparative theme'. The identification of comparative themes aimed to capture the similarities and subtle differences between the principals in each location and to hypothesize the possible influence of culture on the exercise and conceptualization of school leadership. However, no generalization beyond the small group of principals engaged in the research is proposed, and even within this limited sample both individual and group variations were evident. The overall findings are summarized in Figure 8.1.

Leadership processes

It is generally accepted that leadership is exercised in different ways in different organizational cultural contexts. Although less well empirically supported, there also appears to be some differentiation between educational leaders in different societies (Gronn and Ribbins, 1996). For example, a growing number of empirical studies have identified quite distinct conceptions of educational leadership in native indigenous communities, including the work of Bryant

(2003) on Native American Indians, and the study of Maori female principals in New Zealand by Fitzgerald (2003). Moreover, in a comparative study, McAdams (1993) suggested that one of the main distinctions between US and Japanese societies is the Japanese group orientation in contrast to American individualism.

Cheng (1998) proposes that Chinese societies are similar to the Japanese in being more collectivist than individualist, which may indicate that, on the whole, Japanese and Chinese principals are more group- than self-oriented. In such group-oriented societies, the role of the principal often seems to focus on developing and ensuring harmony among staff and enforcing common, standard approaches to governance, organization, curriculum and instruction. In contrast, in many English-speaking and non English-speaking Western societies principals are more inclined to consider the individual needs of both teachers and students in the operation of schools (Cheng, 1998, p. 16). Organizations generally focus on task achievement rather than the maintenance of relationships. Principals in such societies have a tendency to put task achievement before relationships, and to judge staff based on performance and the 'bottom line'. Such principals may be classified, according to our framework, as influenced by *limited relationships*.

Consequently, different cultures deal with conflict and participation in different ways. According to Bond (1991a), the disturbance of interpersonal relations and group harmony through conflict can cause lasting animosity in Chinese cultures. As a result, the Chinese tend to avoid open confrontation and assertiveness. In the school or group context, this is manifested by teachers and principals tending to avoid open disagreement, with the leader's view invariably being accepted (Walker, Bridges and Chan, 1996). In such cultures, principals tend to avoid situations which risk conflict and instead to rely on authoritarian decision-making modes. A possible side effect of conflict avoidance and a requirement for harmonious relationships is that decisions and policies are seldom challenged, or indeed approached creatively, by the group. In such cultures, which we classify as *replicative*, school leaders may more readily accept policies and edicts and tend towards preserving the status quo.

Both Hofstede (1991) and Trompenaars and Hampden-Turner (1997) suggest that cultures attribute status, respect and power according to different cultural norms. In Chinese societies, for example, respect may be attributed to position, age or family background, whereas in New Zealand (at least for white New Zealanders), it is attributed more to personal or on-the-job competence (Trompenaars and Hampden-Turner, 1997). In societies where power is linked to extrinsic factors, leadership tends to be from the 'top' and exercised in an authoritarian or autocratic manner, a point reinforced in the next chapter in a discussion of teacher appraisal.

They also suggest that cultures differ in their stance toward change. In countries such as Australia, there tends to be a reasonably high tolerance of change and people in schools take a proactive stance to engineer its effects on their work lives. Policy and operational changes are challenged, questioned and negotiated at the school level. In other societies, change and uncertainty is accepted, almost as a *coup de grâce*, as the way things are and are meant to be. For example, principals in countries such as China, which tend toward this fatalistic view, tend to rely on established philosophies, responsibilities and power relationships to provide staff with security, while accepting and implementing change, whether they agree with it or not (Dimmock and Lim, 1999; Hallinger, Chantarapanye and Kantamara, 1999).

A comparison of school leadership in Hong Kong, Singapore and Perth (Australia)

Taking a comparative perspective, the following sections focus on the influence of culture on leadership style, teacher involvement and leader–teacher relationships, based on data from our research in Singapore, Hong Kong and Perth (Western Australia). (See Figure 8.1)

Theme 1: leadership style

Sub-theme 1 – Hong Kong: Hong Kong principals see their leadership role as shifting from remote and autocratic to more participative. However, participation has developed among senior teachers as a group and separately among teachers as a group in ways that have enabled principals to retain their hierarchical distance and positional authority and aloofness The Hong Kong principals in our study believed they were moving towards more participative leadership, but only within certain boundaries and to a limited extent. Their instrumental definitions of participative leadership remained grounded in a traditional remoteness from classroom teachers, but included closer working relationships with and through their senior management groups or teams. The principals supported the maintenance of leadership remoteness in line with what they saw as traditional beliefs about the place and determination of authority, and that a level of aloofness was necessary to retain status and order.

In the Hong Kong education context, remote leadership can be taken as 'leadership from a distance (above)' and its apparent intractability in schools may be rooted in the respect traditionally given to the position of the principal, or other senior administrators, by teachers and society in general. As one principal

Theme 1: leadership style		
Hong Kong	**Singapore**	**Australia**
Hong Kong principals see their leadership role as shifting from remote and autocratic to more participative. However, participation has developed among senior teachers as a group and separately among teachers as a group in ways that have enabled principals to retain their hierarchical distance and positional authority and aloofness.	Singapore principals see themselves as hierarchical, but in readily adopting more consultative modes of decision-making, they are balancing the traditional and the modern.	Australian principals face strong tensions in their leadership style between expectations of participative democratic decision-making, on the one hand, and demands of accountability, which focus responsibility on the principal, on the other. Consequently, they feel the need to assert their prerogative as final decision-makers.
Comparative theme 1: Principals in all three societies acknowledge changed expectations of their leadership styles held by others: however, their subtly different responses reflect cultural differences.		

Theme 2: teacher involvement		
Hong Kong	**Singapore**	**Australia**
Hong Kong principals see teachers as moving tentatively from passive acquiescence to more active involvement in school decision-making while still retaining a keen sense of hierarchy. Younger teachers seemed more willing than their older colleagues to challenge and openly contribute in school forums.	Singaporean principals see younger teachers as less reticent about expressing opinions on school matters, whereas older teachers tend to maintain their traditional reluctance to openly contribute and challenge. The increasing tendency for teachers in general to speak more freely in school forums continues to be characterized by the traditional Asian values of respect, non-aggression and non-confrontation.	Australian principals see teachers as primarily driven by self-advancement, and with some loyalty to students rather than to the school. They were split as to whether teachers were willing to challenge and criticize the principal.
Comparative theme 2: Principals in all three societies acknowledge the trend towards teachers' more active involvement in decision-making; however, while Hong Kong and Singapore principals note a difference between older and younger teachers in this respect, and recognize the importance of school loyalty as a factor, Australian principals make no such distinction between older and younger teachers, and think teachers are primarily driven by self-advancement rather than school loyalty.		

(Continued)

Theme 3: principal–teacher relations		
Hong Kong	**Singapore**	**Australia**
An important aspect of Hong Kong principals' leadership style is that they employ a range of strategies to cultivate and preserve harmonious relationships with staff. Preservation of harmony and the suppression of emotional displays are seen as imperatives for maintaining performance, self-concept and loyalty to the school.	Singapore principals place store in the expression of opinion while combining this with a strong desire to maintain harmonious relationships, all within a multicultural context.	The perception of school leadership held by Australian principals was one of independence of mind, standing up for what they believe, and upholding egalitarian virtues. While valuing collaboration and harmony they are not prepared to compromise on their right to express their views.
Comparative theme 3: Principals in all three societies place value on collaboration and harmony in their relationships with teachers; however, the contextual and qualifying conditions for such relationships differ between them: in Hong Kong, harmonious relationships are part of preserving 'face' and loyalty to the school, in Singapore they are seen in combination with the need to express opinion within a multicultural society, and in Australian, they are seen within a context that respects the individual's right to expression of views.		

Figure 8.1 *Society-specific and comparative leadership themes 1–3*

stated: 'When I first came to the school I needed to be a strong leader – everyone expected me to make the decisions because I was the leader' (HK2). In line with such statements the principals believed that leaders were traditionally expected to act autocratically, and that teachers expected them to set the direction and make major decisions. In fact, a number of principals expressed the belief that teachers expected them to be the chief decision-maker, with minimal input from others. This, however, was seen as changing. Two principals captured the essence of the shift thus:

> When I first became a principal you were the most influential person, you were like the head of a big family. A bit of a despot – but now you can't really be like that. (HK5)

> You used to get respect because of position – but this is no longer enough, you must be respected for your ability and performance. (HK1)

Reasons given for the apparent movement towards increased participation, albeit slowly, included the strong policy moves toward decentralizing education governance, especially through school-based management, and, for some principals, increased exposure to Western ideas. In the words of one principal:

An important element of Chinese culture is respect for authority, but this is slowly changing. It is changing because of teachers coming in who have been educated and, to a certain extent, influenced by, Western ideas. (HK4)

The shift toward more participative leadership, however, seemed to be taking a largely hierarchical form. This involved increased participation between the principal and his or her senior teachers, and other administrators, rather than directly between the principal and teachers. One principal described participation in her school thus:

There's a lot of collaboration, but there's not a lot of interaction between levels. My involvement tends to be with the senior level, but for the lower level, teachers form groups, they collaborate among themselves. These groups then give their opinions to the senior teachers who talk with me, so there's plenty of opportunity for people to have their say and eventually for decisions to be discussed, often at staff meetings. (HK8)

Or as another principal explained:

(But) for the collaborative working habit or style, I think it's exclusively at the administrative level. Other than that, for the normal teachers, I think they would rather follow orders. (HK7)

Given such forms of participation, which one principal referred to as 'ordered collaboration' (HK8), principals tended to use their senior staff as intermediaries. In the words of another: 'They use intermediaries, like the assistant principal, to collect opinions and feelings. This must be done by someone the principal trusts' (HK7). This, according to the principals, was preferred, in most cases, by both the teachers and the principals themselves. A key reason for this preference appeared to be that teachers were more willing to express ideas and opinions, or even criticisms, to a senior teacher or their peers, than to the principal, especially in large-group or whole-staff forums such as staff meetings. Principals themselves stressed that they had to have a trusting relationship with anyone who acted as an intermediary. Hierarchically restricted participation also helped prevent conflict and maintain a harmonious working environment.

Although the general themes of remoteness and increased participation varied in terms of strength and structural configuration, they appeared common across all principals.

Sub-theme 1 – Singapore: Singapore principals see themselves as hierarchical, but in readily adopting more consultative modes of decision-making, they are balancing the traditional and the modern   Singaporean principals claimed to be largely working in consultation with their staff, superiors and broader communities. They worked closely with their senior management teams, particularly vice-principals. One principal expressed this general belief as follows:

I believe in consultative management and I have often told my vice-principal that in my mind at least we must be like twins so that if one of us is absent we would know how each other feels and how to react under similar circumstances. (S3)

While discussing leadership style, Singaporean principals also seemed to perceive a difference between school leaders from different ethnic backgrounds. This type of categorizing appeared relatively common when principals talked about students, teachers, parents and the broader community. One principal explained her perception of the difference between principals representing each of the three major ethnic groups in Singapore in the following way:

I think that Chinese principals are more aggressive in the sense that they seek more results, achievements and publicity. And Indians do that also. But I find that Malays, they are happy with the current state of the school and don't make much fuss about new ideas and implementing new programs. Of course we get some who differ from the norm, but generally you can see these trends. (S5)

The Singaporean principals provided numerous examples of how they consulted with staff in most school based decisions. This, however, did not signify that hierarchy was unimportant in their schools. One Chinese principal, for example, explained why hierarchy and position remained important to determining relationships in schools:

We are also mindful of hierarchy because we have the culture of, and respect for, elders. There is some kind of dynamic you know, I'll elaborate a bit. If your supervisor is someone who is older and wiser, it is much easier to go along with the things that they want to do. If your supervisor is someone younger, I know that some principals find it difficult to relate to them. (S6)

In general, Singaporean principals appeared quite capable and comfortable with balancing modern approaches to school management with more traditional approaches. Modern approaches were typified by concepts such as increased teacher involvement and openness, and traditional approaches by respect for hierarchy, loyalty and obedience. In terms of the modern, for example, most principals indicated that they involved teachers, and particularly heads of department (HODs) in decisions that related to workload, class allocation and other 'major decisions'. One principal explained her approach to making decisions with the HODs, thus:

Even the general principles of approach should be decided by the group – it will largely be consultative. So even at a broad level we will initiate a series of discussions and reflections. So there's a lot of consultation going on around the table, but in the end, what finally appears on the paper before the teachers has to be decided in a meeting with all of us present at the same time, so nobody is surprised. (S3)

On the other side of the equation a continued dedication to more traditional approaches to management and relationships in some sections was also obvious. This appeared grounded in traditional 'Asian' values and required principals to balance their staff, beliefs and roles. One principal provided an example of how traditional culture endured and influenced relationships:

> There is one superintendent who is much younger than some of the principals. I know that within the hierarchy there is a tension between the older principals, particularly if they are males, and the superintendent, who happens to be a woman. It can be a very difficult situation for the older male principal because he feels he must 'submit'. No, not the kind of submission found between a husband and wife, but that he has to go along with what is advocated. You may not agree totally with me but Asians, most of the time, would not go against authority. (S6)

As introduced in this theme, part of balancing the modern and the traditional in school operation, management and decision-making is encouraging, and allowing, all members of the school community to contribute ideas and to challenge the status quo. Such issues are covered in more detail under the later themes in this chapter dealing with teacher involvement and teacher–leader relations.

Sub-theme 1 – Australia: Australian principals face strong tensions in their leadership style between expectations of participative democratic decision-making, on the one hand, and demands of accountability, which focus responsibility on the principal, on the other. Consequently, they feel the need to assert their prerogative as final decision-makers While expressing the need for participative decision-making in schools, Australian principals felt they were increasingly pulled toward more autocratic approaches, at least in terms of making final decisions. Such a trend seemed attributable to a number of reasons. The most influential of these appeared to be policy moves stressing accountability, and particularly principal accountability for what happens in the school. As one principal stated:

> I think it was in the early 1990s we had a real democratic push in schools – one where the collective was responsible. But since 1995 onwards, workplace agreements pass all the responsibility to the principal. More principals have said that if their heads are on the line, then they will make the final decision. (P5)

Although there was little doubt that principals felt pressured to take the final decision, at the same time, they also remained dedicated to shared decision-making and believed it essential for school and teacher health. One principal, for example, stressed that schools could not rely only on a small number of decision-makers. While expressing their beliefs of the benefits of participation with teachers, however, they indicated that they continued to have difficulty in getting teachers involved to a desired level. In the words of one principal:

The dependency is on the leader to make all decisions, even small ones – and this is the case in my school – the leader makes the decisions in consultation with the chosen few. And the job is to get participative decision-making going. (P6)

In order to get teachers more involved in running the school and contributing to decisions, Australian principals employed a number of strategies. These included, building staff self-belief, offering resource and psychological support, allowing mistakes without fear of retribution, challenging teachers and structuring their teacher contributions. The principals cited below expressed a number of these opinions in their own words:

I make sure that their (the teachers) self-esteem stays intact, you're not going to get anywhere by running them down and criticising them, encouragement and lots of positives is crucial. So it gets down to positive interactions, individual accountability and making sure that people are supported. That they have the resources and time that the school is able to offer. But they are also involved in the planning and the realization of the goals themselves. (P4)

I focus on quality relationships and everybody in the school is a leader. When teachers come and ask me whether they can do something, I generally ask them, 'Well, what do you think?' (P6)

Given their preference for combining the somewhat contradictory concepts of directive decision-making, and a belief in the importance of staff input into the decisions, the principals sometimes had to walk a fine line between autocrat and democrat. A number seemed to manage this tension through encouraging input, but within certain parameters. As one respondent stated: 'I do it through the administration team (deputy principals) and other people such as the subject teachers. And then you go to staff and justify your reasons and hear their input' (P2). The principals also stressed that whereas they made the final decisions, they still believed that they had to convince their staff of the merit of their decisions; otherwise, the implementation of subsequent changes or innovations would be threatened. There was also mention that middle managers played an important role in both decision generation and dissemination:

To maintain control when power for decisions is given to others you must give clear guidelines, and people have to know what they are doing and why. You need to convey your actions clearly, with a timeline/deadline. (P4)

In sum, Australian principals claimed that they were forced into becoming final decision-makers by increased policy demands for accountability. Despite this, they also claimed a genuine dedication to participative decision-making in their schools, but only for some decisions at certain levels.

Comparative theme 1: Principals in all three societies acknowledge changed expectations of their leadership styles held by others: however, their subtly different responses reflect cultural differences All three groups of principals recognize the changes in leadership style brought about by many contemporary forces affecting school leadership. Hong Kong principals, for example, viewed their leadership role as shifting from autocratic to more participative. While Singapore principals still perceived of their role in hierarchical terms, they have taken on board a more consultative style. Australian principals also clearly accepted the necessity for a more participative, democratic decision-making style, but harboured deep concerns about the plausibility of this within a strong accountability environment.

While similar trends away from autocratic, monopolistic notions and towards more participative, consultative modes of leadership cut across all three cultures, there are subtly different ways in which the trends are manifest in practice.

In Hong Kong, for example, participation tends to take place *within* hierarchical levels rather than *between* them. Thus, there are high levels of participation within senior teachers as a group, and similar levels of participation among teachers as a group. Communication between the groups, however, is channelled through 'conduits', that is, those staff members 'accepted' by their seniors. This pattern enables principals to maintain their hierarchical distance, positional authority and aloofness, while appearing to satisfy demands for more participation.

In Singapore, there seems a ready acceptance to combine traditional with modern notions of leadership. Teacher involvement in consultative leadership is relatively open and does not display the confinement to their own hierarchical level, as in Hong Kong. Three further points are worth making: first, principals emphasise consultative leadership above all else, preferring it to participative or democratic; second, consultative leadership continues to be exercised within traditional parameters of respect for hierarchy and seniority; and third, consultation and involvement is selective, being dependent on what principals see as falling within the purview of department heads and teachers.

Principals in Australia, however, emphasized an altogether different phenomenon. After years of school-based management stretching back to the late 1980s, and the evolution of government policy exacting tough accountability expectations in return, principals felt they confronted a major dilemma. While acknowledging the need for, and wisdom of, participative decision-making, they were aware that the Western Australian government passed a regulation in the mid-1990s that made them, as principals, individually responsible and accountable for decisions and outcomes in their schools. The effect of this on principals appeared, somewhat paradoxically, to reverse the trend towards more open, participative decision-making and towards principals reasserting their prerogative to control decisions. If they are going to be held individually accountable for school performance, then they feel the necessity to exert more rather than less control.

Theme 2: Teacher involvement

Sub-theme 2 – Hong Kong: Hong Kong principals see teachers as moving tentatively from passive acquiescence to more active involvement in school decision-making while still retaining a keen sense of hierarchy. Younger teachers seem more willing than their older colleagues to challenge and openly contribute in school forums Remote leadership holds ramifications for teacher behaviour and openness in school decision-making. Respondents indicated that teachers appeared to be gradually becoming more willing to contribute through offering their opinions and ideas. A willingness to contribute openly seemed more common in secondary than in primary schools, where teachers remained reticent to express themselves in large forums. A primary principal who claimed to be trying to promote participation expressed her frustration thus:

> I encourage them to do it (express opinions), but every time in the meeting you'll find that they are so quiet. Unless on your agenda you appoint certain teachers to report something or to share something, they will not speak; otherwise they will listen quite passively throughout the whole process. (HK7)

She suggested that teachers are reluctant to contribute in open forums because it may be seen as 'disrespectful' to the principal, whereas a primary colleague explained that teachers were reluctant to contribute because it may lead to some type of conflict and that 'teachers will lose face' (HK6). The trend toward more active involvement in primary schools was more prevalent in smaller groups, through intermediaries, or in one-on-one situations with the principal.

Secondary principals believed their schools were becoming increasingly open to teacher input. As one principal explained,

> I think people are more willing to speak up, especially in a small team setting, like the administrative team … and when I invite teachers to complete a self-evaluation form they are quite frank about what they don't like about the school, they are not just saying things to please you. (HK4)

Although secondary principals suggested that recent education reforms had helped make participation more common in their schools, here too, it seemed they were governed by hierarchy and etiquette. Principals agreed that teachers rarely quarrelled openly in large group settings and that schools could be characterized by a brand of 'surface harmony'. Surface harmony, or what one principal labelled 'superficial harmony', can be defined as a school projecting the illusion of harmony to outsiders and, further, that this illusion is actually played out in the school in terms of overt behaviour, such as through conflict avoidance. This does not indicate, however, that disagreement and conflict do not happen in smaller forums and in different ways. In other words, according to the principals interviewed, the water appears calm but that this does not mean the absence of ferment below the surface. Such an atmosphere is obviously ripe for micro-political activity. One secondary principal, while stating that people do not generally 'quarrel (openly) much' in the school as a whole, gave examples of both the positive and negative:

> if you come into my administrative team meeting these days, where the heads of department and heads of functional committees come together, for some issues, we could argue for hours and hours because people do have different opinions ... Some people are not afraid to speak up.
> ... behind the scenes or at the back, people have lots of criticisms, and in the staff room people are complaining so much, they grumble, it's all around you, people are criticising so much, it's very negative. (HK4)

The picture that emerged from the principals was that involvement was increasing, and that open disagreement was more common than five years ago. Most discord however remains 'controlled and polite' and 'less blunt', emerged in small group settings, and tended to be expressed and dealt with privately, either individually or in small groups. This seemed to be because it avoided embarrassment and open conflict, thereby constructing the illusion of surface harmony. As expressed earlier, part of this illusion is that disagreement is acceptable 'inside' but should not be expressed 'outside'; that is to say to teachers not included in the senior management group and/or to parents, community members and government officials. One principal used the example of the Chinese communist party's annual meeting at Bei Dai He[2] to illustrate this point.

> Every summer the Chinese leaders go to 'Bei Dai He' to make policy and work out their differences. While there, they have lots of quarrels, debates, power struggles and politicking – all inside the venue. Then, they iron out their differences and come out as a group and say 'OK, this is our agenda for the country'. This is how things should work out – they call it a 'united front'. (HK5)

So the shift from 'surface' or passive acquiescence, which appears to have been the norm in traditional Hong Kong schools, toward active involvement is subtle, slow and bounded by consideration for hierarchy and image. As with the movement away from remote leadership, a number of factors may be behind the modification of involvement patterns and forms.

One factor identified behind the more general opening up of school decision-making, especially in secondary schools, was that younger teachers seemed more willing to openly contribute and challenge decisions than older teachers. Secondary principals believed that younger teachers, because of their education and more liberal upbringing, were more outspoken, and even less polite when interacting with seniors, than their older colleagues were. In some schools this was seen as a source of tension, especially when older teachers 'disagree with the way the younger teachers express their opinions when discussing issues in a meeting' (HK2). This tension was often more apparent between teachers themselves than between the principal and teachers.

A similar tension between local and expatriate teachers also came out in a number of secondary schools (see Chapter 10). In the words of one principal:

> We have 58 teachers, two are foreigners and the rest are Chinese. The two behave very differently from the 56, very differently. These two, especially the lady teacher, will come up front and just tell me whenever they disagree with me. (They) do this in public or in private – even in the staff meeting. The rest (of the teachers) they are rather quiet, very reserved people – it's very different. (HK8)

Unlike other staff, the principal claimed that she appreciated the challenges, explaining that:

> (after the foreigners spoke up) other staff would come up to me and say that it is wrong for her to say such things in a staff meeting. That's very rude of her, not a respectful thing for her to do to the school head. Then the head of department came and apologized on her behalf, but only after he had asked her to apologize and she would not. She was alienated from her colleagues. (HK8)

The move from quietly accepting what the principal says to at least having some input is a slow one; and seems more advanced in secondary than primary schools and among younger than more experienced teachers. Even as openness in front of the principal becomes more common, it remains framed by restraint, politeness and respect. Interaction is still more likely to happen in private or in small groups, and through the use of intermediaries, usually senior teachers. Just because teachers do not openly complain or disagree with the principal, is in no way an indication that they actually accept what is happening in school or agree with the principal.

Sub-theme 2 – Singapore: Singaporean principals see younger teachers as less reticent about expressing opinions on school matters, whereas older teachers tend to maintain their traditional reluctance to openly contribute and challenge. The increasing tendency for teachers in general to speak more freely in school forums continues to be characterized by the traditional Asian values of respect, non-aggression and non-confrontation Even though Singapore schools are widely recognized as among the most modern, in terms of facilities, innovation and programmes in the Asia-Pacific region, there appeared a persistent reluctance for many teachers to express opinions on school matters. This appeared particularly true of older teachers. Younger teachers, however, seemed to be more willing to express their opinions across a wide range of topics and issues once considered the exclusive domain of the principals and other senior staff. That younger teachers were more willing to expose opinions that sometimes challenged the principal's perspectives was seen partly as the result of government, business and education rhetoric that downplayed the importance of hierarchy and promoted a 'meritocracy'. While other principals agreed that respect for the hierarchy appeared to be less important to younger teachers, they attributed this more to a slippage of traditional values, whether Chinese or Malay. One principal captured the 'anti-hierarchy' perspective thus:

> With offering different opinions or confronting principals, the rules of the game have changed. The new younger breed of teachers don't hesitate to express their views. So nowadays, I think all teachers can confront principals because they've been told that hierarchy is not important anymore. (S5)

The Singaporean principals, overall, claimed that they encouraged all staff to contribute, but that older teachers were more reluctant than their younger colleagues for at least two reasons. First, they had typically been raised to respect their elders and seniors and so were reluctant to openly dissent; and secondly, they felt that they lacked the knowledge and skills necessary to make a worthwhile contribution. On the latter point, one principal explained:

> Older teachers are struggling with rapidly changing ideas. Younger teachers are the ones who always implement new ideas and pick up things well. So that's why I think the hierarchy thing is not so obvious any more, because the older teachers actually come to me and tell me to let the younger teachers take over. (S5)

Although the trend toward younger teachers 'speaking up' more than their older colleagues was quite strong, there was still a general feeling that overall contributions from staff were not all that they should or could be. One principal lamented his teachers' unwillingness to disagree with him on professional issues and claimed that even when he tried to set up special forums, most remained silent, a factor which he clearly attributed to the influence of culture:

> The majority of my teachers would not disagree with me – I think this is part of the Asian culture. Is it the same in Hong Kong? I do encourage my teachers to speak up – I even held a special meeting. I would say the majority of them are very quiet but there are a handful of teachers who raise questions and among these I think one was an expatriate. (S6)

> You may not agree with me totally, but Asians most of the time will not go against authority. Our culture is that we do not normally speak up – even though we are

encouraged to speak up. We have to be sensitive to how we were brought up – this is a very prohibitive side of culture in Singapore. We have learned not to speak up. (S6)

However, one principal offered a different cultural explanation, claiming that his teachers were willing to raise issues and opinions, but that this was done using a non-confrontational style and a respectful tone and manner:

I believe that teachers are always given the opportunity to raise their opinions and views. We do encourage them to speak up. Teachers in my school will raise issues. If they have strong views they will speak up and confront me. Well not so much confront, more like raise up the issue for discussion. They can raise it very strongly too, but in a respectful way. (S2)

This theme reoccurred time and again during interviews with the principals. It was quite plain that regardless of whether contributions came from younger or older teachers, it was important for all that they not be communicated aggressively, or lead to open confrontation, especially with the principal or other senior staff. As one principal explained:

The question is not whether you speak up, but how you do it. The timing and the way you say things should not be aggressive or confrontational – we will open doors for communication. (S5)

This was related to elements of culture that appeared to endure, even across age groups and regardless of position. Such 'politeness' was expected and demanded by both principals and teachers, often as a way of preserving harmony and preventing differences of opinion from turning into disagreements or even arguments. This point is expanded under theme 3.

Sub-theme 2 – Australia: Australian principals see teachers as primarily driven by self-advancement and with some loyalty to students rather than to the school. They were split as to whether teachers were willing to challenge and criticize the principal Australian principals claimed that their staff were driven largely by self-advancement. This indicated that teachers were concerned with their career and personal/family well-being, rather than loyalty to the organization or the principal, although, on the whole, the principals also suggested that teachers were still dedicated and loyal to the students.

The principals appeared divided on whether teachers were willing to criticize them. They suggested that even if the majority were unwilling to challenge them openly, there was always a minority willing to do so, and to do so quite aggressively, and that teachers were sometimes happy for these people to speak on their behalf.

I think the majority don't challenge because of my position, but a few will and you need to be able to justify to these people. (P5)

The majority don't, but there is a minority that feel comfortable to make their points. If enough of them disagree with me they will get the 'mouth' to speak up on their behalf, and if they argue well enough the rest will follow. (P3)

Hierarchies were recognized in the schools, but they seemed to be based more on mutual respect than position and, at least in secondary schools, seemed more functional at the departmental than the school level. Indeed, as one principal pointed out, secondary teachers tended to be more loyal to their departments and heads of department than to the school itself: '[Staff] are very loyal to the heads of department, even when they do the wrong things. High schools have always been faculty based' (P6). He also suggested that the 'Balkanized' structure of secondary schools shielded him from criticism because teachers would rather criticize each other than him. He also reflected a more general trend that teachers were becoming more aggressive, because 'people are tired of change, burnt out'.

Comparative theme 2: Principals in all three societies acknowledge the trend towards teachers' more active involvement in decision-making; however, while Hong Kong and Singapore principals note a difference between older and younger teachers in this respect, and recognize the importance of school loyalty as a factor, Australian principals make no such distinction between older and younger teachers, and think teachers are primarily driven by self-advancement rather than school loyalty

This second theme supports and is consistent with, the first theme; that principals in all three cities acknowledge the willingness of teachers to be more involved in school discussions. In this respect, Hong Kong and Singapore principals are more aligned in regard to the nature of this trend than are their Australian counterparts.

In regard to the role that teachers play in school discussion, principals in Hong Kong recognize a steady evolutionary trend away from passive acquiescence to more active involvement. However, this is a slow rather than dramatic change and it is taking place within a general climate of keen awareness of hierarchy.

Likewise, Singaporean principals identified a trend of teachers speaking up more freely in school meetings and forums, but invariably within a milieu characterized by traditional values of respect, non-confrontation and non-aggression. In both Hong Kong and Singapore, principals identified the younger generations of teachers as exhibiting this capacity to challenge and openly contribute more than older teachers.

Somewhat differently, Australian principals were unable to distinguish between teachers' willingness to challenge and contribute on the basis of age or generation. They differed in their summation of teachers' willingness to do so, some teachers appeared willing to speak their minds, others less so. But in one important respect, Australian principals highlighted an important difference between their teachers and those of their Asian counterparts. Australian principals thought their teachers' motivation to contribute was a combination of loyalty to their students and their own self-advancement. In contrast, Hong Kong principals played up the strong feelings of loyalty to the school held by many teachers.

It may well be that Chinese values of seeing the school as an extended family, deserving of personal loyalty and commitment, are still cherished. Certainly this is reflected in the low incidence of teacher mobility between schools in Hong Kong, and contrasts with a much higher rate of teacher turnover in Australia. However, it is also apparent that the Asian communities of Hong Kong and Singapore are undergoing significant cultural change as they develop world class education systems, promote creativity and higher-order thinking skills, encourage many of their students to seek graduate training overseas, and integrate into the global marketplace. All of this is leading to a more self-confident younger generation that displays different qualities from their older, more traditional parents. Australian principals, on the other hand, in identifying teachers' sense of self-advancement and loyalty to students rather than loyalty to the school, as their main motivators, exhibit the individualism that characterizes Anglo-American societies.

Theme 3: leader–teacher relationships

Sub-theme 3 – Hong Kong: An important aspect of Hong Kong principals' leadership style is that they employ a range of strategies to cultivate and preserve harmonious relationships with staff. Preservation of harmony and the suppression of emotional displays are seen as imperatives for maintaining performance, self-concept and loyalty to the school The preservation of harmony, whether it be real or surface is seen as important by Hong Kong principals as they and policy-makers seek to involve more teachers and parents in open discussion of school operation and improvement. It appears that the opening of schools to broader participation is progressing, but remains bounded by traditional norms.

Although the meaning of harmony differs somewhat among the principals, all principals believe it to be extremely important. One secondary principal's definition of harmony best captured the feelings of her colleagues:

> The sensitive areas of an individual that should not be stepped on – the sensitive areas or issues that a person most treasures should not be disturbed. This can be in personal or school life. You must be very careful not to criticize someone's personality or even what they are saying in the classroom – or they will be very uncomfortable. This must be dealt with very carefully. So to be harmonious to a certain extent means that we need to be conscious about how we interact and this means we avoid arguing. (HK2)

Principals exercise a range of strategies to preserve and cultivate harmony, maintained through suppressing or hiding personal issues, problems and disputes, and largely avoiding open argument or confrontation. The principals interviewed all seemed to agree that open argument and conflict are extremely rare, especially in open forums or with the principal. The main reason for this appears to be that such conflict is dangerous to harmony, whether it is at deep or a surface level. One primary principal explained that 'arguments' may occur about specific professional questions but that in her ten years as principal 'there has never been a personal argument' (HK6). This means that principals must be very careful over how they communicate with staff and, in general, must steer clear of a person's worth. As another principal explained: 'I have to be very, very careful not to use derogatory words that refer to the person himself. You can only talk about the facts, the behaviours, the incidents, the tasks – very specifically – and try to detach this from a person's worth' (HK5).

The principals claimed they were extremely reluctant to criticize a teacher in front of others because the 'teacher will lose face. So I try to avoid criticism in front of others, it's an insult' (HK6). The concept of 'face' seemed to maintain its importance for all principals. This appeared a difficult concept to verbalize and seemed to hold multiple meanings. One principal attempted to define 'face', and differentiate it from 'pride':

> 'Face' means a person's dignity. Behind this, it refers to a person's self-knowledge, whether you really know who you are, what you are supposed to do, how much education you receive, how good your upbringing is ... When you talk about 'losing face' you are not referring simply to being unhappy – it also means that the person loses standing for a number of reasons ... If you are a teacher ... you have a certain identify as a teacher. So if I tell you that you are not doing your job properly it means you do not have enough knowledge and so you are not a worthy person. (HK5)

Another strategy aimed at maintaining harmony was the suppression of outward shows of emotion by the principal and teachers. When talking about an ongoing problem with a teacher, one principal commented that: 'I don't show anger – I feel it, I feel it – I would never shout at people, I have to talk with them in a way to show that I am not satisfied, but not necessarily angry with her' (HK7). Another principal explained why principals must control their emotions, but also explained that at times they were almost expected to show anger to illustrate where they stand.

> Normally a leader shouldn't get too angry, too anxious, too worried, nor too pessimistic in public. You can go back to your office and cry over what's happened behind the door, but not before you get there. In Chinese thinking a great leader is one who will remain serene and calm even when standing in front of a collapsing mountain ... If you lose your temper so much, it means that you can't control yourself – if you can't control yourself, how can you control others – right?

At other times, you are expected to strongly show your displeasure, but not too much. If a teacher, for example, is very irresponsible, causing lots of trouble for his colleagues, and you as the principal don't lose your temper, everyone will say, 'oh, you accept it' ... Yes sure (it's about harmony) if it's strongly against other people's welfare and interests, and then you don't stand up for them, how can you be a leader? (HK5)

Interestingly, both the avoidance of emotional displays, and the occasional outward displays of such seem geared toward preserving group harmony. As one principal explains below, it also appears that the display of positive emotions is suppressed. The quote also introduces the notion of shifting culture, and perhaps culture clash:

Inside my heart, I am considerate, but I guess some of the staff think I should be task oriented. Sometimes I hide my affection ... on the whole, the image, the figure, needs to be demanding. I guess this is in the Hong Kong culture, the Chinese culture; I need to be a demanding leader as this is an accepted characteristic. But because of my counselling background I try to moderate my self and be a more humane leader. (HK2)

Across all areas, Hong Kong principals claimed that in almost all incidences, interaction at, and between, all levels within the school is couched in politeness and carried out in a quiet manner. As stated earlier, however, politeness and conflict avoidance in no way indicate that there is no disagreement, but that this is largely addressed in a non-confrontational way, either one on one or through the help of intermediaries. Principals generally believed that conflict avoidance in schools was indicative of Hong Kong society in general and grounded in traditional culture.

The desire for organizational and inter-group harmony is not without context. Principals see the maintenance of harmony as a key to performance, order, loyalty and the leadership function itself. Harmony was viewed both in terms of smooth interpersonal relations and in terms of organizational cohesiveness. In the words of one primary principal: 'It is very, very important; if they are not working in harmony, one will do this and others will do that, and the school cannot be established and it cannot be a famous school' (HK6). A secondary principal explicitly linked harmony to teacher performance thus:

Harmony and working together is very important, because in a harmonious situation people will relax. Since we all have to work so hard to tackle problems, if there is any conflict between staff, it could be very stressful and affect one's performance. (HK8)

Others tied harmony to staff loyalty, suggesting that teachers are more likely to be loyal to an organization where they do not feel threatened by a fear of 'looking bad' or openly having someone attack their ideas. This relates again to notions of face and teachers feeling comfortable in the school. Harmony, of course, may also be desirable to principals because it shelters them from criticism and open challenge.

Interestingly, principals generally agreed that the preservation of harmony would be discounted quickly if perceived as harming student learning and welfare. When commenting on this relative importance, one principal said: 'On the other hand if you have to sacrifice the benefit of students, that is something that can't be negotiated' (HK7). Another principal commented on the advantages of harmony to students, but again put this in perspective: 'A harmonized atmosphere is important because it inspires students to grow and develop character throughout their life; so in the long term a harmonized atmosphere is better for everyone and also better for the development of students. However, if harmony is at the expense of student achievement it is not right' (HK1).

Although there were indications that some principals were beginning to try and infuse more open discussion into their schools, largely because of exposure to Western literature and the democratizing thrust of current reforms, the openness promoted seemed underpinned by a concern for control, politeness and harmony. In the words of one principal, 'I let them [teachers] voice out their ideas before I try to work things out with them and harmonize the situation … but I don't try to shame them in public or harm them' (HK5).

The value of harmony in schools seems to endure in Hong Kong schools and is consciously cultivated and protected by principals for a range of reasons. Although principals are moving toward opening debate and discussion in schools, concerns for respect and face, at least in public, remain important.

Sub-theme 3 – Singapore: Singapore principals place store in the expression of opinion while combining this with a strong desire to maintain harmonious relationships, all within a multicultural context Like their Hong Kong counterparts, Singaporean principals valued harmonious relationships, while seeking to increase staff participation in discussion and school-based decision-making. The importance of harmony and the related concept of loyalty seemed driven by traditional cultural and religious beliefs. Principals tended to equate the school with the family and used this metaphor to express the importance of loyalty and harmony:

> Loyalty is very important. When I was a young girl I was taught that the family is the core and that it is like your hands. When you look at your hand, your fingers bend inwards, not outwards. The family comes first, then the school, then community and then the nation. You must be loyal to your family and remember that your school is your second family and second home. (S5)

> (Harmony) is of vital importance to me because my belief is that the organization is a very big family. So the appointment of staff is important so that we are one big team and not different parts. (S6)

The dynamics between modern and traditional beliefs emphasize the importance of harmony even as teachers are encouraged to participate. The quote below illustrates a number of general points as suggested by the Singaporean principals. First, the willingness of teachers to contribute seems linked, at least partly, to their direct exposure to 'Western' culture. Second, teachers are encouraged to voice opinions, if under certain informal rules, but many remain reluctant to do so. Third, confrontation is not acceptable – in fact, the long-serving principal cited below indicates that his school never has 'aggressive confrontations' and, as such, maintains harmony.

> Many of my staff have been overseas and influenced by Western culture. We get a lot of people trained overseas and they are pretty open. We've never encountered any big issues that have made us unhappy or made us feel that the administration has to get involved. However, people may have a perception that that they will be penalized if they speak up too much – because of appraisal – but you can never help that. But we do encourage staff to speak up if they think something is not right. Say, for example, at one stage some of the teachers felt that changes were needed to the timetable because they felt certain days were too long. If I feel they have a point we will gather more information and cross-check the situation. We've never had aggressive confrontations. (S2)

Despite encouraging broad participation, Singapore principals tended to use their senior staff as sounding boards before taking issues to the whole staff. As one principal stated: 'You see before I go through with a plan or idea I always call a meeting with all the HODs. We go through the policies of implementation and the heads are encouraged to speak of their views before I go ahead and tell the teachers' (S1). This was not only seen as a way to maximize the effectiveness of any decision made, but also as a way of ensuring that senior staff can present a combined front to the remainder of the school. Like their Hong Kong counterparts, principals also used their senior staff to communicate with teachers.

The multicultural composition of Singapore, and the huge importance placed on a harmonious society by the state also drove the desire for harmonious relationships. Racial and organizational harmony were seen as inseparable – with the latter openly discussed and actively promoted by the government and echoed at all levels, including the classroom level. Some of the intricacies of the multicultural nature of Singapore society and schools, and how principals perceive this, are other themes which emerged from the research.

In Singapore schools harmony is important for cultural, religious, organizational and multicultural reasons and is maintained through the application of ingrained informal rules about how disagreements and opinions should be raised and discussed. As one principal neatly summarized:

> In Singapore we want to promote Singaporean uniqueness but at the same time encourage distinctiveness. There are no restrictions on religious freedom or worship or what you do in respect of your own culture, as long as you do not insult another culture or destroy the harmony between the cultures. (S4)

Sub-theme 3 – Australia: The perception of school leadership held by Australian principals was one of independence of mind, standing up for what they believe, and upholding egalitarian virtues. While valuing collaboration and harmony they are not prepared to compromise on their right to express their views Australian principals valued their right to independent thought and action and held that they would speak up strongly for what they believed and would do the same for others within their school. When discussing 'Australian leadership', and how they and others perceive good leadership in general, two principals explained thus:

> Good leaders are people who have the gift of the gab and are hard punchers – and they are decisive ... Australians like leaders who will not be pushed around by others, regardless of their position. (P1)

> I think that people want you to roll up your sleeves and get involved, unlike in the past when principals were put on a pedestal. They look at the principal as someone who can communicate with young people ... but at the same time they are able to move on things and speak well and make decisions when necessary ... I think the Australianism comes through in that they like to see fairness and equity, providing there is a little lee-way ... I guess you have to be all things to all people, in many regards – flexible, empathetic, down to earth, a practitioner and theorist, a leader, all those things. (P2)

The principals were unanimous that respect for the leader in general was something that had to be earned from staff, and did not automatically accompany a specific organizational or social position, or relate to inherited status. In terms of the school context, the principals held that the same principle tended to hold true, and that they had to earn the respect of their staff. While they certainly considered working together collaboratively was very important in schools, they were not afraid to express their beliefs or feelings at the expense of maintaining a 'smooth, friendly atmosphere in the school'. In fact, one principal claimed: 'Sometimes you need to challenge harmony to change things' (P2). Neither do they expect their staff to remain neutral; in fact, most principals maintain that they expect teachers to question their decisions. This belief is reflected in the following comment by a principal:

> (Leadership is about) active questioning and being able to accept that your decision will be challenged ... This is different from places like Japan and Thailand ... . (P5)

Although the Australian principals as a group strongly espoused egalitarian values and a dedication to equity, they did not believe that everybody should be treated the same. In other words, they supported fairness but not necessarily uniformity.

Comparative theme 3: Principals in all three societies place value on collaboration and harmony in their relationships with teachers; however, the contextual and qualifying conditions for such relationships differ between them: in Hong Kong, harmonious relationships are part of preserving 'face' and loyalty to the school, in Singapore they are seen in combination with the need to express opinion within a multicultural society, and in Australia, they are seen within a context that respects the individual's right to expression of views The three themes discussed in this chapter form a trilogy concerned with principals' leadership in relationship to teachers. Principals in all three selected research locations acknowledge the importance of creating and maintaining harmonious and collaborative relationships with teachers, although Hong Kong and Singapore principals are more closely aligned than Australian principals in the value placed on such relationships.

Principals in Hong Kong adopt a range of strategies aimed at cultivating and preserving harmonious relationships among and with staff, showing a predisposition towards people- or relationship-centred leadership over that which is predominantly task-centred. This, it is believed, is more likely to gain the support of the staff, which will, in turn, lead to their greater loyalty and commitment to the school. Thus preservation of harmony, at least on the surface, involves suppression of emotional displays, which is in turn seen as imperative for maintaining performance, saving 'face', protecting individual dignity and ensuring loyalty to the school.

Singapore principals also value highly the preservation of harmonious relationships, but they are more inclined than their Hong Kong counterparts to emphasize the importance of combining this with the need to encourage the expression of opinion. In this regard, they represent a combination of Asian and Anglo-American values, aware of the overriding reality that they are a multicultural society consisting of three main ethnic groups and the need for sensitivity in expressing views in pursuit of ethnic harmony.

More than their Asian counterparts, Australian principals held a perception of leadership that valued independence of mind, standing up for what they believed and upholding egalitarian values. While valuing collaboration and harmony, they were not prepared to compromise their right to express their views.

Thus, although principals in the three diverse societies value harmonious relationships, subtle differences are detectable. On one dimension, Hong Kong and Singapore principals reflect the Asian-Chinese valuation of collectivism and the common good served by harmony, while in contrast, the Australian principals reflect the Anglo-American characteristic of individualism and the right to speak one's beliefs. On another dimension, their values reflect the particular contexts of the three societies.

Conclusion

This chapter has sought to illustrate the subtle yet enduring influence of culture on school leadership through the words of three different groups of principals from three diverse cultural contexts. The discussion has touched on a number of in-school processes, which focus on staff relationships. The following chapter looks more specifically into an increasingly important area of human resource management – that of teacher appraisal.

Notes

1   It is not the purpose of this book to present in any detail the purpose, structure and methodology of the study. The materials presented in the chapter are taken from:

Walker, A. and Dimmock, C. (2002b). *Development of a Cross-Cultural Framework and Accompanying Instrumentation for Comparative Analysis in Educational Administration.* Final report to the Hong Kong Research Grants Council for Competitive Earmarked Research Grant CUHK 4327/98H. The Chinese University of Hong Kong: Hong Kong.

Further information can be obtained from the authors.

2   Bei Dai He is a Resort city, not far from Beijing, in Hebei Province in China. Bei Dai He is best known as the site where the upper echelons of the Communist Party go to debate and formulate policy. During policy formulation they argue openly and relatively freely among themselves; however, once policy has been agreed upon and is announced, they put their differences aside and present a united front to the population as a whole.

9
Teacher Appraisal in Culturally Diverse Settings

The debate about different approaches to appraisal and its associated processes has been largely restricted to English-speaking Western settings. Little has been written about the place and shape of teacher appraisal and, in particular, the influence of societal culture on teacher appraisal in non-Western educational contexts, with the exception of the recent collection of essays edited by Middlewood and Cardno (2001). These authors address a number of universal concerns and contentious issues, including the challenges of achieving the optimal balance between the accountability and development functions of appraisal, and between the needs of the organization and those of the individual. They also address the influence of context, culture and tradition, and how these pose serious dilemmas for school leaders illustrated with a number of international case studies drawn from the USA, the UK, New Zealand, South Africa and Singapore. However, studies such as these are only beginning to scratch the surface, and the gap in the knowledge base has become more conspicuous with globalization and the spread of 'common' educational and managerial practices. For example, as from the year 2000, all Hong Kong schools had to implement a teacher appraisal scheme. As schools in different societies are pushed toward such implementation they are increasingly exposed to 'foreign' appraisal practices and ideas.

This chapter is divided into three major sections. The first provides an overview of teacher appraisal from an international and cross-cultural perspective, raising the question: 'Does one size fit all?' In the second section, we consider some important tenets of appraisal espoused in the UK and the USA, questioning their cultural suitability for schools in Chinese societies. The analysis is bounded by those aspects of Chinese culture connected with work and organizations, and particularly appraisal. Likewise, the choice of specific aspects of appraisal for discussion is by necessity highly selective. We therefore put aside discussion of many of the emerging issues (see *Education Update*, 1999) and concentrate on what appear to be the dominant approaches currently influencing schools, some of which may be incompatible with certain Chinese cultural values. In the final section we discuss a number of issues that deserve to be addressed if teacher appraisal is to be meaningfully transported across cultural boundaries, suggesting a number of ways forward for future research.

Teacher appraisal: does one size fit all?

Teacher appraisal is a contentious and divisive issue regardless of the context within which it operates. It is not unusual for educators around the globe to openly and/or covertly resist involvement in appraisal schemes for a multitude of reasons, ranging from a fear of negative information becoming public to a complete lack of trust in the appraiser or supervisor. Debates related to the form appraisal should take – and which constituent elements it should include – are widely debated across cultures. Teacher appraisal is also a relatively recent phenomenon in many school systems around the world, especially in South-East and East Asian societies such as Hong Kong, Taiwan and mainland China which have little history of teacher appraisal. Schemes that have existed have tended to be limited to the occasional, summative, external inspection of teachers seeking promotion. In the distant past, most systems did not require schools to develop any formal procedures for evaluating teacher performance.

Formal recognition of the need for teacher appraisal arrived in parts of Asia in the late 1980s, usually as part of broader reform efforts aimed at decentralization and increased school level accountability. On the whole, these reform efforts mirrored earlier or in-train reform packages initiated in Western countries such as Australia, the UK or US (Walker and Dimmock, 2000a). Such reforms were often part of a larger neo-liberal approach to public sector restructuring. Approaches to teacher appraisal were often included in broader reform packages and, as such, reflected Western values and ideals, and promoted appraisal as a vehicle for both teacher development and teacher quality assurance.

Given that schools in East Asia had little history of teacher appraisal, and the fact that 'international' models of appraisal were (and are) so easily available, educational departments and schools tended to look to existing Western approaches as the answer. The growth of teacher appraisal in Hong Kong provides a case in point (Mo, Conners and McCormick, 1998; Walker and Dimmock, 2000c). In the early 1990s a group of schools were charged with developing their own appraisal models. To help them, the Education Department provided guidance in the form of workshops and the distribution of a handbook (Advisory Committee on the School Management Initiative, 1992). The model presented in the handbook appeared to clone approaches then in vogue in Western countries such as the UK (for example, see Bell, 1992) and were roughly based on a traditional clinical approach to supervision.

From the outset, the appraisal component of the reform in Hong Kong caused dissension and dissatisfaction in schools and had limited impact in or beyond the schools involved. By 1998 it was decided that all schools should implement a teacher appraisal scheme and, again, a guide was produced and distributed to schools (School Management Initiative [SMI] Section, 1998). The contents provide an example of the appraisal schemes widely adopted and show that they draw heavily on traditional Western, mainly North American and British, approaches and processes. For example, three objectives of appraisal proposed, namely, *accountability*, *staff motivation* and *professional development*, are the standard purposes found in many supervision or appraisal texts in countries such as the UK and the USA (see Sergiovanni, 1995). The document then goes on to explain the procedure which schools may follow when developing an appraisal system, a number of processes which may be adopted and a collection of answers to common 'appraisal' questions. Key elements of the content are listed briefly below:

- The booklet suggests to schools that teacher appraisal should focus on performance rather than personality and the criteria should wherever possible be based on concrete performance indicators (SMI, 1998, p. 5). The underlying message then is that appraisal should not be based on who the teacher is, or their relationship with others, but rather on what the teacher does in the school and classroom. Except for some mention of peer appraisal it is clear throughout the document that appraisal is seen very much to have an individual focus.
- The booklet explains the difference between summative and formative evaluation, suggesting that an appraisal system needs to address both (SMI, 1998, p. 6); and that different systems can be established in schools to meet what is seen as these different purposes. Advice is provided for appraisers when communicating with teachers. Recommendations are similar regardless of the form of appraisal being conducted and focus on the need for open communication and a free-flowing exchange of views.
- A basic three- or four-stage clinical supervision process is suggested as a means of conducting formative appraisal (along with some suggestions for conducting peer appraisal for developmental purposes). The basic aim of the process is to support teacher professional development. Recommendations on process include that the appraiser should 'show appreciation and recognition' (p. 8) and 'understand the appraisee's feelings, problems and expectations' (p. 9).
- The booklet acknowledges the importance of an open school culture, conducive 'communication (which) encourages the teachers to express their views, engage in discussion and respect different views' (p. 13). It also suggests that appraisers need qualities that fit with such a culture (p. 35).

The above summary provides a flavour of the dominant approach to existing and proposed teacher appraisal in Hong Kong schools and other societies through the Asia-Pacific region. The approach and advice provided reveal the considerable influence of Western appraisal methods and philosophies. The adoption of Western models of appraisal is unsurprising given the 'hangover' effect of colonization, increasing globalization, that most of the available literature in the area is from the UK or the USA (Dimmock and Walker, 1998a), many of the consultants who aid policy development and training are short-term Western visitors; and that most local university staff and a large number of school and administrative personnel are educated in countries such as the UK, the USA and Australia (Walker and Dimmock, 2000c).

When considering the suitability of appraisal schemes for the Chinese context, we put aside what can be thought of as the general principles of appraisal and concentrate on the processes involved in the implementation of an appraisal scheme. The principles of appraisal include generic tenets such as: all teachers should be accountable for what they do; all teachers need information (feedback) which can help them perform better in the classroom; or schools need mechanisms for determining the most appropriate persons for promotion and for contract renewal. Such principles can be regarded as universally acceptable and are difficult to argue with, regardless of the values underpinning beliefs and actions. In other words, such all-encompassing principles cut across cultural differences and, in most instances, are the domain of policy-makers and are mostly accepted, if not openly welcomed, by teachers and principals alike.

General principles and policies become problematic at the implementation and operational level – it is here that cultural considerations particularly come into play. Implementation issues relate predominantly to the processes comprising an appraisal scheme. Process issues include: whether the scheme focuses on individuals or groups of teachers; who should be the appraisers; the relationships necessary for appraisal to be successful; the skills required by appraisers; or the need for open communication and 'impersonality' (Chow, 1995). The shapes of such processes do not stand alone and are anchored in the cultural beliefs, values and norms shared by a group, organization or society. This shared culture then influences the acceptance and efficacy of the particular appraisal processes. Therefore, a process such as giving open feedback, which is suggested as an integral part of Western-based appraisal schemes, may be incongruent with the values in other cultures and do little to improve teaching.

Our 'suitability' discussion targets a number of appraisal process areas. These are organized under: the focus of appraisal, appraisal roles and positioning, and the relational dynamics and communication that underpin the appraisal process. We suggest that the efficacy of many of the practices as envisaged in Western contexts may be questionable when set in Chinese cultures and the reflection of this culture in schools.

Cultural suitability

The focus of appraisal

Typically, the form of appraisal being advocated in schools throughout South-East and East Asia follows a clinical supervision model, where the appraiser and appraisee proceed through a three- or four-stage cycle. Although there are many variations on the model, the cycle roughly comprises a pre-observation conference, classroom observation and a post-observation conference or appraisal interview (SMI, 1998). This process, with minimal variation, is often promoted for both judgemental and developmental purposes. As typically implemented, the clinical model places the individual at the heart of the appraisal process. Such a practice may sit uncomfortably in Chinese cultures, which tend to be more group- than self-oriented (Hofstede, 1991).

Group orientation   The most notable difference between English-speaking Western societies, such as the USA, and Chinese societies relates to what we refer to in Chapter 2 as the *group-oriented/self-oriented* dimension. This refers to the degree to which people see themselves or their collective group as more important (Adler, 1997). In group-oriented societies, good relationships and interpersonal and organizational harmony are pre-eminent considerations and tend to mediate organizational relationships and influence behaviour patterns (Redding, 1990). Chinese societies, such as Hong Kong, Taiwan and mainland China are identified as highly group-oriented societies, in which: 'The significant point of reference for (Chinese) people is the collectivity rather than the individual self and the interests of the collective supersede those of the individual. A sense of identity is achieved via membership of and reference to the group rather than self-reference' (Westwood and Kirkbride, 1998, p. 567). On the other hand, self-oriented societies, such as Canada, Australia and Britain, tend to emphasize the 'I' above the 'we' (Shaw and Welton, 1996). Whereas people in group-oriented societies value relationship over task, in self-oriented societies, the task is held to prevail over personal relationships and, hence, appraisal systems have developed along individualistic lines.

   Taken to the school level, in schools where group relationships outweigh tasks, teachers are pushed to adapt to the group needs and norms, to control their emotions and avoid confusion, competition and conflict. Such behaviours are associated with the primary moral precept of harmony – which is viewed as a fundamental outgrowth of collectivism (Westwood and Kirkbride, 1998). Therefore, the maintenance of harmonious relationships within the group or school becomes the basis of interaction and teachers subdue individual desires and interests in the cause of harmony. Cross-cultural psychology suggests that this group orientation in Chinese societies contrasts with the self-orientation and egocentrism of many Western cultures. In practical terms, Chow (1995) stresses that self-oriented cultures emphasize getting ahead and being a good teacher/leader, whereas group-oriented cultures stress belonging and being a good, equal group member.

The mismatch then of appraisal systems developed within individualistic cultures and imported into collectivist societies becomes apparent, raising doubts about their suitability. A system based on the judgement of individuals appears incongruent with a group-oriented culture. If teachers are predominantly concerned with 'fitting into' and supporting the group, individual performance becomes secondary and any individual judgement or advice means less than a person's role in the wider group. Since group-oriented cultures are characterized by the avoidance of conflict and competition, two-person, face-to-face appraisal discussions tend to remain at a surface level only with both parties extremely reluctant to risk saying or doing anything that might lead to confrontation. We return to this point later in the chapter.

When relationships are valued over tasks, as in many Chinese organizations, related Western notions of objective measures, impersonality and personal achievement become troublesome when deciding upon what form appraisal should take. A group orientation, to some extent, militates against task performance-based, impersonal and impartial judgements or opinions in appraisal situations.

Objectivity   The application of objective measures is taken as necessary in many performance appraisal or management schemes in Western countries. Basing appraisal on such objective measures may be antithetical in Chinese schools – where valuing relationships takes precedence over task. Huo and Clinow (1995) submit that appraisal systems in Chinese organizations avoid using too many objective techniques or instruments. The authors hold that the Chinese tend to have a higher tolerance of subjectivity, and that as long as they feel they can trust the leaders who conduct the appraisal they will accept subjective evaluations on their performance. As Huo and Clinow (1995) note: 'They feel comfortable with a straightforward form of appraisal, even if it means some loss of precision or sophistication' (p. 10). Such perspectives are supported by Hofstede's (1980) assertion that Chinese societies can be classified as having low *uncertainty avoidance* cultures, which implies that citizens are comfortable with less formality and formalization, and with fewer explicit organizational rules, policies and procedures.

Effort/achievement   Typical appraisal schemes designed to measure and reward achievement rather than effort may also be difficult to implement in schools in Chinese societies. There are at least two reasons for this. First, the Chinese tend to value effort over achievement (Lee, 1996). This makes it difficult to rate teachers' performance outcomes, or achievements, on objective instruments, such as those suggested by central bodies. It also makes it difficult to challenge a teacher's performance, even if it is weak, if they have committed the required effort to their work. Second, achievement in collectivist cultures holds different meanings from those held in individualistic cultures. According to Yu (1996, p. 29) achievement motivation in Western cultures reflects middle-class Western values that are 'self-oriented, person-oriented, or individual-oriented'. In other words, as we have seen above, achievement is seen in relation to the individual not the group. In group-oriented cultures, on the other hand, achievement motivation is based on achievement for the family or the group, not for oneself (Westwood, 1992). If achievement is conceptualized in terms of the group rather than the individual, individualized forms of performance appraisal may be ineffective in many schools in Chinese contexts. At the very least, they risk painting an inappropriate picture of performance.

Goal-setting   A related issue is that many suggested forms of appraisal call for individuals to formally set their own, individual achievement goals. As noted above, Huo and Clinow (1995) suggest that the Chinese appear more comfortable working without clear goals or criteria, whereas individualistic societies prefer more explicit, formalized rules to ensure impartiality. While a lack of such rules may appear disadvantageous or even 'wrong' from a Western perspective, in group-oriented cultures it affords the flexibility and adaptability seen as necessary for maintaining harmony and making decisions on relational grounds. To ask teachers in schools to set 'individual' achievement goals may be impractical and have little influence on performance. It may be that a form of small group goal-setting would be more appropriate in collectivist societies.

Given the group orientation of Chinese societies and organizations, it may appear that some type of group appraisal process would be more efficacious. Interestingly, team- or group-oriented teacher evaluations have attracted attention in the USA and the UK over the last decade. For example, Glatthorn (1997) suggests co-operative professional development (CPD) as one of the main developmental tenets of 'differentiated supervision'. In CPD, groups of teachers work together to decide their own appraisal focus and goals, collect their own appraisal data and are charged with demonstrating how they have met their goals. Although such approaches may well hold promise for appraisal in schools in Chinese societies, it would still require adaptation for a number of reasons. First, Chinese teachers tend to hold seniority and status in very high regard, so they are often more willing to accept comments from superiors than peers. This may militate against easy acceptance of more democratic modes of appraisal such as CPD. Second, the Chinese are generally uncomfortable with disclosing their inner self and to criticizing or praising their own performance, even in a group context. As a result, they are reluctant to be observed by peers and will attempt to hide any inadequacies. Given these factors, it may be that a suitable form of appraisal for schools in Chinese societies would combine a group emphasis with the stronger presence of the principal to judge progress.

This raises the question of who is best suited to conduct appraisals and how various school actors are positioned within the process.

Appraisal roles and positioning

A contentious issue in Western societies is the issue of who should conduct the process and what roles various school actors should take (see Webb, 1994). The intricacies underpinning the problem in Chinese cultures are, however, quite different. In Chinese societies, relationships are guided largely by seniority, as reflected in terms of position, connection and age. Hence, relationships tend to be ordered and governed on hierarchical grounds. Within such relationships, implicit norms and rules govern aspects such as openness, obedience and *face*. The way in which hierarchies are played out in schools in Chinese societies will have a significant effect on the question of who appraises and how the process is conducted. Hierarchy therefore has a major influence on the appraisal process.

Hierarchy

According to Cheng (1995), groups and organizations in Chinese societies are more likely to be ordered around hierarchical sets of relationships and the rules which govern them than are their Western counterparts. Hierarchical structures with uneven power distributions are prevalent and accepted in most Chinese social structures, including groups and organizations (Jackson and Bak, 1998). In Chapter 2 we used the power-distributed/power-concentrated dimension to refer to this phenomenon. The dimension concerns how less powerful members in institutions and organizations perceive and cope with the inherent inequities involved in the distribution of power; that is, how the culture institutionalizes inequity. The followers, as much as the leaders, enforce a society's level of inequality. In societies which can be classified as power-distributed, such as the USA, inequality is treated as undesirable and efforts are made to reduce it wherever possible. In power-concentrated cultures, such as China, inequalities are accepted as natural and are legitimized in customs, relationships and institutional policies. Thus, people in power-concentrated cultures tend to be more accepting of unequal distribution of power (Walker, Bridges and Chan, 1996).

One of the main characteristics of power-concentrated societies is the ingrained respect for seniority and hierarchy. In schools, this means that formal leaders are granted respect by virtue of their hierarchically superior position, rather than because of their expertise. Similarly, teachers who are older, particularly males, are often granted respect because of their age, regardless of their position. Such values shape relationships, which, in turn, can influence the appraisal process.

One result of power-concentration in schools is that teacher participation in school-level decisions and managerial tasks is less common, while authoritarian leadership tends to be more common (Walker, Poon and Dimmock, 1998). As a result, many Chinese leaders have little practice in making decisions and submitting them to scrutiny (Bond, 1991a). Redding and Wong (1986) claim that the Chinese are trained to be obedient to superiors from childhood and normally, at least at a surface level, accept instructions without challenge. Studies on authoritarianism (Yang, 1970) and compliance offer empirical evidence which supports the traditional values of respect for authority and conformity associated with prescribed social structures and behaviour patterns. In practice, this acceptance of authoritarian leadership leads to a situation where only formal leaders are deemed qualified to evaluate others' performance. Chinese teachers tend to comply with superiors in the interests of harmony, even if they disagree with them. This is not to say that there is never disagreement, but when it surfaces the leader must still be given *face*. Hence, if a teacher disagrees with the leader, he or she may first agree with what has been said and only then will differences be voiced, and usually in an indirect, private way. This often entails using an intermediary or third party. In the rare instances that face-to-face confrontation is inescapable, the teacher will use only very mild language (Bond, 1991a). The relational dynamics bred from respect for authority aim to maintain a harmonious group environment – a pre-eminent consideration in Chinese groups.

Conversely, leaders in Chinese organizations have difficulty in openly singling out a staff member as better or worse than others, as this may cause animosity and sabotage relationships. Consequently, one of the purposes of appraisal – to promote more capable teachers to positions of authority – may be nullified. This may result in promotions being made on the grounds of seniority or connections, even if the best person does not get the job (see Walker and Dimmock, 1999a; 1999b; 2000b). The way leadership is played out in Chinese organizations, however, is not as straightforward as an all-powerful figure, the leader, tactfully criticizing teachers in an appraisal discussion.

Reciprocity

The trade-off for the obedience and respect granted to leaders is an equally powerful obligation for the leader to reciprocate. As Bond (1991a) explains: 'In a culture system that gives wide-ranging power to those in authority, there must be a reciprocal emphasis on compliance and loyalty of those subject to authority' (p. 82). Westwood and Kirkbride (1998) further explain that the moral and philosophical basis of the Confucian ethic includes 'a legitimized and expected set of reciprocal relationships – emperor/minister, father/son, husband/wife' (p. 568). Such implicitly scripted relationships are captured by the key Confucian values of *Li* and *Jen*. *Li* refers to the ethic of propriety and prescribes social relationship structures, which discourages individuals from challenging or disturbing the role system. The concept of *Jen* verifies that individuals should not be considered as separate entities but as inextricably bound to social context, the family and the organization (Westwood and Kirkbride, 1998). Again, these 'rules' aim to maintain harmony, which in turn calls for reciprocity.

In simple terms, reciprocity dictates that in exchange for obedience and conformity, leaders must care for and protect their followers. In practice, this means that leaders should not embarrass or openly criticize teachers. Nor can they place others' jobs, careers or standing at risk (Walker and Dimmock, 2000b). Reciprocity dictates that both parties must be given *face*. For example, during an appraisal meeting, the leader gives the teacher *face* through praising the teacher's performance and, likewise, the teacher attempts to give the supervisor *face* by agreeing with them. The requirement for harmonious relationships then implies that both teachers *and* formal leaders are expected to yield to established structures and the accompanying behavioural prescriptions which include, conformity, reciprocity, compliance, uniformity and obedience. According to Bond (1991b), comparative data suggests that the Chinese readily conform and so are less likely to take the initiative, proffer opinions, take risks or depart from established procedures without a superior's approval. In appraisal terms, such behaviour is unlikely to lead to open discussion of strengths, weaknesses or developmental needs, thus turning any discussion into a 'polite' one-way conversation.

Seniority

Given the complications that arise from authoritarian leadership and the Chinese predisposition towards group orientation, it again appears as if peer appraisal may present a viable alternative. However, this may not necessarily hold true because implicitly regulated hierarchical relationships stretch beyond formal leadership roles. Most often, distinctions are also made in terms of age and seniority. Many Chinese are uncomfortable in criticizing older colleagues. For example, in a study of appraisal beliefs in Hong Kong and the People's Republic of China (PRC), Chow (1995) reported that 70 per cent of respondents believed it impolite to say negative things about people of a more advanced age. This issue becomes even more complicated if the appraiser is younger than the teacher being appraised, and is female.

Beliefs about seniority, hierarchy and harmony combine to challenge the suitability of Western approaches to peer evaluation, such as those currently in vogue in UK schools. Teachers are reluctant to participate in peer appraisal because involvement tends to be accompanied by the authority to evaluate others' performance. Since the outcome of a low performance rating can be problematic, 'many Chinese employees would rather not participate in such a process lest friendship with co-workers be ruined' (Huo and Clinow, 1995, p. 10). In other words, teachers are not willing to risk disrupting harmonious relationships through appraising or criticizing each other. This need not imply that peer appraisal will not work in Hong Kong schools, but it does point to the need for greater consideration of what shape it might take, and who might be involved.

In sum, power concentration and a group orientation play an important role in Chinese organizations, such as schools. Westwood and Kirkbride (1998) provide a concise summary of the cultural context within which appraisal needs to be implemented in organizations in Chinese societies:

> Chinese organizations are configured by a legitimized hierarchy based upon status overlaid with a system of reciprocal personal relationships and rituals. It is the tacit (Confucian) social ethic and the prescribed set of relationships that orders and controls the system, not an abstract and impersonal rule system – as in the Western bureaucratic model. Acceptance of, and compliance to, this form of structure and governance has been deeply rooted in Chinese organization and persists down to the present day. (p. 568)

Relational dynamics and communication

So far we have established that values important in Chinese societies, such as hierarchy and harmony, can influence the efficacy of certain approaches to appraisal. It is clear that Confucianism stresses the importance of relationships and the conscious effort required to maintain them – all people, all things, have a purpose and a station in life. The belief is that if everyone understands their purpose and station, and performs their duties well, they will work harmoniously. Harmony then gives rise to the conscious exercise of 'proper behaviour' and a concentration of formal power into ordered hierarchies. It should be noted here that proper behaviour as the basis of harmony does not mean that people do not think poorly of their superiors, or always agree with what they do. Rather, it means that they will not easily or openly disagree with someone in a hierarchically superior position, or even someone who is older. In this way, the demand for outwardly amiable relationships might be best thought of as 'surface harmony'.

As we have also suggested, decisions in Chinese organizations are often based on the person rather than the task. This relates to an implicit assumption, or hope, that performance is in some way linked to relationships, such as loyalty. Relationships are governed by the notion of *guanxi*. In simple terms, *guanxi* refers to 'the status and intensity of an ongoing relationship between two parties' (Westwood, 1992, p. 51). The quality of *guanxi*, which people consciously attempt to develop, then guides relationships according to an implicit set of rules. When two people have established *guanxi* it can make them extremely reluctant to say 'no' to any request from the other party, or to openly disagree with each other. Within relationships, the Chinese are often socialized to mask their true feelings in personal interactions, often by nodding and smiling. In Western appraisal terms, the shape of such relationships influences the essential communicative elements of feedback and personal exposure.

Feedback

A key element of teacher appraisal in Western societies is the importance of providing open, honest feedback on performance to the individual being appraised. Feedback is taken as essential to effective appraisal, regardless of the type of appraisal being conducted – be it formative or summative, or whether the appraisal is conducted by a superior or with peers. Hofstede (1995) holds that the Western management literature reasons that employees' performance will improve if they receive direct feedback about what the superior thinks of them. While agreeing that this may be true in individualist cultures, he argues that such direct feedback destroys the harmony that is expected to govern interpersonal relationships in collectivist countries. In even stronger terms, Hofstede believes that direct feedback can cause irreparable damage to the employee's 'face' and ruin his or her loyalty to the organization (Hofstede, 1995).

Chow (1995) provides some support for Hofstede's assertion and suggests that giving open, honest feedback can be problematic in Chinese organizations, since the supervisor is often reluctant to provide critical feedback to teachers because he/she does not want to embarrass them by exposing any weaknesses in their performance. In fact, Herbig and Martin (1998) suggest that the Chinese will go to extreme means to avoid embarrassing another person, whether friend or foe. This, again, relates to the Chinese concept of *face*, referring to the ways people seek to present themselves in interactions, so that others 'will attribute to them positive characteristics so as to gain a good impression and the esteem of others' (Westwood, 1992, p. 51).

While 'looking bad' as a result of an appraisal is a universally embarrassing experience, one which applies in Western contexts, too, it has even greater significance in Chinese cultures (Westwood, 1992). In Chinese organizations, issues of *face* govern social relationships through providing powerful social sanctions. *Face* can only be gained or preserved if a person behaves in an appropriate manner according to the situation and the position of the other person in the relationship. Face is a multifaceted concept. Bond and Hwang (1986) identified six variations of *face* behaviour, including enhancing one's own face, giving face to another, losing one's own face, damaging another face, saving one's own face and saving the face of another. Any disruption of *face* risks unsettling the harmony of the group and therefore the smooth operation and effectiveness of the organization. Appraisers may therefore be extremely reluctant to provide honest feedback on teaching performance, thereby seriously impairing the efficacy of the appraisal process, at least in Western terms.

This point is again borne out by Chow's (1995) study of appraisal beliefs in private sector companies in Hong Kong and the PRC. She reported that negative feedback from a supervisor could cause serious problems within an organization and that 'giving face' and losing face' discourages frank and honest discussion in the appraisal interview because participants do not want to disrupt the co-operative (harmonious) atmosphere. If, as it is reasonable to assume, the same is true in schools, school principals often find it difficult to provide candid feedback for fear it will cause themselves or the teacher to lose *face*. The same holds for peer appraisal where teachers are reluctant to openly criticize colleagues for fear of making them lose *face*. Consequently, any comment about performance or development tends to be superficial, perhaps failing to lead to improved performance.

Hofstede (1995) suggests that 'giving feedback', as conceptualized and practised in Western organizations should be challenged for East Asian societies. He suggests that feedback might be more appropriately given indirectly, 'through the withdrawing of a favour, or via an intermediary person trusted by both supervisor and employee' (p. 157). In other words, it may be necessary to adapt appraisal from Western approaches relying on direct face-to-face feedback between appraiser and appraisee to suit more specific cultural contexts.

Hierarchy and feedback

The Confucian notion of hierarchy and the associated concept of reciprocity discussed earlier, also play an important role in giving feedback. Superiors are bound to give staff face. The concept of *face,* then, is multifarious and relates up, across and down hierarchical relationships. For example, if a supervisor invalidates a teacher's claim to face, such as to say he or she is underperforming, group harmony is damaged. An effect of this may be that the supervisor loses face. Since the act of criticism is considered aggressive, the supervisor can no longer support a social identity as a kind or considerate person and so loses respect. Anyone who does not wish to be considered socially illiterate will sidestep any behaviour that could lead to such an episode.

On the other side of the *face* equation, Chinese teachers are generally reluctant to admit to their own weaknesses or problems, typically responding in ways suggesting that they do not have any problems. Consequently, appraisal approaches grounded in self-appraisal may encounter difficulties. Exposing problems may not only be seen as a sign of weakness but, and perhaps more importantly, may also indicate that people are not contributing sufficiently to the goals of the group or organization. Again, this unwillingness to expose problems seems typical, whether the type of appraisal is summative, formative, top-down, self or peer.

A micro-society, such as a school, whose membership is geographically stable and whose numbers are relatively small, will therefore have a stronger code of behaviour about face-saving, as anonymity will be unusual in such a society (Bond, 1991a). In addition, the act of saving another's face promotes cohesiveness among group members that helps and forms a type of protective cocoon around members. Even when criticism is given it is usually hedged with numerous qualifiers. The appraiser might deprecate his own abilities, clearly disqualifying himself as a competent critic or as an aspirant for the appraisee's position. Finally, the content of the criticism would probably be stated indirectly and with many linguistic qualifications.

Clearly, there is a need for everyone in all cultures to be careful when criticizing others, regardless of how strongly the demands of the situation warrant such criticism. For criticism here involves unfavourable comparisons of a person's performance against socially defined standards. With a heightened reluctance to criticize in Chinese culture, comes the development of social skills that preserve the faces of others and the use of linguistic skills in diluting criticism. In these respects, the original purpose of appraisal – as conceived in Western terms – may be lost.

Avoiding conflict and confrontation

In summary, Western literature on performance appraisal suggests that skills, such as listening, giving and receiving feedback, counselling and dealing with emotions, are necessary for success (Huo and Clinow, 1995). Chinese school leaders, however, may be reluctant to pursue two-way communication or to provide counselling, a fact which can be explained by the power-concentration found in Chinese societies. As mentioned above, in Chinese cultures seniority means managing authority from the top (Bond, 1991a) and to challenge the authority of superiors is not considered appropriate for subordinates (Hofstede, 1980). More importantly, in providing feedback, the potential for interpersonal discord between supervisor and teacher tends to increase. Since both supervisors and teachers in Chinese societies want to avoid such direct confrontation, it is understandable that they will try to minimize the frequency of such conflict-prone encounters in the workplace and preserve harmony.

Torringtan and Tan (1994) point out that in Chinese communities any form of unpleasant confrontation that may upset relationships is avoided. The same authors claim that this is the reason why open appraisal is not readily practised above a perfunctory level in many Chinese organizations and that, as a result, Western appraisal schemes even when 'officially' implemented seldom reflect the real situation. Upsetting relationships means upsetting harmony – a key collectivist value that determines interpersonal relationships.

The centrality of maintaining harmonious relationships in Chinese organizations clashes with the Western notions that some variation of views and convictions, openly expressed, can be productive and lead to fresh ideas

155

(Fullan, 1993). In Chinese organizations, Western notions of power-sharing, typified by public explanations and exchanges, debates, voting and documentation, are unusual. Harmony for the Chinese does not assume participation (Bond, 1991a). Most forms of open dispute or disagreement are alien to Chinese cultures where harmony is paramount. In Chinese organizations, the norm is to consciously avoid directly contradicting others, especially formal leaders or more senior colleagues. To avoid loss of face and to preserve harmony there is no need to say 'no'; people feel comfortable with saying 'yes' which indicates understanding, but not agreement (Bond, 1991a).

In most situations, the Chinese are reluctant to confront others. Open disclosure and critical reflection are uncommon in interpersonal interactions such as appraisal meetings or classroom observations. Disclosure which may lead to confrontation is avoided, as it might be perceived as a threat to authority and hierarchical relationship. Chung, McMahan and Woodman (1996) conclude that confrontational meetings, negotiation and even third party interventions that demand an open critiquing of others can prove highly problematic in Chinese organizations. If teachers are unwilling to openly critique their own performance – much less others – during appraisal meetings, it appears unlikely that worthwhile discussion will result.

In summary, the emphasis on harmonious relations and the concept of 'face-saving' can discourage open communication, self-critique and feedback during the appraisal process. Therefore, the need for openness and confidentiality, as promoted by Western appraisal models, may not fit neatly with Chinese culture.

The way forward

While not claiming to be exhaustive, the above discussion indicates that the societal cultural values of Chinese communities may not fit the assumptions and practices of the imported or Anglo-American approaches to appraisal currently being promoted and adopted in many schools in different corners of the world. It is therefore reasonable to question their efficacy in schools and to search for more culturally appropriate approaches. The following questions and discussion hope to stimulate discussion about developing more culturally sensitive teacher appraisal models.

- A major difference between Chinese, and indeed other East Asian societies, and most English-speaking Western societies is that the former elevates the place of relationships, whereas the latter elevates task and performance. An important question for schools in Chinese societies, therefore, is whether they persevere with a 'hostile' task model or try to adapt/develop a model that elevates relationships. To do this, greater understanding is necessary of how the Chinese see the relationship between the two. It may be overly simplistic to assume that just because relationships are pre-eminent, that task accomplishment is unimportant. Rather, it might be that task accomplishment is seen as deriving from ordered, hierarchical relationships. An area then that deserves further investigation in searching for a more culturally appropriate model of appraisal is the link between relationships and task and whether this could provide a platform for judging or improving performance.

- The dedication to collectivism in schools in Chinese societies casts serious doubts over the effectiveness of instituting teacher appraisal schemes that focus predominantly on individuals. Consequently, it appears that a type of group appraisal model may be more suitable. Coincidentally, much Western literature increasingly recognizes group or peer approaches to appraisal. It may be that such approaches, which challenge traditional one-on-one schemes, hold promise for developing more culturally sensitive approaches to teacher appraisal. If we accept that this is so, the question then moves to what type of group appraisal is most appropriate. Given the level of respect for authority and seniority and the accompanying influence this has on open interaction, there appears to be a number of options. One is to group teachers according to their perceived place in the school. For example, all new teachers, or all more experienced teachers, could be grouped on the basis that teachers would interact more easily with those of equal status. A second option may be to allow teachers to form their own groups, thus allowing them to work with those with whom they are most comfortable. Either of these types of configurations may be suited to developmental appraisal, but it is unlikely that they would be effective for judgemental purposes.

- It may be that schools need to consciously separate developmental and judgemental appraisal. The separation of these functions would allow for more collectivist approaches to appraisal for professional development and for more hierarchical approaches to judgemental appraisal. Given the reluctance of leaders to openly criticize teachers, it may be that appraisers from outside the school would be more able to take this role. Although this could be construed as a step backwards according to recent thought, the introduction of an 'outside' appraiser could overcome issues of openness and objective judgement. We do not suggest that this is *the* answer, but that it should at least be considered. The use of 'outside' appraisers also gives rise to the use of intermediaries within the school.

- Whereas the Chinese are reluctant to provide feedback which may lead to confrontation or loss of face, they appear willing to receive such feedback through a third party. It seems that feedback, even when negative, can be given as long as it is not in a direct setting. Intermediaries may be used as links between the principal and teacher for commenting on the latter's performance. They may be mid-level staff, with experience as senior teachers. Given the respect for seniority, it could also be possible for schools to develop structured mentoring programmes, where senior staff capitalize on their seniority to advise and develop younger teachers.

Conclusion

In summary, the key to a culturally sensitive teacher appraisal system may involve a model that separates judgemental and developmental purposes. Teacher development may best be pursued in carefully selected groups, each interacting with the principal through agreed intermediaries. Judgements may best be made by qualified people who are somewhat removed from the ordered relationships within the school and its departments. There needs to be an acceptance that feedback and exposure will often be given in roundabout ways and will be non-confrontational. Approaches based on Glatthorn's (1997) differentiated supervision philosophy may hold some promise in this direction. The aim should be to meet different needs in different ways while taking full account of culture.

Developing culturally sensitive approaches to teacher appraisal is complex and it would be audacious to suggest that we have done more in this chapter than highlight important and serious issues which appear to have been over-looked. We have attempted to recognize the influence societal culture can play in teacher appraisal. The continued penetration of Anglo-American teacher appraisal policies and practices into different cultural contexts may well result in failed attempts at implementation.

The next chapter focuses on the dilemmas that school leaders face in respond-ing to the ever shifting educational landscape and the many – and often – conflicting demands and expectations placed on them. This is an important area of research aimed at achieving a deeper understanding of how school leaders both conceptualize and manage the tensions and dilemmas they face.

10

Leadership Dilemmas and Cultural Diversity[1]

This chapter explores and analyses two themes and their relationship. The first theme is the notion that principals tend to perceive at least part of their work lives as dilemmas. The second is that both the perception/conception of dilemmas, and their subsequent management or resolution, tend to be culturally influenced. In support of both themes, we report a study carried out with a group of principals in Hong Kong.

Schools throughout the world operate in an increasingly complex and confusing environment. School leaders in particular are exposed to the problems, paradoxes and dilemmas associated with shifting educational landscapes. Recent research into the dilemmas perceived by school principals presents a picture of leaders torn between opposite, often contradictory, directions as their roles become less circumscribed and more subject to debate in times of societal change (Dimmock, 1996; Walker and Quong, 1998). MacBeath (2003, p. 323) describes the situation as the intensification of dilemmas in 'changing hyper complex societies'.

Major social upheaval and hypercomplexity can be attributed to a number of forces, including globalization and the clash of external sources of influence with indigenous cultures and traditions. The movement of people across the globe and the growing multi-ethnic and multicultural nature of many Western societies is a further factor. The increase in complexity and associated problems have also been exacerbated by concentrations of poverty and socio-economic disadvantage in certain geographic areas, such as the West and the South in the USA, where some schools have between 45 and 50 per cent socially disadvantaged ethnic minority student populations (Seashore Louis, 2003). As Seashore Louis (2003) points out, in the American context these challenges pose a number of serious dilemmas for school leaders. First, not only are they faced with meeting the special needs of ethnic minority and disadvantaged students, but they must also satisfy the more conservative and academically oriented demands and expectations of middle-class parents, or else lose their patronage to more affluent schools as a result of market forces and parental choice. Secondly, faced with the inexorable pressure to raise standards, principals run the risk of worsening the already low morale of many teachers battling against low student achievement brought about by problems of socio-economic disadvantage largely beyond their immediate control. And, thirdly, managing the needs of a diverse community of stakeholders with conflicting values and expectations can pose a serious problem for school leaders. These socially related dilemmas are not confined to pockets of poverty in American society, but have been mirrored in most advanced societies. Dempsey and Berry (2003), for instance, in citing the major dilemmas identified by Australian principals, list a number directly associated with students (including bullying, violent and disruptive behaviour; a conflict of family and school values; and child custody battles) and with external relations (including overly demanding parents and cultural diversity within the school community).

School leaders also face dilemmas that can be directly attributed to contradictions in educational policy. Reminiscent of the situation in the UK, Moos and Møller (2003), for example, in their discussion of school leadership in Danish and Norwegian schools, identify the tension between, on the one hand, those policy initiatives within the neo-liberal tradition (characterized by the abolition of local regulation of the administration and financial management of schools in the interests of market competition and consumer choice), and, on the other, those policies within the neo-conservative tradition (characterized by greater central control of the curriculum and inspection processes in the interests of accountability and the drive to improve educational standards). Such tensions give rise to a range of associated dilemmas facing school leaders. The pressures of the so-called New Public Management (NPM) and external accountability, for instance, give rise to the dilemma of 'power over' versus 'power through' teaching staff: of the hierarchical control and obedience characteristic of managerial accountability, set against the need to build trust and commitment, facilitate collaboration and sustain professional autonomy. This is epitomized in the dilemmas associated with teacher appraisal, 'because appraisal is intended to serve two fundamental purposes: holding people accountable for their performance and supporting the improvement of that performance' (Cardno, 2001, p. 145). Tensions are also likely to arise between the need for school leaders to satisfy both the needs of the organization (with a leadership emphasis on tasks and outcomes) and the needs of individuals (with an emphasis on maintaining and promoting harmonious relationships). It is what Schratz (2003) in his analysis of school leadership dilemmas in three German-speaking countries – namely Germany, Austria and Switzerland – describes as the tension between *sollen* (duty) and *wollen* (desire), as 'personal needs can rarely if ever be correlated 100% with organisational needs' (p. 409).

Problems or dilemmas facing school leaders have been classified by Cuban (2001) as either 'tame' (those amenable to resolution) or 'wicked' (those which are either extremely difficult if not impossible to resolve). Unfortunately, dilemmas are increasingly of the latter kind, either in consequence of the profound social and global changes and pressures, or as a result of major policy changes and initiatives, as outlined above. In the words of Moos and Møller (2003, p. 354), 'the collision of those trends leaves schools and school leaders with an unclear basis for their praxis and unclear consequences for their decisions'. It is therefore unsurprising that calls are being made for more insightful methods for understanding how school leaders make sense of, and manage, their work lives (Dimmock and O'Donoghue, 1997). One way of accomplishing this is to invite principals to conceptualize their working lives in terms of the dilemmas they face. While a small but growing body of research on how principals perceive their lives in terms of dilemmas has recently begun to appear, such work has to date been restricted to the study of principals in Western countries. Little if any research has been conducted on whether and how school leaders in other cultural contexts perceive their work lives in terms of dilemmas. Accordingly, this chapter attempts to redress this situation through mapping the perceptions of a small number of school leaders for whom dilemmas figure significantly in their work lives in the Asian setting of Hong Kong (Walker and Dimmock, 2000b).

The concept of leadership dilemmas is introduced in the context of emerging research literature on cognitive dimensions of educational administration. Existing literature is referenced in conceptions of dilemmas almost exclusively from Western cultural paradigms, thereby ignoring dilemmas faced by principals in non-Western settings. We then report on a study which identifies the dilemmas experienced by a group of Hong Kong principals. Using a framework generated in part by inductive analysis, dilemma situations recounted by these school leaders are analysed, their sources, coping mechanisms and outcomes are identified, and the relationships between these phenomena are examined.

Contemporary interest in studying dilemmas pertaining to the principalship stems from at least three interrelated sources. The first is an accepted recognition that schools are not rational organizations. Traditional conceptions of schools and school life tend to underestimate the reality of individual differences in values, goals, interests, motivations and understandings of the organizations in which they work and of their roles. The second stimulus for studying principalship dilemmas is the multitude of reforms influencing schools over the last decade. Dimmock (1996) and Cuban (1994) hold that unless we can gain a practical understanding of values conflicts 'deeply rooted' in the work of principals, as well as the ways in which they have learned to manage these, schools are unlikely to engage in sustainable reform. Both authors advocate further analysis of dilemmas as a way of probing principals' own cognition, or their 'perception of the social and political frames within which they work' (Dimmock, 1996, p. 140; Hallinger, Leithwood and Murphy, 1993).

A third justification for advocating the study of principal dilemmas is the increased emphasis on values and values conflict in educational administration (Begley, 1996; Campbell-Evans, 1993; Greenfield and Ribbins, 1993). Begley and Johansson (1997) explicate the values perspective in the following way: 'School administrators increasingly encounter situations where consensus cannot be achieved. In some respects, this renders obsolete the traditional rational notions of problem *solving* because administrators must respond to values conflict situations that arise, but there may be no solution possible that will satisfy all' (p. 5, emphasis in original). In our schema, such values conflict situations are classified as dilemmas and are investigated using an inductively developed framework.

Dilemma analysis seeks to gain insight into how principals make sense of, conceptualize and approach the difficulties, contradictions and problems they face in leading schools. Research into this area is relatively recent and has moved towards a better understanding of how principals construct knowledge within their particular contexts (Heck and Hallinger, 1997).

Dilemma analysis in context: alternative approaches to understanding principalship problem-solving and sense-making

Dilemma analysis is one way of investigating how principals make sense of and approach difficult situations in their work lives. How principals approach problem-solving has long been of interest to researchers and organizational theorists. Early attempts to investigate principal problem-solving employed rational decision-making frameworks and relied heavily on positivist methodologies. As understanding and sophistication increased, researchers widened the net of perspectives, frameworks and methods for studying the principalship. These included multiple variations of the classical rational model, incorporating political and micro-political perspectives. While recognizing the existence of multiple perspectives on leadership problem-solving, we do not attempt to discuss these here. Rather, we discuss emerging cognitive perspectives on the study of educational administration which we regard as complementary to our dilemmas approach to understanding an important part of the work lives of Hong Kong principals.

Duke (1996) divides educational leadership research using cognitive perspectives into two distinct strands. The first is represented by Gardner's (1995) investigation into how the mind influences ideas and thinking. The other, which relates more directly to our approach, is best represented by Leithwood's (1995) interest in how leaders solve problems and arrive at decisions. Such studies attempt to account for contextual influences on cognition and stress that values pervade the process of problem-solving (Heck and Hallinger, 1997).

Within this emerging tradition, researchers (e.g. Begley, 1996; Begley and Johansson, 1997) have concentrated on the relationship between social cognition and values, and principals' problem-solving and decision-making (Hallinger and Heck, 1996). Leithwood's (1995) work, for example, conceptualizes principals as problem-finders and problem-solvers. Cognitive perspectives emphasize the importance of values, and their origins, in making leadership choices. Work examining the place, role, influence and effect of educational leaders' values on school operation has been widely investigated (for example, see Begley and Leithwood, 1990; Walker, 1997). According to Leithwood

(1995, p. 118) cognitive research into the principalship is grounded in 'how the mind works in terms of hypothetical structures and relationships explaining why people attend to some aspects of the information available to them in their environments'. In short, it is rooted in how principals think about practice.

Cognate research has investigated the categorization and resolution of values conflicts faced by school principals. One such approach (Leithwood, Begley and Cousins, 1994) posits that school leaders encounter two general types of values conflicts. The first type involves contention between two or more values 'for recognition in the formulation of a solution' (p. 108). Within this category, values conflicts take three different forms: conflicts between two or more people other than the principal; conflict between the principal and other staff; and values conflict concerning the principal alone. The second general source of values conflict occurs between the principal's own strongly held values and actions. This is manifest in a principal's inability to act in a manner consistent with his or her own values. According to Leithwood, Begley and Cousins (1994) principals resolve values conflicts, formally or informally, either through what they call 'deep and strong' ways, for example, careful explanation and referral to formal organizational procedures (typically used by expert problem-solvers), or through 'surface and weak' strategies, such as seeking out others' interpretations of the conflict or consulting others about solutions (typically used by less expert problem-solvers).

As part of a broader study on administrator values Begley and Johansson (1997) adapted Hodgkinson's (1978) values typology to uncover the type, frequency and intensity of values conflicts encountered by principals, and the specific values underpinning their response to values conflict situations when 'personal, professional, and/or organisational values compete for precedence' (p. 5).

Despite advances in understanding gained through investigation into leaders' cognitive processes, much 'problem-solving' research has relied on principals' reactions to 'problems set in a static, fictionalised context ... rather than in a dynamic context' (Hart et al., 1997, p. 4). Heck and Hallinger (1997) support this position and call for research into principal problem-solving to move beyond external measurement of internal processes; and for greater recognition that 'personal values, political pressures and organisational concerns' are translated into action to solve day-to-day problems (p. 9). This is echoed in the recent research study into the tensions of school leadership in Ghana, where an understanding of leadership decisions and processes is unlikely to be derived from the application of Western-based theories and principles, but rather through a 'need to see the interlocking set of relationships in a Ghanaian school as a complex activity system' (Oduro and MacBeath, 2003, p. 453).

The dilemma analysis used in our empirical study attempted to investigate how principals approach 'actual problems' within the 'dynamic and real-world' context of Hong Kong.

Studying principalship dilemmas

While the concept of dilemmas is not new and has previously targeted the moral and ethical aspects of teachers' work (O'Donoghue, Aspland and Brooker, 1993), little empirical work has been carried out to date on the principalship. Glatter (1994, p. 2) makes this point, supporting Cuban's call for a practical grounding of dilemmas claiming researchers, 'rarely examine real situations of conflict and tension in which there are genuine dilemmas to confront' (p. 2). This situation is beginning to be addressed by researchers such as Dimmock (1996) in Australia, Grace (1994) and Day et al. (2000) in Britain, and Murphy (1994) in the USA.

Although many dilemmas are perennial (Glatter, 1994), they are, by nature, individual contestations between important values. While mostly underpinned by conflicting values, dilemmas often surface in organizational structures and relationships. A number of researchers have attempted to clarify the nature of dilemmas. Berlak and Berlak (1981), for example, recognized dilemmas which embraced sociological, political and educational dimensions. Winter (1982) conceptualized dilemmas in sociological terms as contradictions, classifying them as ambiguities, judgements and problems. He distinguished three types according to the degree of control an individual feels he/she has over a situation. For example, ambiguities are defined as beyond the control of the individual, judgements can be dealt with using skill, care and knowledge, while problems are only partially amenable to control since taking action in one aspect leads to problems in other domains.

Winter's category of 'problems' approximates to the conception of 'dilemma' adopted in this study. However, while Winter's (1982) categories are useful, they are restrictive in limiting understanding of dilemmas to the degree of controllability individuals possess in handling them. The schema also attempts to categorize dilemmas into discrete categories, thereby denying their possible interactive or interrelated nature.

Further clarification of the nature of educational problems and their more extreme form of dilemmas is provided by Holmes (1965) who suggested that their origin lay in asynchronous changes taking place in education and society. Dimmock (1996) applied this idea to principalship dilemmas related to restructuring in Australia stating, 'a dilemma in restructuring may be conceptualised in terms of asynchronous change *within* and *between* ... norms and values, institutional practices and structures, and resources' (p. 144, emphasis in original). For the purposes of this chapter we define dilemmas as conflictual situations that demand irreconcilable choices because of the existence of competing, deeply rooted values. As previously recognized, while dilemmas are grounded in values, they often emerge from structures, resources and relationships, and interactions between these. Dilemma situations contain elements of contradiction, conflict, paradox and inconsistency in the ways they are perceived, and in how they may be solved, since the selection of a course of action, or inaction, to deal with one aspect automatically leaves other aspects unsatisfied or more problematic.

Despite the increasing volume of research into values conflicts and principalship dilemmas, little of this work has explored dilemmas faced by principals in Asian settings. This reflects part of a wider neglect of the influence of culture on educational leadership (Dimmock and Walker, 1998a), which has a number of consequences. First, unless research is conducted to identify the dilemmas of principals in non-Western countries, it is likely that the all-too-prevalent assumptions that Western-generated research findings are applicable to all settings, will continue to be made (Walker, Bridges and Chan, 1996). Secondly, if one considers the different cultural and social contexts of different communities the prospect of universally shared values becomes untenable, implying that the shape of leaders' lives and the meanings attached to leadership will expectedly vary (Dimmock and Walker, 1998b). Thus, the form of values conflict which underpins dilemmas in various contexts cannot be purposefully investigated if research exclusively reflects an ethnocentric bias towards Western traditions and Judaeo-Christian thinking and logic (Begley and Johansson, 1997). Put simply, dilemma research conducted purely in Western contexts disenfranchises large groups of principals, denies the identities of important racial, ethnic and national groups, and risks restricting understanding to narrowly, even arrogantly, defined parameters.

A robust case exists for a research focus on dilemmas experienced by principals in different countries, the importance of studying and identifying these dilemmas, schema for categorizing dilemmas and, finally, ways in which principals cope with the dilemmas they face. As suggested by Cuban (1992; 1994), we need to learn first hand the practical dilemmas faced by principals, how they cope and the various outcomes brought about by particular actions or inactions. There is also a need to map the multidimensional nature of dilemmas by identifying their sources and the conflict of values which underpin them. The study purported to meet this agenda by widening the research focus to examine the dilemmas faced by principals in Hong Kong (for explication of the Hong Kong context see Dimmock, 1998; Dimmock and Walker, 1997; Walker and Dimmock, 1998).

Method

The investigation aimed at identifying the characteristics of principals' dilemmas by addressing four guiding questions: what dilemmas, if any, do Hong Kong principals face in the course of their work lives? What are the sources or roots of their dilemmas? How do the principals manage or cope with dilemmas? And what are the outcomes of their coping or managing strategies? Importance was also attached to the relationships between the four questions.

A qualitative approach using naturalistic methods of inquiry was adopted as the methodological paradigm for the study. According to Miles and Huberman (1994, p. 7), qualitative research aims 'to explicate the ways people in particular settings come to understand, account for, take action, and otherwise manage their day to day situations'. In addition, Lincoln and Guba (1985) suggest that naturalistic inquiry is most appropriate when multiple constructed realities exist. The dilemmas experienced by a group of Hong Kong principals constitute such multiple realities.

The principals

Fifteen principals were selected for interview using, first, *criterion* and, then, *snowball* or *chain* sampling over a period of approximately six months. *Snowball* or *chain* sampling aims to identify 'cases of interest from people who know people who know what cases are information rich' (Miles and Huberman, 1994, p. 28). Initially, a group of principals with good English language proficiency and who were active in the educational community were asked whether they would be willing to talk about their life in schools and any difficulties they faced. A number of them agreed to a preliminary interview. A full exposition of the interview protocol is set out later in this methodology section.

The number of principals interviewed was not determined beforehand and sampling was completed only when data from new respondents was replicating that from earlier participants. The aim of the study was not to uncover all possible dilemma situations. By definition, what is a dilemma for one principal may not be for another. Besides, the aim of this study, in line with naturalistic inquiry, was not to generalise to broader populations. Rather, it was to uncover situations and relationships between constructs which serve as explanations of reality. As Firestone (1993) notes, 'the most useful generalisations from qualitative studies are *analytic*, not sample-to-population' (cited in Miles and Huberman, 1994, p. 28, emphasis in original).

The principals interviewed ranged in their experience of principalship from three to 17 years. They had been in their present schools for varying periods from one to 17 years. The 15 principals included 12 males and three females. Four were principals of secondary schools and 11 were principals of primary schools. All of the principals interviewed were heads of aided schools.[2] The secondary schools had approximately 1200 pupils, while most of the primary schools had enrolments of around 1500 students attending on a split shift morning/afternoon basis. The study did not set out to differentiate between the dilemmas faced by primary and secondary principals. There is, however, one difference between primary and secondary schools which is worth mentioning. The structure of primary schooling involves separate morning (AM) and afternoon schools (PM) which share the same building (this dual sharing is not found in the secondary system). The participating principals represent both

AM and PM primary schools as well as secondary schools, thereby presenting a range of dilemma situations and perspectives.

The interviews

Data were collected through face-to-face interviews which took the form of a 'conversation piece, not an inquisition' (Simons, 1982, p. 37; Taylor and Bogdan, 1984). To overcome minor language difficulties experienced by some principals, six of them were interviewed in pairs by one interviewer, and the remainder were interviewed individually either by one or both interviewers.

Interviews were conducted in three phases: open-ended, semi-structured and structured. In the first phase (open-ended), principals were invited to talk about their lives in schools in general terms and the difficulties they believed they faced. This phase was largely unstructured and conversation was used to encourage principals to think about their work lives in school. Once they were comfortable with the conversation, the second phase was introduced whereby semi-structured questions were used as prompts to seek out whether they experienced problems, difficulties and dilemmas. The prompts were always influenced by the principals' own stories. If necessary, the researchers provided a generic, simplified definition of a dilemma situation in a Hong Kong school (using stories from other principals) to help them understand the concept. It should be noted that at this stage, some of the principals did not perceive their lives in terms of dilemmas. Their right to this opinion was made clear throughout our conversations. When this happened, we invited the respondents to clarify their perceptions and terminated the interview. The phenomenon of a small minority of principals who conceptually did not recognize dilemmas is worthy of separate and subsequent investigation. For the majority of principals who did conceptualize their work lives in terms of dilemmas, we moved forward to the third phase of the interview. In short, we only moved to phase three, as described below, when principals could themselves readily identify and recognize dilemmas and were willing to accept that dilemmas were an important part of their work lives.

The third phase of the interview delved into the principals' dilemmas, including the background to the dilemmas, how they had coped with, or managed the situations, and what, if any, outcomes had resulted. A more structured interview was adopted, specifically targeting the guiding questions set out earlier. All interviews were tape-recorded and subsequently transcribed.

Analysis

Analysis occurred at each stage of data collection. That is, analysis took place after the first interview; this analysis was then used to shape the second interview and so on (Bogdan and Biklen, 1992). This process of inductive analysis meant that formal analysis is almost complete by the end of data collection. The sequence of 'interview followed by analysis' enabled interpretations to emerge and to be cross-checked on an ongoing basis. Through inductive analysis, an iterative process facilitated the cross-checking of data against the rudimentary framework, enabling the framework to be progressively refined. The result was the construction of a number of 'dilemma maps' for aiding analysis of the dilemmas. The analytic framework emerged from a combination of the principals' own accounts of their dilemmas and the researchers' interpretations. The maps, in turn, allowed the relationships between dilemma situations, their sources, how principals managed the dilemmas and the outcomes of the dilemmas to be explored in greater detail. The framework is discussed below.

Framework for analysing dilemma situations

Constructing dilemma maps involved the fracturing of dilemma situations in order to seek relationships and connections. The maps allowed the principals, first, to reflect upon the intricacies of their own dilemmas, including how they made sense of, and coped with them. Secondly, the maps were useful for the researchers in attempting to interpret principalship dilemmas in terms of their sources, coping strategies and outcomes. The framework is shown in Figure 10.1. It is presented before the analysis of dilemmas section, but it should be borne in mind that the framework was refined through an iterative process of inductive analysis.

Data collection and analysis began with the principal describing his/her work life, and particularly the major challenges (phase one of the interviews). It gradually moved to whether the principal perceived these as dilemma situations (phase two of the interviews). The situation was then 'unpacked' by identifying the elements of the dilemma (phase three of the interviews). The principal was asked how he/she makes sense of the dilemma in terms of its constituent elements, that is, the factors which comprise the dilemma, such as staff dissatisfaction or policy imposition. Discrepancy between the principal's perception and the researchers' interpretation were noted. Once the dilemma situation and the constituent elements had been clarified, we sought to explore the sources of the dilemma. These, for example, involved conflicting values, structural arrangements, and teaching and learning beliefs.

The next stage was how the principal had coped with or managed the dilemma – the action or inaction taken and how the constituent elements and sources of the dilemma may have influenced this. Why had the principal coped with the dilemma in a particular way? The final stage of the analysis considered the outcomes of the dilemma, and the consequences of how it was managed. Four outcomes of the dilemmas emerged as experienced by principals in this study: the creation of another dilemma, the return of the existing dilemma, a magnification in complexity of the existing dilemma and a lessening of the dilemma. Consideration of outcomes allowed both the practitioner and researcher

Figure 10.1 *A way of mapping dilemmas*

to 'backward track' the dilemma and consider, in tandem with the elements, sources and coping strategies. Although not pursued in this study, this process may also aid discussion and whether the dilemma could have been managed differently.

From the array of dilemma maps constructed, three were selected for presentation on the basis of their analytic interest. In line with the sampling procedure and methodology employed, we do not claim that these dilemmas are typical or representative of other Hong Kong principals' dilemmas. We do claim, however, that they provide a legitimate and authentic picture of how this group of Hong Kong principals conceive their dilemmas. In the following section we present a more detailed analysis of dilemmas faced by three of the principals interviewed.

Three dilemma situations of Hong Kong principals

Dilemma 1: The expatriate teacher

The sources of this dilemma present a coalescence of cultural, structural, and teaching and learning beliefs (Figure 10.2). An expatriate teacher had his own

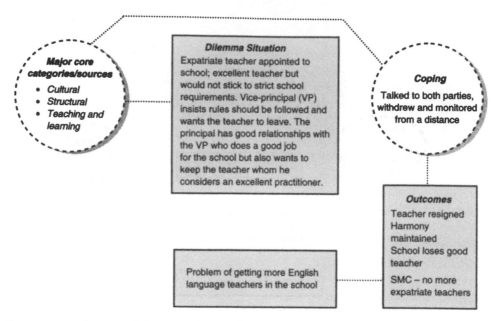

Figure 10.2 *The case of the expatriate teacher*

strong ideas about how to conduct his teaching in the school. These clashed with the conformist position of his immediate supervisor, the vice-principal (VP), who regulated the 'accepted ways of working' in the school. The principal interpreted the dilemma as stemming from the educational training of the expatriate teacher, emphasizing openness and autonomy, an approach which clashed with the traditional customs of this Chinese school which placed value on order, hierarchy, harmony and avoidance of open conflict. Disagreements quickly escalated to open conflict, placing the principal in a dilemma. He had worked with the VP for many years and respected her dedication and work, and, as he added, 'she was senior to the teacher'. Above all, the principal saw it as very important to maintain a close, harmonious relationship with the VP. On the other hand, the principal felt the teacher was an asset to the school and was a very good practitioner. Although the principal talked to both parties, proposing compromise, the conflict became more bitter and attracted the attention of other staff. He felt that no more formal action than this could be taken while expressing a continued concern for maintaining harmony. Eventually, life for the teacher became so uncomfortable that he resigned. As a result, harmony was maintained with the VP and other staff, but the principal was left disappointed and grappling with contradictory feelings. In the principal's words:

> I was sorry to see the teacher go because of his excellent classroom ability, but in a way I was relieved because it released some of the fighting which had been disrupting the panel (department).

Most staff agreed that he had to go in order that we have a more harmonious situation between the teachers. In Chinese we say 'two tigers cannot get on together'.

Initially, the principal managed the dilemma by discussing the situation with those involved in an attempt to reach some form of compromise. When this failed, he withdrew from active involvement and stood back, counselling the VP when necessary. He then concentrated his action on communicating with the VP, but could do little for the teacher. His main concern seemed to be to maintain good relations with his senior staff. Despite the coalescence of dilemma sources, the dominant coping strategy related to cultural values and maintaining relationships, rather than technical considerations of teaching and learning. The principal did not ignore the situation, or abdicate total responsibility; staff knew he was concerned and that the VP had his support. This strategy probably contributed to the teacher's resignation, but for all that, there was not a clear and satisfactory resolution to the dilemma. For the principal, in both personal and organizational terms, the dilemma had adverse outcomes. He was unhappy that he had a lost a good teacher and, as a result of the conflict, the School Management Committee (SMC) decided to avoid future conflicts by discontinuing the practice of accepting expatriate teachers from a non-profit-making, religious organization. This left the principal in the difficult position of being unable to staff the school to the standard he desired. The particular coping strategy solved part of the principal's dilemma, but left him feeling disappointed and actually posed for him a new set of dilemmas which had not previously existed.

Dilemma 2: A controversial promotion

The coalescence of sources of this second dilemma germinated from a combination of structural, cultural and personal factors (Figure 10.3). The supervisor requested the principal to promote a teacher who was a relative of his. Neither the principal nor other teachers believed the teacher deserved such promotion. In structural terms, the school supervisor has considerable formal and informal power in terms of staffing and school operation, as do other members of the SMC. If this structural arrangement had not existed, the dilemma situation would have been avoided, and the principal alone would have been able to make the decision as to whom to promote based on performance criteria. The principal explained that he was conscious that the supervisor and SMC had the power to fire him. Although he was never threatened with this action, the fact that he was aware of this authority over him appeared to accentuate his dilemma. The principal explained, 'by law – Hong Kong law, if half the members of the SMC are dissatisfied with the Headmaster, he is fired'. The final element of the dilemma was perhaps the most influential, especially in terms of how he coped. The principal saw

171

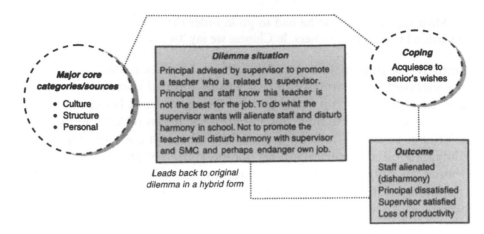

Figure 10.3 *The case of the related supervisor*

the dilemma in terms of respecting hierarchy, maintaining harmony and preserving relationships with both teachers and the supervisor. He saw himself in a no-win situation: to promote the teacher would alienate staff and to refuse would, at the least, disturb his harmonious relationships with his superiors. He linked the need for harmony to Chinese cultural values: 'I think harmony is culture. Harmony is central to Chinese culture, I honestly believe that in our Chinese society, harmony comes first.' What appeared then to give him the most dissonance was the possibility of harmony being disturbed by conflict. Whichever way he turned, harmony was bound to suffer. If he promoted the teacher, he would lose the respect of other teachers, but would satisfy the supervisor and SMC. If he did not promote the teacher he might incur the wrath of the supervisor and SMC, but enjoy the confidence of his staff. He expressed his feelings, thus:

> The need for harmony makes me feel lonely as a principal. I was annoyed that I was pushed to promote one teacher by one of my managers ... this made me very upset. I tried to put forward my point that we want equity, we want performance. I put all of these to my supervisor – to gain harmony.

The principal chose a coping strategy which acquiesced with the request from his supervisor. Somewhat misleadingly, he thought this to be a 'compromise'. His choice of coping strategy illustrates the apparent importance of hierarchy and respect for position so deeply embedded in Chinese society. The primordial consideration was maintenance of harmony with the supervisor, his superior, rather than faith kept with his staff. This was, however, an unsettling decision for the principal in that it had detrimental effects on his relationships with teachers, teacher–teacher relationships and even on how he felt about himself. He explained his position, thus:

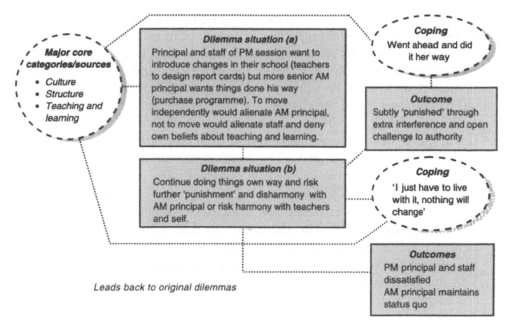

Figure 10.4   *The case of two principals*

The rest of the teachers felt uncomfortable with the decision. I tried to explain it, but how can you explain? I can't say a teacher got promoted because he was related to a school manager ... it is not fair to them – to the rest of the teachers, because promotion is not based on performance.

As a consequence he believed that he had lost some trust and respect from staff and that teachers were no longer 'as happy and co-operative as they once were no longer working as much like a team'. In short, because of his decision, the operation of the school had been adversely affected. He believed the harmony between the teachers had been disturbed, and that this now presented him with another dilemma, namely, how to recapture the harmony. He felt that the coping strategy had eventuated in an unsatisfactory outcome, from both a personal and organizational viewpoint, and that in some ways he was back to his original dilemma of balancing harmony and positive relationships with both the supervisor, the SMC and the teachers. Indeed, his original dilemma was still existent, but was now more complex.

Dilemma 3: Obeying a more 'senior' principal

This dilemma derived from a tension between cultural values and the principals' beliefs about teaching and learning, the dilemma situation manifesting in the bi-sessional school structure (Figure 10.4). The dilemma would not have emerged had it not been for this structure. The principal, a recent graduate from a local university, believed that the school could better meet the needs of the students by revamping the student reporting system to be more flexible in reflecting individual differences. She secured the agreement of most of her staff. However, the AM principal, her senior in terms of age, experience and the informal hierarchy, disagreed with what he saw as progressivism. When the PM principal went ahead and introduced the change, she was, as she put it, 'informally, but obviously punished'. Her dilemma was now accentuated, since if she continued doing things her own way she risked further 'punishment', while if she discontinued the practice, she risked a lowering of staff morale. As the principal stated, 'if I do everything he (the AM principal) says, my teachers would not be happy'. The principal's chosen coping strategy was to back down and accept the seniority and power of the AM principal, claiming 'I just have to live with it, nothing will change'. This did not imply that she would never try anything new again, but that the situation would always exist, and that she was aware of, and concerned about, the possible consequences. As the principal stated, 'if I do not keep harmony (with the AM principal), I will be punished'.

The principal's management of the dilemma, namely, accepting the statues quo, produced an outcome which not only had the effect of confirming the power of the AM principal, but adversely affected the morale of the PM teachers. As she put it:

> Gradually I think that my teachers feel that they are inferior in a sense and that the AM teachers are their bosses. So we have to ask their permission for everything before we can do it. At least we have to consult the principal and if he likes it then we can do it, if not, then we have to stay as we are.

As was the case for dilemma 2, the roots of this dilemma reflected cultural, structural and professional dimensions. The initial coping strategy was to press on with the change, driven by a commitment to certain teaching and learning beliefs, and to maintain staff harmony and morale. The outcome of this strategy, while unintended, was an adverse effect on the otherwise harmonious relationship with the senior principal, which in turn, according to the PM principal, lead to informal but overt punishment – therefore escalating the dilemma. The new situation caused the principal to rethink her position, at least temporarily, and to fall back into line with the AM principal's beliefs. Her reaction was driven equally by fear of sanction and respect for seniority. This, in turn, harmed staff morale and harmony and created a loop back to the initial dilemma, leaving it unresolved and even more complicated.

A further element hidden beneath the more obvious dilemma situation was that the PM principal was attempting to introduce what were perceived as progressive, Western-based, ideas into a more traditional Chinese cultural setting. This phenomenon was reflected in a number of dilemmas (including dilemma 1) where tensions arose between new and traditional approaches to school operation and teaching and learning.

174

Discussion

In this section we address the nature, source, coping strategies and outcomes of principals' dilemmas in Hong Kong.

The sources, elements and outcomes of the dilemmas were multifaceted and were difficult to disentangle. Nevertheless, there appeared to be a number of commonalties which we now discuss. First, the dilemmas did not stand alone; that is, they were normally complex and related to multiple sources. Indeed, it seems that few dilemmas would have been perceived as such if not for these multiple sources which were difficult to distinguish. When seen in this light, dilemmas are a contributory factor to the confused and complex nature of school leadership (Patterson, 1992). A typical example of this complexity was provided by the combination of cultural values, structural arrangements and teaching and learning beliefs which underpinned most of the three case dilemmas cited in this chapter. In dilemma 2, for example, the governance structure of the school led to pressure being placed on the principal, thereby creating the initial tension. The tension, however, was also related to, and complicated further by, the principal's values of harmony and respect for hierarchy, values found to be very pre-eminent in Chinese culture. Cheng and Wong (1996), for example, suggest that in Chinese societies, group harmony is seen as more important than individualism (also see Hofstede, 1980). It is assumed that maintenance of group harmony is in the best interests of the individual. They continue, 'This is quite different from the Western notion of the individual–group relationship where the group cannot thrive unless and only after individuals in it thrive' (Cheng and Wong, 1996, p. 38). The need for harmony is intricately woven into most dilemma situations in Hong Kong, reflecting a primary desire across Chinese societies for harmonious relationships (for example see Bond, 1991a; Kirkbride, Tang and Westwood, 1991). According to Bond (1991a), the disturbance of interpersonal harmony through conflict can cause lasting animosity in Chinese cultures.

If most of the dilemma situations we uncovered were rooted in the need for harmony, they were equally involving of respect for hierarchy and seniority. According to Cheng (1995), groups and organizations in Chinese societies are more likely to be ordered around hierarchical sets of relationships and the rule of behaviour which govern them, than are their Western counterparts. Fei (cited in Cheng and Wong, 1996, p. 38) holds that Chinese societies are governed by a hierarchy 'where people are born into a certain position in the social hierarchy, and behave accordingly. This is in contrast with societies in the West where, in an *association configuration*, social structures and norms are formed acceding to *ad hoc* needs among individuals' (emphasis in original). The values of harmony and hierarchy are about maintaining relationships and power structures. In Chinese societies, and as reflected in the dilemmas we studied, relationships are paramount and play a predominant role in peoples' lives. Redding (1977), in fact, suggested that organizational behaviour in East Asian organizations was relationship-centred, whereas in the West it tends to be 'ego-centred' (for a discussion of the influence of culture on school adminis-tration, see Cheng and Wong, 1996).

The principal in dilemma 2 was torn between his desire for harmony with his superiors and with his staff, a perceived no-win situation. He was also con-cerned that the teacher was not upholding satisfactory standards of perfor-mance in the school, while at the back of his mind, he was mindful that the SMC had authority to terminate his own employment. As with other dilem-mas, it was difficult to disentangle the various sources. Some sources were more overt than others. In dilemma 2, the supervisor's direct request for the teacher's promotion and the candidate's inadequate performance were overt; yet other sources, such as fear of termination of his own contract if he upset the SMC and respect for harmony were more covert and personal to the prin-cipal. Other sources resulted from pressures external to the principal, but these often appeared to combine with the principal's own values system to produce the dilemmas. Values conflicts, either between the principal and others, or within the principal's own set of values, were pre-eminent in all dilemmas.

In summary, the dilemmas appeared to be rooted in a complex mix of factors, including school structure, personal considerations and beliefs about teaching and learning. In all cases they were underpinned by conflicts of values which, in the context of Hong Kong, naturally reflected a number of dominant Chinese values (see Bond 1996; Hofstede, 1991). Furthermore, some of the dilemmas were heightened by elements of a 'culture clash'. That is, they were caused or accentuated by the attempt to import Western beliefs and values about education into a traditional Chinese cultural setting. When these 'dif-ferent' values clashed, new dilemmas resulted or existing ones worsened. Evidence of such is seen in dilemmas 2 and 3.

Emergent patterns were discernible in how principals coped with their dilem-mas and the ways in which coping strategies related to the sources of a dilemma. The range of coping strategies reflected in the cases (including those not reported here) included – transferring a problem teacher to another school, attempting to compromise, withdrawing from direct involvement (or 'hoping it will sort itself out'), acquiescing with superiors' wishes, adopting a laissez-faire, fatalistic attitude of inaction, creative insubordination (Haynes and Licata, 1995), appealing to school tradition and mission, resorting to logical and emo-tive argument, and delaying decisions. Coping with dilemmas was never easy and involved unwinnable choices based on competing values. Although the dilemmas we examined were multifaceted in terms of their sources and elements, coping mechanisms were more strongly associated with the predominant cul-tural values. Even these cultural values appeared to be implicitly arranged in a hierarchy, with harmony, hierarchy, seniority, and age, rather than teaching and learning beliefs or personal reasons, predominant. For example, in the case of dilemma 1, the basic cultural value was the need for harmony with the more senior teacher; in dilemma 2 and eventually in dilemma 3, it was the need for respect for, and harmony with, the supervisor and the SMC. Coping strategies in these cases suggest the existence of a hierarchy of values in this Chinese society, with hierarchy, seniority and harmony predominant.

While harmony appeared paramount in consideration of all dilemmas, the problem for principals was to achieve a balance of harmony within themselves, within their school, between and with teachers, and with their superiors and the wider community. Achieving harmonious relationships between so many constituents was a problem of image-building. While the achievement of harmony was at the centre of most coping strategies, it demanded a delicate balancing act by principals, as exemplified in dilemma 3. Coping strategies invariably necessitated choices be made as to who were the most important constituents with whom to maintain harmony. In addressing this aspect, most principals adhered to the formal system of seniority in their communities. Further study of this aspect is important, as is indicated by Begley and Johansson's (1997) study attempting to identify the types and levels of values used by Canadian and Swedish principals for solving problems.

This study suggests that coping mechanisms assumed many different forms, frequently derived from cultural characteristics and usually resulted in the status quo being maintained. These conclusions raise a number of questions. First, if the pursuit of harmonious relationships is the predominant driver of coping strategies, even when dilemma sources are multifaceted, how does this influence the prime function of the school – teaching and learning? Secondly, if principals tend to cope with dilemmas through allegiance to the system of seniority, can they secure the commitment of teachers towards school improvement? In other words, what implications follow for teacher empowerment, involvement and dedication to the school? Thirdly, is it possible for principals to develop alternative coping strategies, when the powerful cognitive and practical influence of cultural values, such as harmony and seniority, are held in such high esteem? Fourthly, how does allegiance to such cultural factors affect principals' feelings about their jobs and work lives? Finally, are principals' dilemmas and coping strategies likely to change with the introduction of restructuring policies designed to reconfigure the roles, rules and relationships in Hong Kong's school system?

Principals' coping strategies resulted in a number of outcomes, none of which appeared entirely satisfactory or proved a resolution of the dilemma. The outcomes resulting from the cases can be grouped into four categories. The first category centred on the creation of a new dilemma (dilemmas 1 and 2); the second category resulted in a return to the existing dilemma situation (dilemma 3); the third category involved a magnification of the complexity of the existing dilemma (dilemma 2 and 3); and the fourth involved a lessening of the dilemma (dilemma 1). Outcomes, like dilemmas, were multidimensional, often involving new dilemmas, variations of existing dilemmas, or returns to the original dilemma. Dilemmas could proliferate and were rarely resolved, either in organizational or personal terms. In some dilemmas the outcome of one dilemma situation led to multiple organizational dilemmas, in others to a personal dilemma (unloading an incompetent teacher on another school) and in the case of dilemma 2, to both organizational and personal dilemmas. However, this distinction between organizational and personal dilemmas, while convenient from an analytical point of view, may be dubious, since we found that few principals differentiated in this way. This itself may be worthy of further study. Dilemmas could not be completely resolved and principals were invariably left feeling dissatisfied and frustrated. Moreover, their attention was continuously attracted by new developments in dilemma situations, the endurance and prolongation of which may also be worth further examination. The multidimensionality and growth of dilemmas support recent suggestions that many principals' lives are unpredictable and constantly beset by tension (Walker and Quong, 1998).

Conclusion

The study reported in this chapter set out to identify and examine dilemmas faced by school principals in Hong Kong. Research on principals' dilemmas has previously been confined to Western settings. Most dilemmas appear multifaceted in terms of their source and their constituent elements. In almost all cases, the sources of dilemmas comprise a combination of, structural, professional, cultural and relational drivers. Cultural values, mainly related to harmony, seniority and relationships, are prominent in interacting with other sources to cause or complicate dilemmas and to configure coping strategies. In no case could a dilemma situation be attributed to a single source. Dilemmas appear to grow from dilemmas, with one situation feeding another, thereby increasing its complexity and making it more difficult to manage. In some cases, the outcomes resulting from management strategies lead directly back to the original dilemma. In this study of Hong Kong principals, their management and coping strategies are most commonly related to specific deep-seated cultural values, in particular, the need to maintain harmony in relationships with others in the school community.

This raises the important issue of the emergence of various approaches and models of dilemma management and the training implications for school leaders. Dempsey and Berry (2003) see the way forward in terms of developing ethical perspectives, both formally (the training of principals in ethical theory) and informally (through peer-based support and collaborative networks), whereas Cardno (2001) advocates the development of school leaders' decision-making skills based on the principles of double-loop learning. Both report success in their respective management training programmes for principals, but such initiatives are in their infancy and are rooted in Western philosophies and their application in Western school cultures. We advocate more international studies of the type undertaken in Hong Kong in order to generate the possibility of cross-cultural comparisons between principals' perceptions of the major challenges confronting them.

Note

1   The authors wish to express their appreciation to the Chinese University of Hong Kong for supporting this research through a Direct Grant, and to the Hong Kong Institute of Educational Research (HKIER) for their support of the project. We also wish to acknowledge the support of the Research Grants Council of Hong Kong for its support through an Earmarked Grant (CUHK 4327/98H) and to thank the principals who so generously gave their time to be involved in the study.
2   The majority of primary and secondary schools in Hong Kong are public rather than private. However, only a small number are managed directly by the government (these are called 'Government schools'). Aided schools are run by voluntary agencies, such as religious and charitable organizations, called sponsoring bodies, under a code of aid ('Aided schools'). The code of aid sets out the procedures to be followed in return for public funds. The sponsoring body, which must be an incorporated non-profit-making organization, contributes the initial cost of furnishing and equipping the premises, nominates the first supervisor and has input into subsequent changes of management committee membership. Each aided school has its own management committee, which employs staff and is responsible to the Director of Education for the operation of the school and quality of education provided. One manager is registered as the supervisor, whose main role is to be the point of contact between the management committee and the Department of Education. Supervisors and the management committee have scope for exercising considerable influence in all facets of school operation should they so desire.

11
Leadership of Culturally Diverse Schools

This chapter explores the leadership of culturally diverse schools. It adopts a broad view, first explaining the growth of multi-ethnic schools, and the development of multicultural education. The perspective adopted is that successful leadership of culturally diverse schools is predicated on providing an authentic multicultural education and curriculum. Accordingly, the chapter explores various connotations of multicultural education. It then draws out some key implications for school leaders in building and sustaining schools of diversity that provide genuine multicultural curricula. The chapter concludes with some implications for the training and development of school leaders in culturally diverse settings.

Background to multicultural education

A major justification for adopting a cross-cultural approach to educational leadership is the creation of a broader international knowledge base and the fostering of comparisons between countries, systems and practices. Such comparisons not only broaden knowledge of other systems, but *ipso facto*, improve understanding of one's own system. In other words, a cross-cultural approach to educational leadership that adopts an international perspective may, in turn, contribute to an understanding of educational issues at home, particularly those of a cultural nature.

Cross-cultural analysis is most often associated with cultural differences between societies and how such differences impact on educational practices and processes, including leadership. These studies may focus on international comparisons, for example, between Japan, China, the UK and America, as outlined in earlier chapters. Increasingly, however, culturally sensitive educational issues occur within societies, especially those thought of as multicultural. Throughout history, there have been waves of human movement. Some have sought to conquer and colonize, others have wanted refuge and a new life. Few societies have remained homogeneous by escaping the diversification caused by the settlement of different peoples. For the past three centuries, people from the so-called Old World have moved to settle in the New World of America, Canada and Australasia. For longer than that, the Chinese have been colonizing other parts of Asia. More recently, the Old World, represented by Europe, has received large influxes of people from the less developed world. Possibly, the sources and patterns of migration have become more diverse in the second half of the twentieth century, partly due to the recent influx of refugees and asylum seekers from post-conflict societies around the world, creating what Johnson (2003) describes as the 'diversity imperative'. Over decades and centuries, these patterns of human movement have made an increasing number of societies truly multicultural. The implications of multiculturalism for schooling and for school leadership have assumed major importance.

It has been argued earlier that researchers in educational leadership have devoted surprisingly little attention to the influence of societal culture (Cheng, 1995; Dimmock and Walker, 1998a; 1998b; 2000b; Hallinger and Leithwood, 1996a). The field suffers a strong ethnocentricity and bias towards Anglo-American values, ideas and empiricism compared with, for example, the cognate fields of international business management and cross-cultural psychology. This neglect is even more glaring in the case of multiculturalism within societies and the implications for school leadership and organization. Put simply, the growing global trend towards multicultural societies – including America, Canada, the UK, much of Europe and Australia and an increasing number of cities around the world, including New York, London, Hong Kong and Singapore – creates changes in demographics and, in particular, in the racial and ethnic composition of populations. These changes, in turn, are reflected in more culturally diverse school communities and teaching staff. Children with widely different cultural backgrounds attend the same schools, sit in the same classes and experience the same curricula, posing challenges for teachers and school leaders alike. Yet, this important phenomenon has, to date, attracted minimal attention among scholars in the field of educational leadership.

Multicultural education is essentially concerned with accommodating diversity and ensuring that all students, regardless of race, gender and religion, have an equal opportunity to learn and to be successful in school. The term has come to assume a broad frame of reference owing to its diverse origins in different countries. In America, for example, it has its roots in the period of social protest precipitated by the Civil Rights movement of the late 1960s and 1970s. Ethnic groups, first African Americans and later Hispanics and Native Americans, began to make a number of demands. These included a curriculum that was more relevant, the hiring of more teachers and administrators from their ethnic backgrounds, and community control of neighbourhood schools (Banks and Banks, 1993).

Early responses to these demands tended to be superficial, selective and piecemeal, focusing mainly on the celebration of ethnic holidays and heroes, and addressed to members of the biggest minority group. However, they gave rise to the development of programmes such as desegregation, bilingual education, special needs education and the use of mainstreaming that were designed to eliminate discrimination (Sleeter and Grant, 1987). Later, the Women's Rights

Movement identified the absence of women as school administrators and the lack of visibility of women's issues in textbooks and curricula, thereby raising issues of inequality and imbalance similar to those highlighted by ethnic groups (Banks and Banks, 1993).

Multicultural education in the USA thus emerged from the mix of programmes and practices that educational institutions implemented in response to the needs and demands of historically victimized groups. What began as a stop-gap plan linked to concerns about racism, expanded to become a serious reform movement that also addressed discrimination according to sex, class, religion and disability.

This broad frame of reference has generated a great variety of ways in which educators now use the term 'multicultural education' and implement its strategies. In one school district in America, multicultural education may describe a curriculum that accommodates the needs and experiences of a particular minority group, while in another, it may describe a programme related to issues of bilingual education or gender. Speaking from a Dutch perspective, Leeman (2003) advocates the use of the closely related term 'intercultural education', because it implies a 'reciprocal influence' and a need to prepare all students, not just those from minority backgrounds, for living in an ethnically and culturally diverse society.

The goals of, and approaches to, multicultural education

Despite these variations, practitioners generally agree that the major goals of multicultural education should include the following (Banks and Banks, 1993, pp. 46–48):

- development of sensitivity, understanding and tolerance towards diversity;
- reduction in forms of prejudice and discrimination that members of some groups experience due to particular racial, cultural, social or physical characteristics; and
- assistance to students in acquiring the knowledge, skills and attitudes needed to function successfully both within their own ethnic or social group and in the mainstream culture.

In the same vein, Davidman and Davidman (1994, cited in Cunningham and Cordeiro, 2000, p. 104) suggest a number of goals for multicultural education among which are:

- educational equity, empowerment, cultural pluralism;
- intercultural/interethnic/intergroup understanding and harmony;
- knowledge of various cultural and ethnic groups; and
- the development of an inquisitive multicultural perspective across all levels of the school community.

Empowerment acknowledges the place of parents as teachers of culture and, as such, promotes their active involvement in schools. Cultural pluralism promotes cultural diversity as a key component of society and calls for teachers to help students respect diversity in school and beyond.

After an extensive review of the multicultural literature, Sleeter and Grant (1987; 1993) identify five main approaches that together form a taxonomy for defining the term multicultural education and examining its use. The five approaches are:

- teaching the culturally different;
- human relations;
- single-studies;
- multicultural education;
- critical multiculturalism.

These approaches form a continuum which traces the development of multicultural education in the USA from the relatively simple, conservative and practical approaches to reform, epitomized by the 'teaching the culturally different' approach, to the more complex, radical and transformative approaches represented by critical multiculturalism, as outlined by McLaren (1994).

This continuum is instructive and provides a helpful framework for review. The following section is based on the major goals and strategies of each approach and its limitations as a means of elucidating the ramifications for school leadership.

The first approach, teaching the culturally different, attempts to assimilate minority students into the mainstream culture by building bridges within the existing school programme. It aims to help the minority acquire the skills, language and knowledge expected of the majority. While the use of transitional bridges to build on, rather than replace, the student's cultural capital is a positive step toward improving the educational opportunities for minorities, the approach is limited in several ways. First, it places greater emphasis on modifying institutional practices (for example, instruction) to make them more compatible with students' preferred methods of learning than on changing curricula or reforming structural characteristics that perpetuate inequality. Secondly, by placing the burden on minorities to change in order to become competitive with the majority, the inequality may even be reinforced. There is no suggestion that the majority re-examine its prejudices and extend or modify its knowledge and values.

The human relations approach focuses on the feelings and attitudes students have about themselves and each other, and aims to foster tolerance and appreciation of diversity. While this approach encourages group identity and pride for minority students and works at reducing stereotypes and biases, it too has limitations. The positive effect of developing such interrelationships tends to be diminished by the fact that they are being promoted within the existing mainstream social system with little attempt to address issues of inequality and social injustice.

The single-group studies approach involves the in-depth study of the experiences, contributions and concerns of a particular ethnic, gender or social class group. Unlike the previous two approaches, it encourages critical analysis of issues like racism and oppression and provides alternatives to a curriculum perspective that is reflective of the majority. However, by focusing on a single group, this approach may tend to become biased and overlook multiple forms of diversity.

The multicultural approach promotes cultural pluralism, social justice and equality by reforming the total school environment to reflect the diversity of all students regardless of whether they attend an inner city multiracial school or a suburban single race school. Choice of curriculum content and materials, student grouping, native language usage, patterns of classroom organization, and teacher interactions and relationships with students and their communities, are important features (Nieto, 1992). There are few objections to this approach. The main limitation is the difficulty in implementing such a broad-based reform on many fronts and developing staff accordingly.

The fifth approach, critical multiculturalism, is both a culmination of the other four approaches and the 'ideal' end point of a continuum that assumes an increasingly complex, political and visionary set of goals. Critical multiculturalism shares with the 'teaching the culturally different' approach the belief that teaching should build on the cultural-linguistic capital that students bring with them to school and should develop mastery of basic skills. It shares with the human relations approach, the concern for developing positive self-concepts and co-operative relationships among diverse groups of students. It shares with the single studies group approach the emphasis on social justice issues and representation of the interests of oppressed groups. And, finally, the approach embraces the practices of the multicultural education approach by sharing its fundamental goal that schools and classrooms should accommodate, reflect and celebrate diversity (Sleeter and Grant, 1993).

Critical multiculturalism extends the goals of the multicultural education approach by teaching students to become analytical, critical thinkers capable of examining forms of oppression based on race, gender, class or disability. Advocates of this approach see schools as places that reproduce the inequalities of the dominant culture and, as such, have the potential to become training grounds for preparing a socially, politically aware and active citizenry. This preparation involves practices that enable students to:

- understand and actively practise the principles of democracy;
- learn how to critically examine their own life circumstances in order to confront and explore myths and stereotypes about controversial politically sensitive issues of race;

- develop social skills in order to make informed decisions; and
- become involved in the process of coalescing individuals across the lines of race and class to fight against oppression (Nieto, 1992; Sleeter and Grant, 1993).

In successfully accomplishing these emancipatory goals of student empowerment and social transformation, McLaren (1994) suggests that teachers must create and deliver a critical pedagogy that students can use both at school and in the home. Such a pedagogy not only bridges both mainstream and minority cultures, but also challenges and critiques the racist principles, which, according to McLaren (1994), are embedded in American society. Central to this underlying philosophy of critical pedagogy is the dialectical concept of similarity with difference. Kanpol and McLaren (1995) stress the need for schools to adopt the notion of a border pedagogy based on Giroux's model which allows teachers and students to explore, understand and accept differences while concurrently unifying similarities between race, class and gender.

The limitations of critical multiculturalism lie in the fact that much of the literature recommending the approach provides little mention of instructional models or material on how to articulate its goals and practices. Without such information, the approach remains idealistic but impractical. A further limitation may be the highly political nature of its philosophy and its call for a radical transformation of education that schools, principals, teachers and parents, no less the state, may be neither ready nor willing to entertain.

In addressing multiculturalism, two of the many important processes that schools need to engage are curriculum redesign and staff development. It is instructive to explore these further since they have repercussions for school leadership. Both processes are important in Sleeter and Grant's taxonomy (1987; 1993). They also figure prominently in another taxonomy, namely, that of Banks (1994). Curriculum redesign offers an accessible approach for practitioners to use to begin a multicultural programme. In this regard, Banks (1994) identifies four main approaches to multicultural curriculum reform and arranges each in a hierarchy, like Sleeter and Grant, from the basic levels of contribution and addition to the more challenging levels of transformation and social action. The four approaches – arranged in hierarchy – are as follows:

- Level 1, the contributions approach – focuses on heroes, holidays and discrete cultural elements.
- Level 2, the additive approach – content, concepts, themes, and perspectives are added to the curriculum without changing its structure.
- Level 3, the transformation approach – the structure of the curriculum is changed to enable students to view concepts, issues and themes from the perspective of diverse ethnic and cultural groups.
- Level 4, the social action approach – students make decisions on important social issues and take actions to help solve them.

185

While Banks suggests that teachers begin at the lower levels and gradually move towards the higher levels, evidence shows that most practitioners tend to stay at the contribution and additive levels, which demand less commitment of time, training and resources. Thus what passes for multicultural education in many classrooms becomes the non-rigorous equivalent of 'food, fiestas, and festivals' (Ladson-Billings, 1995, p. 128). Authentic curriculum integration and redesign demand greater commitment.

With the contributions approach, for example, content is limited mainly to special days, weeks or months related to ethnic events and celebrations. During these celebrations teachers involve students in isolated lessons with little preparation or follow-up. This approach often results in trivialization of ethnic culture, patronizing exposure to strange customs and reinforcement of stereotypes (Banks, 1994).

Similarly, the additive approach involves the addition of content to the curriculum via a book, unit or course without changing its goals or structure. According to Banks (1994), this adding on of bits and pieces of ethnic content not only reinforces the idea that minority groups are marginalized, but also tends to evade significant issues such as racism, poverty and oppression.

In both approaches – the contributions and additive – multicultural education does not become an integral part of the core curriculum but, rather, as Nieto (1992) describes, an add-on of 'exotic knowledge' or a 'frill' that often cannot be afforded due to time constraints and pressures to fulfil curriculum imperatives.

School leadership and multicultural education

The taxonomies outlined above raise many issues, some of which are central to school leadership and management. Among these are the following:

- To what extent should schools be proactive in their attempt to change, as opposed to simply reflect, societal values in respect to multiculturalism?
- Which of the approaches is realistic and appropriate for a particular school or group of schools to adopt?
- What are the respective roles of school leaders, teachers, parents and curriculum developers in adopting and implementing the particular approach adopted?

In response to the first and second questions, it is necessary to consider the political and societal context of the school. For example, in societies where the government conducts a proactive campaign against oppression and racism, and where there is explicit recognition of an ethnic minority or cultural problem, a school may feel it appropriate to adopt a stronger, more critical response to multicultural education. Such a response may correspond to Banks's (1994) Level 4 social action approach or Sleeter and Grant's (1987; 1993) Level 5 critical multiculturalism. Schools in those American states, for example, where the governments actively campaign to confront and eradicate racist inequality, particularly concerning Blacks and Hispanics, would fall into this group.

In other societies, governments may take the view, rightly or wrongly, that no serious racial oppression or inequality exists and thus the aim of government policy is to preserve the peaceful and harmonious coexistence and integration among the races. Schools are deemed to play a role towards this end. These governments may consider a more benign non-confrontational and less aggressive policy towards racial equality/inequality appropriate. In such cases, the appropriate response from schools may be indicated by, say, Banks's Level 3 transformative approach or Sleeter and Grant's Level 4 multicultural approach. Schools in Singapore exemplify this situation. For the most part, peaceful coexistence between Chinese, Malays and Indians in Singapore is apparent, such that any attempt by schools to change the status quo through a more radical multicultural agenda would almost certainly be interpreted unfavourably by the government.

The extent to which a school's policy on multiculturalism is aligned with government policy on racial and ethnic issues is, of course, variable, being dependent on the political persuasion and regime in power. In societies with less liberal governments, it is difficult for schools to depart from close alignment with government policy. In more liberal regimes, however, schools may feel they have greater discretion for social engineering by either adopting a more socially active multicultural approach than is reflected in government policy, or conversely, by adopting a more conservative approach than the government. This implies that in contemporary multicultural society, there is a need for schools to define and articulate their multicultural policy in the context of broader societal and governmental policy. Principals – as leaders of their school communities – have a key role to play in this respect.

This is not to argue that multiculturalism becomes the only or even the main preoccupation of school leaders. Rather, it is to recognize that it deserves a key place in the competencies and role expectations expected of contemporary school leaders. It is when attention turns to school adoption and implementation of approaches – as foreshadowed in the third of the questions posed above – that issues concerning leadership are particularly highlighted. This is because adoption and implementation connect leadership of multicultural schools with school mission and aims, curriculum reform, teaching and learning, the organization and grouping of students, teacher professional development, resource allocation, school culture, decision-making, counselling and support, and the hiring and evaluation of teachers. The leadership implications of each of these for multicultural education are discussed below, developing the six-point framework of key qualities for school leaders initially outlined in Chapter 6.

1 Leadership of multicultural school communities

If multiculturalism is to influence the curriculum, teaching and learning in a school, then it is important that principals as leaders first engage their communities in a process that represents the school standpoint on multiculturalism. Parents, teachers and other members of the school community, after reflecting on the relevance and significance of multiculturalism for the school, might choose to formalize their position in terms of a general statement incorporated in the mission and aims of the school. In executing the role responsibilities in this way, a key quality or competency of the school leader is the capacity to mould a multicultural community together as a harmonious group on the one hand, and yet to recognize, celebrate and respect cultural diversity and richness on the other.

2 Leadership of the educational programme and multiculturalism

It has already been remarked (see Chapter 6) that if a school is serious about addressing multiculturalism, then curriculum redesign is fundamental. As pointed out by Banks (1994) and Sleeter and Grant (1987; 1993), adding increments to the mainstream curriculum, such as special days to celebrate ethnic food or festivals, is likely to offer no more than an interesting distraction from the normal curriculum. If, however, the aim is to go beyond tolerance and towards understanding of, and respect for, other races and cultures, then themes and ideas of a multicultural nature need to be embedded in subjects across the whole curriculum, including integrated cross-curricular designs. Banks (1993) refers to 'content integration' as the process whereby examples, data and information are drawn from a variety of cultures to illustrate the core concepts, principles and generalizations in subject areas.

A framework for redesigning the curriculum might be provided by incorporating specific learning outcomes for multiculturalism into relevant subject areas. Evaluation and assessment would also need to reflect multicultural themes, including the diversity of learning styles and objectives among culturally diverse student groups. In this regard, school leaders and heads of department can ensure that teachers incorporate such approaches into their syllabuses, lessons and assessments. School leaders require the values, knowledge, skills and attributes to oversee the curriculum design and development process to ensure that it reflects the school's mission with respect to multiculturalism.

Educational leadership is not just concerned, however, with curriculum structure and content. Attention is also given to instructional methods and learning processes. School leaders can promote particular instructional strategies that favour and support multiculturalism. Here, Banks (1993, p. 17) refers to 'knowledge construction' as the process whereby teachers can help students understand how knowledge is created and interpreted through such factors as race, ethnicity, gender and social class. They can also engage in 'prejudice reduction', that is, developing strategies to help students acquire positive cross-cultural and racial attitudes.

Teachers can promote multiculturalism through their choice of particular teaching/learning methods used in classrooms. As Feinberg (1998) astutely reminds us:

> Learning-through-culture is to be distinguished from simply learning about cultures other than one's own. It is a concept that recognizes that there are distinctive ways in which cultures constitute both the process and the product of thinking and that these in turn become distinctive elements of learning. It is important not to confuse the fact that there may be culturally different ways of learning and culturally different things to learn. (p. 146)

In order to promote teaching that is culture-sensitive, principals of multicultural schools may encourage student-centred strategies, such as peer learning and collaborative approaches that require students to work together. Peer tutoring, co-operative learning and project work provide opportunity for students of different cultures to learn together and from each other. In addition, where such collaboration is centred on curriculum problems, as in the case of problem-based learning (PBL), students of different ethnicities are united in pursuit of a common goal that is problem resolution. Other appropriate teaching methods include the use of role play and drama as ways to connect with the emotions, feelings and attitudes of students with respect to multicultural issues. In relation to the whole issue of instruction and learning, Banks (1993, p. 17) refers to 'equity pedagogy', meaning the use of instructional techniques that promote cooperation and include the learning styles of diverse groups.

An example of culture-sensitive teaching strategies, or what Banks refers to as 'equity pedagogy', is provided by Rothstein-Fisch, Greenfield and Trumbull (1999). These authors describe the problems faced by many teachers in the USA who have Latino children from Central and South America in their classes. These immigrant children bring collectivist values with them to school, making it invaluable for their teachers to understand the ramifications of collectivism in an otherwise individualist society. Collectivism emphasizes the interdependence of family members, children are taught above all, to be helpful to others and to contribute to the success and welfare of the group to which they belong – beginning with the family. Even the knowledge of the physical world is placed within a social context. In reality, American schools tend to foster individualism, viewing the child as an individual who needs to develop independence and value individual achievement. While collectivism emphasizes the social context of learning and knowledge, individualism emphasizes information disengaged from its social context (Hofstede, 1991). As Rothstein-Fisch, Greenfield and Trumbull (1999) comment, 'When collectivistic students encounter individualistic schools, conflicts that are based on hidden values and assumptions can occur' (p. 64). They go on to illustrate how children from collectivist cultures can misinterpret the teacher's expectations when asked questions. They also show how teachers can incorporate more collectivist values by allowing children to do tasks in pairs and groups, and by allowing the children to introduce elements of their social life and background into science lessons. They conclude,

> When teachers understand and respect the collectivist values of immigrant Latino children, the opportunities for culturally informed learning become limitless. Our examples in classroom management, reading, math, and science demonstrate that educators can design instruction responsive to diverse groups that does not undermine home-based cultural values. (Rothstein-Fisch, Greenfield and Trumbull, 1999, p. 66)

As important, however, is that teachers come to realise that their own practices are cultural in origin rather than the 'only right way to do things'.

School leaders need to encourage teachers to explore these cultural differences as opportunities to expand their repertoire of teaching techniques and classroom management. As Cunningham and Cordeiro (2000) note: 'Teachers who accept cultural pluralism constantly ask themselves how to help students respect and appreciate cultural diversity in the classroom, school and society' (p. 105).

3 School organization and structure reflects multiculturalism

School leaders can enhance multiculturalism through the formal system of student grouping adopted in the school. This means that streaming and setting by ability gives way to broader social issues concerned with mixing ethnic and multicultural groups in the same classes. Within classes, teachers can exercise the same prerogative by mixing different ethnic and cultural groups to form collaborative groups. Racial and ethnic mixing can also be encouraged through extra-curricular activities, involving sports teams, clubs and societies which themselves respect the values and traditions of diverse cultures.

4 Human resource management and development and multiculturalism

School leaders have strong capacity to influence the approach to multiculturalism in their schools through appropriate personnel and human resource management. First, the policy and practice used in the selection and appointment of staff can ensure that teachers are hired whose career record reflects a disposition towards, and a commitment to, multicultural schooling. Secondly, given the particular ethnic and cultural student intake to the school, it is prudent to have a teacher and administrator profile that at least in part reflects this cultural mix. If such a staff mix is not possible, parents and community members can be more heavily involved in curriculum development, policy decisions and the development of suitable pedagogical techniques and methods. Even if schools can achieve a more representative teacher and administrator cultural mix, it is no guarantee that the ideas and values of the relevant cultural constituencies will be represented. There needs to be a heightened awareness on the part of school leaders that teachers from various ethnic or cultural groups may bring with them very different ways of interacting and communicating. For example, teachers socialized in certain cultures may be unwilling to openly comment on or criticize the actions or decisions of others, particularly those of the principal and others in positions of authority. Hiring 'representatives' of various cultures therefore is no guarantee that diverse values and ideas will be expressed and thus explicitly represented. Inescapably, a sensitivity to, and knowledge of, working and communicating with teachers, fellow administrators, parents and community members from diverse cultures becomes a key facet of school leadership.

Thirdly, enthusiastic and informed leadership is needed to motivate teachers. This is particularly important in schools that have taken decisions to go beyond the basic levels of curriculum provision as indicated in the taxonomies of Banks (1994) and Sleeter and Grant (1987; 1993). Comprehensive curriculum redesign entails the commitment of considerable time and resources on the part of leaders and teachers. Again, for schools with a culturally diverse group of staff, it is important for leaders to recognize that motivation can take very different forms. Although it is true that each individual may be enthused or motivated in different ways, various cultural groups can perceive motivation differently.

Fourthly, a crucial part of the additional resource commitment concerns professional development. Teachers will require professional development in understanding different cultures and their values, in designing curricula reflective of multicultural schooling, in adopting a range of new teaching and learning techniques and in creating new forms of assessment, that are all culture sensitive. The North Central Regional Educational Laboratory (1995) suggests a set of six principles which may guide professional development in schools:

1 School policies and practices demonstrate respect for and acceptance of culturally and linguistically diverse students.
2 Curriculum, instruction, and assessment build on students' culture, language, and prior experiences.
3 Educators set high expectations for all students and provide opportunities to reach them.
4 Students gain knowledge about a variety of cultures and languages.
5 Schools construct culturally responsive and high-achieving learning environments through active partnerships with parents, families, and community leaders.
6 Professional development helps educators examine their own beliefs and fosters understanding of culturally and linguistically diverse groups.

Finally, leaders can consolidate and connect curricular and pedagogical practice supportive of multiculturalism through a staff appraisal and evaluation system that reflects the knowledge, skills and attributes necessary for the successful implementation of school policy on multicultural schooling. Where possible, reward systems for teachers involving their promotion and additional responsibility can be grounded in their successful practice and promotion of school policies with respect to multicultural education.

5 Culture-building, resource allocation and multiculturalism

Changing the school culture to reflect the values of multiculturalism is a key responsibility of leadership. Culture is partly built and influenced through leaders modelling and demonstrating their own values in interacting with others, making appropriate public pronouncements, establishing supportive reward and discipline systems, and treating and valuing students from all races and ethnicities. Banks (1993, p. 17) refers to 'an empowering school culture', whereby a learning environment is created in which students from diverse racial, ethnic and social groups believe that they are heard and are valued, and experience respect, belonging and encouragement.

Resource allocation can also provide an indicator of the relative importance given to multiculturalism within a school. Both the level of resources devoted to multicultural activities and the distribution of them in support of a multicultural curriculum, provide a barometer of the school's seriousness in this regard.

6 School governance, decision-making and multiculturalism

Finally, how schools organize themselves to promote multiculturalism, and respond to, and prevent multicultural problems is a key concern of school leaders. Problems can be foreseen and alleviated through the representation of different ethnic and cultural groups on school governance and decision-making bodies. Democratic decision-making processes that are inclusive of all members of the school community are important. Support and counselling systems within the school are also helpful in this regard. It has already been remarked that multiculturalism is enhanced where the ethnic and racial mix of teaching staff reflects that of the student intake.

School governance issues also stretch beyond traditional school boundaries into the wider community and toward greater inter-agency collaboration. Although such inter-agency links have traditionally been weak (Capper, 1996), such collaboration provides a powerful means of understanding, interacting and empowering different cultural groups. Capper suggests that community-based inter-agency collaboration can promote the involvement of traditionally disempowered groups across the gamut of human welfare service provision. Connections deliberately and consciously forged between the school, systems, agencies and informal community service organizations that have long been seen as peripheral to schools can be harnessed to promote meaningful multiculturalism in schools.

The implications for school leadership training and development

Evidence pointing to the vital importance of a multicultural perspective in schools is unequivocal. However, building cross-cultural leadership is also beset by problems (Shields , Laroque and Oberg, 2002). Leaders' perspectives are often too narrow, failing to reject 'deficit thinking' about ethnic minority students and parents in favour of more positive 'capacity-building' strategies. Also 'with the best intentions [they frequently] make unwarranted assumptions' (p. 130); for example, that surface harmony indicates an absence of underlying conflict, when it may well be present but not immediately evident because of a reluctance or fear on the part of ethnic minorities to express an opinion that may result in more social discord. Moreover, as stated earlier, many multicultural initiatives are little more than cosmetic add-ons, rather than being 'intrinsic to learning to live in a civil society' (p. 130). It therefore follows that there is a need for effective training and continued professional development in multicultural education for all school staff – and particularly for school leaders as major catalysts of school improvement.

A review of the literature reveals surprisingly little in the way of training and support for leading and managing multicultural schools. In reviews of the various continued professional development programmes for serving headteachers in the UK (e.g. Newton, 2001, on HEADLAMP; Collarbone, 2001, on LPSH), attention is drawn to the generic, cross-phase nature of the training with insufficient regard to specific school context, as well as the unquestioned assumptions of the leadership models and theories which underpin such programmes. As we noted in Chapter 4, there is a strong case for arguing that leadership theory for diversity may require new paradigms and ways of thinking. It is also worth noting that of the 24 leadership development programmes currently provided by the NCSL, none specifically addresses leadership for multicultural education.

The situation in the USA is similar. In a trenchant critique of the US licence schemes for school principals, Hess (2003) draws attention to the weakness of overly generic programmes, when it should be a question of having the right leader for the right situation, rather than a particular type of leader for all situations. He states: 'There is legitimate concern that leaders be sensitive to the cultural needs of the organizations they lead. However, administrative preparation today devotes little or no attention to such considerations' (p. 9). As a consequence, there are major barriers to diversity, partly due to a lack of recruitment of school leaders from diverse ethnic and cultural backgrounds, and partly due to a lack of adequate support and professional development in multicultural leadership for serving principals.

The gap in training provision in the USA is noted by Henze et al. (2002, p. 4), and as a result the four-year Leadership for Diversity Project was launched for school principals in 1995. Research has since been undertaken in 21 case study schools across the USA with ethnically diverse student populations. What has emerged from these studies is a leadership framework for developing positive interethnic relations. Drawing on project research data, Norte (1999) identifies five distinct categories of intervention used by effective principals in multicultural schools:

- *Content*: vision, mission statements aimed at promoting social justice and cross-cultural understanding, and how these are manifested in the school curriculum.
- *Process*: how people put the content into practice through collaborative working and participation between teachers, parents, students and the wider community.
- *Structure*: the configurations of time, space and people to facilitate the processes, for example by way of organized meetings and the creation of cross-cultural groups.
- *Staffing*: generating understanding and cultivating positive staff attitudes through recruitment strategies and staff development programmes.
- *Infrastructure*: the physical setting, ensuring accessibility and the creation of a safe, comfortable environment.

Also from a US perspective, Johnson (2003) draws up a similar leadership framework for building a whole-school approach to diversity, based on strategies in each of the following five key areas: school management; teacher in-service training and development; curriculum and instruction; building partnerships with parents; and pastoral care and student development.

There have also been recent developments in Europe, including the Intercultural Education Project initiated by the Dutch government in 1994 (Leeman, 2003). Running for a period of four years, this project drew attention to *direct* leadership strategies that can be taken to manage diversity, including a revision of the curriculum and teaching strategies to reflect the needs of a multicultural student population. However, attention was also drawn to equally important *indirect* approaches designed to promote a positive school climate, including the creation of a safe and democratic school environment, opportunities for inter-ethnic contact and co-operative learning groups, and a clear repudiation of bullying or any form of discrimination.

Such insights, combined with the six facets of strategic leadership for multi-ethnicity discussed earlier in Chapter 6, provide the basis for creating a training and professional development framework for leaders of multicultural schools. They have a high degree of legitimacy not only because they are rooted in research evidence but also because they draw on the insights of experienced and highly successful school leader practitioners. Unlike so many discredited prescriptive recipe book solutions to complex problems, they also emphasize the importance of school context and the need for professional dialogue, networking and support systems. However, as Leeman (2003) points out, the challenges ahead are considerable. In the Netherlands, with the end of the Intercultural Education Project in 1998, the impetus must now be sustained within the devolved framework of school-based management, and its future is far from certain for two reasons: from the perspective of popular support, multiculturalism is still seen as a low priority; and from an internal school perspective, moral tasks (including intercultural education) are seen as less pressing and urgent than satisfying school improvement targets (Leeman, 2003, p. 36).

Conclusion

This chapter has highlighted the fact that school communities in many countries and states have become, and are becoming, more multi-ethnic and diverse. Migration is not new, but over the last half century its magnitude has increased and it has taken on a more complex form than hitherto. Migration to parts of Europe, North America and Australasia has continued unabated, driven by persecution, wars, poverty, disparities in economic wealth, the global economy, multinational corporations, education, rising personal wealth, jet travel and even the Internet, transforming these peoples into truly multicultural societies. The increasing phenomenon of mixed marriage and the offspring that result, is a further consideration in the creation of multicultural societies. In some countries, the result of racial and ethnic diversity has been racism and racial oppression, while in others, it has been relatively peaceful coexistence, with occasional underlying tension.

Schools as micro-social systems tend to exhibit the tensions prevalent in wider society. Education is seen by individuals and ethnic groups as a vehicle for social and educational opportunity and advancement. It is also viewed as a means by which social relations between disparate groups, and society more generally, can be engineered and transformed. Schools, together with other organizations, carry these responsibilities. Of central importance is the attainment of a critical balance between, on the one hand, forces recognizing and respecting cultural divergence, and, on the other, those aiming for cultural harmony and convergence that is part of a united society. This chapter has addressed the central issue of the different meanings that multiculturalism has for schools and schooling, how schools mediate and respond to these meanings, and in particular, the role and responsibilities of school leaders in that process.

Attention has also focused on the fact that the important issue of school leadership training and development for a multicultural society has only recently begun to attract attention. Effective training and support for the leaders of multi-ethnic schools is clearly an important priority, requiring the provision of more differentiated programmes which are relevant to specific contexts and individual needs and priorities. Equally important is the creation of collaborative support networks to break down a sense of isolation, to facilitate the sharing of problems and ideas, and to disseminate good practice.

12
Developing Educational Leadership in Culturally Diverse Contexts

In a globalizing and internationalizing world, it is not only business and industry that are changing. Education, too, is caught up in a new world order. Growing numbers of school and university students are studying overseas. Universities are seeking international collaboration. International education agencies and consultants abound. Increasingly, the global transmission of policies and practices ignores national and cultural boundaries. The business of education is fast becoming just that – a business – operating on a globalized and internationalized scale. Internationalized universities and schools are likely to be a significant development – in one form or another – in the twenty-first century.

While the terms 'globalization' and 'internationalization' are closely related (indeed, they could be seen as synonymous), some may recognize subtle distinctions between them. 'Globalization' generally refers to the spread of ideas, policies and practices across national boundaries, while 'internationalization' relates to the adoption of outward-looking perspectives in stark contrast to ethnocentrism.

On the other hand, a scrutiny of the most recent journals in educational administration, management and leadership reveals an alarming ethnocentricity (Dimmock and Walker, 1998a; 1998b). Especially is this the case in the UK and the USA, where researchers seem preoccupied with homespun issues. In the former, the research agenda seems largely dictated by government policy, with academics responding, reacting and critically evaluating the implications of such policy. In the latter, the country's nature, size, and complexity helps explain a certain parochialism. In both countries, the pace of educational innovation in the last decade has been nothing short of breathtaking, a phenomenon which has probably contributed to their ethnocentrism.

Meanwhile, the spread of policies and practices across national boundaries and cultures has continued with gathering pace. Efforts to restructure schools by emphasizing school-based management, devolution and increased accountability to the central bureaucracy, have become the keystones of reform in many countries. Likewise, curriculum trends in different continents have targeted outcomes-based education and social-constructivist approaches to teaching and learning. These similarities are neither fortuitous nor coincidental. They are the result of many complex forces shaping the globalized world: they include the electronic and print media, jet transport, international conferences, international agencies, multinational corporations and overseas education.

When measured against these contextual developments, the study of educational leadership and management has generally failed to keep pace theoretically, conceptually and empirically with practice. Even studies completed by agencies such as the Organization for Economic Co-operation and Development (OECD) and the United Nations Educational, Scientific, and Cultural Organization (UNESCO) generally fail to provide in-depth international comparisons, preferring instead separate country studies as their more usual format.

The argument is simply that as a field of study, educational management and leadership needs to reflect the globalizing and internationalizing of policy and practice. To do that, we need a comparative branch to the field that is rigorous and reflects cross-cultural dimensions (Dimmock, 2000a). The reasons and benefits are manifold. First, the transfer of policy across boundaries that continues to ignore societal culture is likely to heap up many future problems. Second, while scholars and practitioners remain largely ignorant about societal, economic, political, demographic and cultural differences between systems, they are likely to draw fallacious conclusions regarding the appropriateness of importing and transferring policy and practice. Third, by understanding the contexts and education systems of other countries, we may come to a better understanding of our own.

Accordingly, it seems appropriate in concluding this book to outline a number of key propositions that summarize our conclusions about the state of the art in respect of a cross-cultural, international perspective of educational leadership and management. These propositions, *inter alia*, might assist in the shaping of relevant and future research agendas.

Key propositions underpinning a future research agenda

Five propositions, which echo the key themes discussed throughout this book, emerge to help map future directions in cross-cultural research into educational leadership and management.

Proposition 1: In order to make valid and informed judgements about the effectiveness and performance of other education systems and about the transfer of ideas, policies and practices across national and cultural boundaries, there is a need to develop a systematic, robust comparative branch of educational leadership and management

A relatively new phenomenon emerged in the 1990s, namely, the reciprocal interest of Anglo-American and Confucian societies of East and South-East

Asia in each others' school systems. Asian educators and politicians, aware of the need for their economies to compete in the global marketplace, realized that their school curricula needed to emulate the West in its emphasis on creativity, technology and problem-solving. For their part, Western nations, intrigued by the apparently superior performance of students from Confucian-heritage societies on international tests, wondered whether they could learn from the East. Moreover, education policy as well as practice in both the curriculum and administration fields increasingly covers the globe as policy-makers and practitioners improve their communication and global knowledge. Whether in Beijing, Bradford or Baltimore, the pattern of responsibility and power for running schools is being reconfigured, often in similar directions. In addition, these developments have brought a new 'internationalism', a genuine willingness on the part of some scholars, policy-makers and practitioners to learn from the experiences of others, if for no other reason than they may come to understand their own situation better.

We could perhaps be optimistic, given the above scenario. Such euphoria, however, would be misplaced. When comparisons between systems are made on superficial grounds with minimal understanding of the deep historical and cultural roots underpinning them, they are misleading and often dangerous. Both the formulation of policies and practices and their outcomes and consequences can only truly be understood when viewed in relation to culture and context.

In our efforts to contextualize and to arrive at more valid and sophisticated judgements about the transferability of policy and practice, we need robust comparative models and empirical data. To date, educational leadership and management as a field of study has failed to develop such models as well as an empirical base in the form of a comparative and international dimension in line with emerging practice.

Proposition 2: The concept of 'culture' demands clarification, specification and measurement

In championing the case for 'culture' as a root concept in a comparative approach to educational leadership and management, there is a need to be mindful and cautious about its problematic nature. As Morris and Lo (2000) point out, culture is a 'ubiquitous, overused and overdefined' concept. In addition, contemporary societies are often fragmented and pluralistic, characterized by subcultural and minority groups. As societies become increasingly multicultural, their traditional homogeneity may be threatened. There are dangers, too, in portraying complex societal differences in terms of oversimplified dichotomies, such as Western/Asian. As much variation occurs within Western and Asian societies as between them. These are all formidable challenges to a cross-cultural approach.

It is not the purpose here to address each of the above problems. Suffice to say that greater conceptual clarity is needed in respect of 'culture', even though it may be difficult and unrealistic to expect universal agreement on what precisely is meant by the term. Most scholars, for example, agree on values, norms and beliefs lying at the heart of the concept, and that these are expressed in a myriad of ways through thoughts and behaviours. Some, however, prefer to reserve the term just for those values and beliefs that are enduring and long established, while others are prepared to include modern or recent values, and to distinguish them from the traditional. There are also difficulties in distinguishing cultural from political values. Decentralization and devolution, for example, can be seen as politico-managerial phenomena or, if they are endemic throughout a society and strongly supported, even as part of the culture.

At the very least, there is an obligation on scholars to clarify such issues as those discussed above and to offer a position. We also believe that in due course, with the development of models and frameworks based on universally identified cultural dimensions, greater clarity and agreement over the nature and meaning of 'culture' will emerge.

Proposition 3: What is seen as 'appropriate' school leadership and management in a particular society is at least partly a function of accepted ideas and practices of curricula, teaching and learning. Since the latter appears to be culture dependent, it follows that what is assumed to be effective or suitable leadership and management in one system, may not be in another

If the main purpose of school is the delivery of curricula in ways that enable all students to realize their potential, then leadership and management need to be responsive and adaptive to the requirements and characteristics of teaching and learning. It became increasingly apparent in the 1990s that teaching and learning are culture dependent. As Watkins (2000) says, different cultures may have different answers to the questions 'What do you mean by learning?', 'What strategies do you use to study?' and 'What is a good teacher?' If answers to these questions differ cross-culturally, then we should not expect the knowledge base, let alone the leadership style of principals, to be universally applicable. The same point holds true, even more starkly, in societies such as mainland China, where the curriculum has an explicit political and ideological function to produce obedient loyal citizens to the socialist state. In short, the principal in mainland China has a different purpose from his counterpart in more liberal Taiwan, the UK or Australia and therefore requires a different knowledge base to understand practice.

According to Watkins (2000), societies differ in the relative emphasis they place on five learning phenomena – diligence (achievement); the development of understanding (deep approaches to learning); memorizing without understanding (surface approaches); dependency placed on the teacher; and the learning environment. In all societies, student self-esteem and low dependency on the teacher (internal locus of control) are associated with achievement and deep approaches to learning. It is the significant differences between societies, however, that we need to highlight. An important implication of these insights is that policy-makers, academics and school leaders need to be culture-sensitive to differences in learning and teaching. In contrasting the Chinese learning environment with the Anglo-American, for example, the latter's emphasis on getting the student on-task, improving classroom management techniques and coping with behavioural problems is less relevant in the Chinese context. In general, students in Chinese societies are brought up to respect their teachers and hence they possess greater degrees of obedience, docility and willingness to learn than is the case in UK or US classrooms. Teachers can therefore devote more time and effort to teaching and learning. Indeed, even notions of 'good teaching' differ, with Chinese students expecting teachers to be good moral models, warm-hearted and friendly, while Western students expect their teachers to set interesting learning experiences. There are also pointers to other cultural differences in the role of questioning and student grouping.

Chinese societies attribute academic success more to hard work and diligence than to ability. Partly for this reason, Chinese educators see creativity and understanding as slow processes requiring effort, repetition and attention. The contrast with Anglo-American notions of creativity associated with insight and spontaneity, is stark. For the Chinese, understanding and creativity are built up slowly; rote memorizing is a means of securing understanding rather than the antithesis of it. As Watkins (2000) also points out, Anglo-American students are typically motivated by intrinsic factors connected with ego and individualist assumptions, whereas Chinese students tend to be motivated by a more mixed range of extrinsic and intrinsic factors, significant among which are collectivist notions of duty and obligation to the family. Again, school leaders and teachers would need to understand these cultural differences in order to motivate their respective students and provide support and advice to their teachers. Academics also need to pay heed, recognizing that effective educational leadership, no less than teaching and learning, may not look the same in all countries.

Proposition 4: When globalized education policy is imported into the host system, the way in which it unfolds can be explained by its fusion with the local politico-cultural context, which may itself comprise different but interlocking arenas

The way in which globalized education trends mix with local politics and culture to explain the unfolding of policy is a theme of major significance. Any notion that globalized policy, mostly emanating from the West, is imported into host systems and straightforwardly adopted before being implemented at school level, is a gross oversimplification. As Morris and Lo (2000) illustrate in the case of Hong Kong, a 'Western' curriculum reform with origins in outcome-based education – the target-oriented curriculum – created fierce political activity leading to fragmentation and competition among local groups in three arenas. Interestingly, their recognition of three local arenas – a policy-making arena consisting of a state bureaucracy conducting its business largely in private; a national political arena consisting of a number of interest groups, including teachers, the media and politicians conducting its debates very publicly; and a schools' arena directly involved in implementation – may hold true for many other systems.

Each arena fulfils different functions. The policy arena, for example, is 'global, private and rhetorical'. The policy-making arena symbolizes the government's vision for education and is hotly contested, consultative and public. Processes and events in the schools' arena are influenced by events in the other two arenas. Thus fierce political activity in the national arena may affect how teachers respond in school. Morris and Lo's (2000) analysis destroys the myth that globalized policy is simply adopted by policy-makers and smoothly transitioned down to school level where problems are suddenly confronted. Importation of globalized policy may ignite fierce contestation among protagonists and former partners at each of the three levels, especially at national and school level. The case study shows in particular how globalized policy, when conflicting with traditional cultural values, can metamorphose a formerly passive teaching staff into a politically charged group of professionals.

Proposition 5: With the importation of policy and practice into different cultural contexts, tensions may arise between the local indigenous culture and the tenets and practicalities of the reform policy, depending on the leadership and management capabilities of the principal

Evidence points to the crucial role of the principal in transplanting new pedagogy and curricula into traditional indigenous cultures. In their Hong Kong study (Morris and Lo, 2000), for example, the implementation was generally unsuccessful. It was the principal of the Hong Kong primary school who engineered his school's adoption of the target-oriented curriculum (TOC), a major curriculum reform introducing fundamental changes based on student-centred teaching and learning and new forms of assessment. The new curriculum contradicted traditional Chinese beliefs of student passivity, obedience and examination orientation. Teachers therefore struggled to make the transition. Above all, they had little say in how the scheme was implemented, because the principal maintained his traditional Chinese autocratic style of leadership. It was the demands placed on teachers by the new reforms in concert with the principal's unrelenting traditional leadership style that brought matters to a head. The staff was transformed from a state of apolitical acquiescence to high political activity, where conflict, bargaining and negotiating became the new established order. In consequence, the school culture dramatically changed. It must also be acknowledged that prior to its implementation in the school, the TOC had already been subjected to much political and professional debate in the national arena, a point not lost on the teachers. The moral is clear: when challenging reforms are imported from other cultures, they demand strong but sympathetic leadership and management from principals to mediate their introduction to the local cultural setting.

This negative Hong Kong experience of implementing a major curriculum reform can be contrasted with the success of three Thai schools, primarily due to the directors (principals), reported by Hallinger and Kantamara (2000a). These authors report that the introduction of school-based management, parental involvement and new teaching–learning technologies into selected Thai schools was an attempt by the government to lessen the 'compliance' culture. As Hallinger and Kantamara point out, these reforms present stiff challenges in their countries of origin, let alone in the strongly hierarchical cultures of Asia. Successful reform in the three schools is attributed to the three directors who adopted participatory leadership styles, to group orientation and teamwork, and to a combination of pressure and support for change as well as the fusion of spirit and celebration in traditional Thai style. The moral for success here is the subtle combination of traditional Thai leadership with new 'Western' approaches demanded by the nature of the reforms. In other words, the school directors used their hierarchical position to win support for more participatory decision-making. Achieving the 'right' balance between traditional mores and new demands seems to be what matters.

A more adept leadership is required in the globalized world of the new millennium. School leadership in many parts of the world, including Asia, lacks an 'indigenous knowledge base'. By the same token, the field demonstrates an over-reliance on 'Western' ideas, policies and practices. Attempts to reform education by importing ideas from one society to another must consider the overall contexts of the societies involved and display greater cultural sensitivity. A future research agenda should focus on the interactions between traditional cultures and new global change forces. A comparative, cross-cultural approach promises a rewarding way forward. Hopefully, the chapters of this book have made a significant contribution towards that goal.

Specific issues and implications for future research

Empirical studies on leadership and schooling in the Asia-Pacific region and other regions outside North America, Northern Europe and Australasia, are relatively few. With globalization and the growing reciprocal interest between Asian and Western societies in the effectiveness of leadership and schooling, there is a need to chart a future research agenda.

In regard to methodology, rigorous and systematic comparative studies are needed that take full account of cultural contexts and influences. In this regard, authentic and well-validated frameworks and dimensions need developing by which to compare, first, societal cultures and social practices, and, secondly, school structures and practices (see Dimmock and Walker, 1998a; 1998b). Country-by-country descriptions will not do. Authentic comparison and explanation needs to be underpinned by generic frameworks and dimensions. In turn, there is a need for reliable and valid instruments – of both a qualitative and quantitative kind – for data collection in the field. Stevenson and Stigler (1992) have shown how large-scale studies involving schools in a number of cities in America and Asia can yield exciting benefits to knowledge and cultural-comparative insights, hitherto unrecognized. Equally, there is a need for in-depth, small-scale case studies comparing schools in different cultures. Cross-cultural collaboration between researchers would be a good start.

In regard to content, relatively few studies of effective schooling in Asia have been published in English. More studies of the primary sector to complement Stevenson and Stigler's work are needed. The dearth of cross-cultural comparative studies is even greater in the secondary sector. There is also a need for comparative studies to adopt an holistic approach that encompasses values and culture transmitted by parenting, socialization and the home, the curriculum, teaching and learning, and school organization and leadership. Schooling is influenced by all of these – to omit any of them is to obtain a partial picture. Finally, the appeal of a holistic sociocultural approach to effective schooling – one that emphasizes context by linking school, home and values – is that it presents an alternative to, and complements, the positivistic, measurement-oriented, student achievement focus of traditional school effectiveness studies.

An important purpose of this chapter has been to recognize the possibilities and prospects of future research in the field of cross-cultural educational administration and leadership. The following questions are illustrative of the directions in which future research could head.

- To what extent is it appropriate to transpose policies and practices of school improvement from one society to another without consideration of cultural context?
- How do sets of dominant values and practices associated with cultures and subcultures affect the meanings attributed to the implementation of, change in schools and school systems? For example, what meanings do the key concepts such as 'collaboration', 'micro-politics', 'school-based management' and 'accountability' have in different cultural settings?

- In what ways do societal cultures and subcultures influence the practice of school leadership? For example, in what ways does culture influence relationships between the school and its environment and processes within the school, such as appraisal, teamwork and shared leadership?
- How can the development of cross-cultural research and understanding in educational administration and leadership inform the issues associated with multi-ethnic schools within societies? For example, in what ways might an improved knowledge base on cross-cultural education have application to how multi-ethnic schools can better understand and serve their diverse communities?
- To what extent can the development of cross cultural research contribute to a better understanding of globalization and its relationship to policy formation, adoption, implementation and evaluation?

Conclusion

In summary, we have argued that educational leadership and management as a field of study and research has failed to keep pace with current events leading to the internationalizing and globalizing of policy and practice. We expressed concern that unlike other fields, such as international business management and cross-cultural psychology, our field has generally failed to develop models, frameworks, methodologies and analytical tools by which to understand these dramatic changes and their effects on school leadership and schooling in different societies. Equally, we are conscious of the limitations of existing models and theories which tend to be ethnocentric, and by generally failing to distinguish cultural boundaries, to assume a false universalism. We contend that a focus on culture as an analytical concept promises more robust comparisons between school administration and policy across different geocultural areas. Such cross-cultural comparisons can embrace a wider rather than narrower perspective, incorporating school leadership, organizational structures, management, curriculum, and teaching and learning, in order to present holistic and contextualized accounts.

We have also argued that a better understanding of societal and ethnic cultures is necessary in order to develop insights and theories that will inform the leadership of culturally diverse or multi-ethnic schools. As such schools increase as a result of demographic trends and movements, and the problems experienced become ever more complex, the justification for developing this aspect of educational leadership is readily apparent.

In concluding this book, the salient message is indefatigably that if the field of educational leadership and management is to develop methodologically and analytically it must take greater cognizance of the diversity and characteristics of context and culture within which leaders function.

References

Abercrombie, N. et al. (1994). *Contemporary British Society: A New Introduction to Sociology*. Cambridge: Policy Press.

Adler, N. (1997). *International Dimensions of Organizational Behavior (3rd edn)*. Cincinnati, OH: International Thompson.

Advisory Committee on the School Management Initiative (1992). *Staff Appraisal in Schools*. Hong Kong: Hong Kong Education Department.

Ah Nee-Benham, M. K. P. (2002). 'An alternative perspective of educational leadership for change: reflections on native/indigenous ways of knowing'. In K. Leithwood and P. Hallinger (eds), *Second International Handbook of Educational Leadership and Administration* (pp. 395–426). Dordrecht: Kluwer Academic.

Argyris, C. and Schön, D. (1978). *Organizational Learning: A Theory of Action Perspective*. Reading, MA: Addison-Wesley.

Aspinwall, K. and Pedler, M. (1997). 'Schools as learning organizations'. In B. Fidler, S. Russell and T. Simkins (eds), *Choices for Self-managing Schools* (pp. 227–242). London: Paul Chapman Publishing.

Au, L., Wright, N. and Botton, C. (2003). 'Using a structural equation modelling (SEM) approach to examine leadership of heads of subject departments (HODs) as perceived by principals and vice principals, heads of subject departments and teachers within "school based management" (SBM) secondary schools: Some evidence from Hong Kong'. *School Leadership and Management*, 23(4), 481–498.

Bain, A. (2000). 'The school design model: strategy for the design of 21st century schools'. In C. Dimmock and A. Walker (eds), *Future School Administration: Western and Asian Perspectives* (pp. 131–166). Hong Kong: Chinese University Press.

Ball, S. J. (1987). *The Micro-politics of the School: Towards a Theory of School Organization*. London: Methuen.

Banks, J. A. (1993). 'Multicultural education: development, dimensions, and challenges'. *Phi Delta Kappan*, 75(1), 22–28.

Banks, J. A. (1994). *Multiethnic Education: Theory and Practice*. Boston, MA: Allyn and Bacon.

Banks, J. A. and Banks, C. M. (1993). *Multicultural Education: Issues and Perspectives*. Boston, MA: Allyn and Bacon.

Begley, P. (1996). 'Cognitive perspectives on the nature and function of values in educational administration'. In K. Leithwood, J. Chapman, D. Corson, P. Hallingar and A. Hart (eds), *International Handbook of Educational Leadership and Administration* (pp. 551–588). Dordrecht: Kluwer Academic.

Begley, P. and Johansson, O. (1997). 'Values and school administration: preferences, ethics and conflicts'. Paper presented at the Annual meeting of the American Educational Research Association, March, Chicago, IL.

Begley, P. and Leithwood, K. (1990). 'The influence of values on school administrator practices'. *Journal of Personnel Evaluation in Education*, 3, 337–352.

Bell, L. (1992). *Managing Teams in Secondary Schools*. London: Routledge.

Berlak, H. and Berlak, C. (1981). *Dilemma of Schooling, Teaching and Change*. London: Methuen.

Biggs, J. (1994). 'What are effective schools? Lessons from East and West'. *Australian Education Researcher*, 21(1), 19–39.

Bogdan, R. C. and Biklen, S. K. (1992). *Qualitative Research for Education: An Introduction to Theory and Methods* (2nd edn). Needham Heights, MA: Allyn and Bacon.

Boisot, M. (1995). 'Preparing for turbulence: the changing relationship between strategy and management development in the learning organisation'. In B. Garratt (ed.), *Developing Strategic Thought: Rediscovering the Art of Direction-giving* (pp. 49–65). London: McGraw Hill.

Bond, M. (1991a). *Beyond the Chinese Face*. Hong Kong: Oxford University Press.

Bond, M. (1991b). 'Cultural influences on modes of impression management: implications for the culturally diverse organisation. In R. Giacalone and P. Rosenfield (eds), *Applied Impression Management: How Image-making Affects Managerial Decisions* (pp. 195–215). Newbury Park, CA: Sage.

Bond, M. (1994). 'Trait theory and cross-cultural studies of person perception'. *Psychological Inquiry*, 5, 114–117.

Bond, M. (ed.) (1996). *The Handbook of Chinese Psychology*. New York: Oxford University Press.

Bond, M. and Hwang, K. (1986). 'The social psychology of the Chinese people'. In M. Bond (ed.), *The Psychology of the Chinese People* (pp. 213–265). Hong Kong: Oxford University Press.

Bottery, M. (1999). 'Global forces, national mediations and the management of educational institutions'. *Educational Management and Administration*, 27(3), 299–312.

Boud, D. and Garrick, J. (1999). *Understanding Learning at Work*. New York: Routledge.

Bourdieu, P. (1977). 'Cultural reproduction and social reproduction'. In J. Karbel and A. H. Halsey (eds), *Power and Ideology in Education* (pp. 487–511). Oxford: Oxford University Press.

Bourdieu, P. and Passeron, J. (1990). *Reproduction in Education, Society and Culture* (2nd edn). London: Sage.

Bridge, W. (1994). 'Change where contrasting cultures meet'. In R. Gorringe (ed.), *Changing the Culture of a College* (pp. 83–96). Blagdon: Combe Lodge Reports.

Brislin, R. (1993). *Understanding Culture's Influence on Behaviour*. Orlando, FL: Harcourt Brace.

Brooke-Smith, R. (2003). *Leading Learners, Leading Schools*. London: RoutledgeFalmer.

Brotherton, C. (1999). *Social Psychology and Management*. Buckingham: Open University Press.

Bryant, M. (2003). 'Cross-cultural perspectives on school leadership: themes from native American interviews'. In N. Bennett, M. Crawford and M. Cartwright (eds), *Effective Educational Leadership* (pp. 216–228). London: Paul Chapman Publishing.

Bush, T. (1998). 'Organisational culture and strategic management'. In D. Middlewood and J. Lumby (eds), *Strategic Management in Schools and Colleges* (pp. 32–46). London: Paul Chapman Publishing.

Cacioppe, R. (1999). 'Using team–individual reward and recognition strategies to drive organizational success'. *Leadership and Organization Development Journal*, 20(6), 322–331.

Campbell-Evans, G. (1993). 'A values perspective on school-based management'. In C. Dimmock (ed.), *School-based Management and School Effectiveness* (pp. 92–113). London: Routledge.

Capper, C. A. (1996). 'We're not housed in an institution, we're housed in a community: possibilities and consequences of neighborhood-based interagency collaboration'. In J. Cibulka and W. Kritek (eds), *Coordination among Schools, Families, and Communities: Prospects for Reform* (pp. 299–322). New York: State University of New York Press.

Cardno, C. (2001). 'Managing dilemmas in appraising performance: an approach for school leaders'. In D. Middlewood and C. Cardno (eds), *Managing Appraisal and Performance: A Comparative Approach* (pp. 75–92). London: RoutledgeFalmer.

Cardno, C. and Piggot-Irvine, E. (1997). *Effective Performance Appraisal: Integrating Accountability and Development in Staff Appraisal*. Auckland: Longman.

Chan, S. L. (1993). 'Approaches to learning of medical and business students in a Guangzhou university'. Unpublished Master of Education thesis, University of Hong Kong.

Chen, C. C. and Van Velsor, E. (1996). 'New directions for research and practice in diversity leadership'. *The Leadership Quarterly*, 7(2), 285–302.

Cheng, K. M. (1995). 'The neglected dimension: cultural comparison in educational administration'. In K. C. Wong and K. M. Cheng (eds), *Educational Leadership and Change: An International Perspective* (pp. 87–102). Hong Kong: Hong Kong University Press.

Cheng, K. M. (1998). 'Can educational values be borrowed? Looking into cultural differences'. *Peabody Journal of Education*, 73(2), 11–30.

Cheng, K. M. and Wong, K. C. (1996). 'School effectiveness in East Asia: concepts, origins and implications'. *Journal of Educational Administration*, 34(5), 32–49.

Child, J. (1981). 'Culture, contingency and capitalism in the cross-national study of organisations'. In L. Cummings and B. Shaw (series eds), *Research in Organizational Behaviour Vol. 3*. Greenwich, CT: JAI Press.

Chow, I. (1995). 'An opinion survey of performance appraisal practices in Hong Kong and the People's Republic of China'. *Asia Pacific Journal of Human Resources*, 32(3), 67–79.

Chung, M. L., McMahan, G. and Woodman, R. (1996). 'An international comparison of organization development practices: the USA and Hong Kong'. *Journal of Organizational Change Management*, 9(2), 4–19.

Collarbone, P. (2001). *Leadership Programme for Serving Headteachers: A Review*. Nottingham: NCSL.

Cuban, L. (1992). 'Managing dilemmas while building professional communities'. *Educational Research*, January, 4–11.

Cuban, L. (1994). 'Reforming the practice of educational administration through managing dilemmas'. Unpublished manuscript, Stanford University, CA.

Cuban, L. (2001). *How Can I Fix It? Finding Solutions and Managing Dilemmas: An Educator's Road Map*. New York: Teachers College Press.

Cunningham, W. G. and Cordeiro, P. A. (2000). *Educational Administration: A Problem Based Approach.* Boston, MA: Allyn and Bacon.

Darling-Hammond, L. (1997). *The Right to Learn: A Blueprint for Creating Schools that Work.* San Francisco, CA: Jossey-Bass.

Davidman, L. and Davidman, P. T. (1994). *Teaching with a Multicultural Perspective.* New York: Longman.

Davies, B. (2002). 'Rethinking schools and school leadership for the 21st century: changes and challenges'. *International Journal of Educational Management,* 16(4), 196–206.

Davies, B. and Ellison, L. (2003). 'The new strategic direction and development of the school'. London: RoutledgeFalmer.

Day, C. et al. (2000). *Leading Schools in Times of Change.* Buckingham: Open University Press.

DeDreu, C. K. W. D. and Van de Vliert, E. V. D. (eds) (1997). *Using Conflict in Organizations.* London: Sage.

Dempster, N. and Berry, V. (2003). 'Blindfolded in a minefield: principals' ethical decision-making'. *Cambridge Journal of Education,* 33(3), 457–477.

DES (1985). 'Education for All: The Report of the Committee of Inquiry into the Education of Children from Ethnic Minority Groups', cmnd. 9453, London: HMSO (the Swann Report).

Dimmock, C. (1995). 'Restructuring for school effectiveness: leading, organising and teaching for effective learning'. *Educational Management and Administration,* 23(1), 5–1.

Dimmock, C. (1996). 'Dilemmas for school leaders and administrators in restructuring'. In K. Leithwood, J. Chapman, D. Corson, P. Hallinger and A. Hart (eds), *International Handbook of Educational Leadership and Administration* (pp. 135–170). Dordrecht: Kluwer Academic.

Dimmock, C. (1998). 'School restructuring and the principalship: the applicability of Western theories, policies and practices to East and South-East Asian cultures'. *Educational Management and Administration,* 26(4), 363–377.

Dimmock, C. (2000a). *Designing the Learner-centred School: A Cross-cultural Perspective.* London: Falmer Press.

Dimmock, C. (2000b). 'Hong Kong's school reform: importing Western policy into an Asian culture'. In C. Dimmock and A. Walker (eds), *Future School Administration: Western and Asian Perspectives* (pp. 191–224). Hong Kong: Chinese University Press.

Dimmock, C. (2002). 'Cross-cultural differences in interpreting and doing research'. In M. Coleman and A. R. J. Briggs (eds), *Research Methods in Educational Leadership and Management* (pp. 28–42). London: Sage.

Dimmock, C. and Lim, H. W. (1999). 'School restructuring in Hong Kong: the perceptions of middle managers'. *Asia Pacific Journal of Education,* 19(1), 59–77.

Dimmock, C. and O'Donoghue, T. (1997). 'The edited topical life history approach: a new methodology to inform the study of school leadership'. *Leading and Managing,* 3(1), 48–70.

Dimmock, C. and Walker, A. (1997). 'Hong Kong's change of sovereignty: school leader perceptions of the effects on educational policy and school administration'. *Comparative Education,* 36(2), 277–302.

Dimmock, C. and Walker, A. (1998a). 'Towards comparative educational administration: the case for a cross-cultural, school-based approach'. *Journal of Educational Administration,* 36(4), 379–401.

Dimmock, C. and Walker, A. (1998b). 'Comparative educational administration: developing a cross-cultural conceptual framework'. *Educational Administration Quarterly,* 34(4), 558–595.

Dimmock, C. and Walker, A. (2000a). 'Developing comparative and international educational leadership and management: a cross-cultural model'. *School Leadership and Management,* 20(2), 143–160.

Dimmock, C. and Walker, A. (2000b). 'Globalization and societal culture: redefining schooling and school leadership in the 21st century. *COMPARE,* 30(3), 303–312.

Dimmock, C. and Walker, A. (eds) (2000c). *Future School Administration: Western and Asian Perspectives.* Hong Kong: Chinese University Press.

Dimmock, C. and Walker, A. (2002). 'Connecting school leadership with teaching, learning and parenting in diverse cultural contexts: Western and Asian perspectives'. In K. Leithwood and P. Hallinger (eds), *Second International Handbook of Educational Leadership and Administration* (pp. 326–395). Dordrecht: Kluwer Press.

Dimmock, C., O'Donoghue, T. and Robb, A. (1996). 'Parental involvement in schooling: an emerging research agenda'. *Compare,* 26(1), 5–20.

DiPaola, M. F. (2003). 'Conflict and change: daily challenges for school leaders'. In N. Bennett, M. Crawford and M. Cartwright (eds), *Effective Educational Leadership* (pp. 143–158). London: Paul Chapman Publishing.

DiTomaso, N. and Hooijberg, R. (1996). 'Diversity and the demands of leadership'. *The Leadership Quarterly,* 7(2), 163–187.

Dreachslin, J. L., Hunt, P. L. and Sprainer, E. (2000). 'Workforce diversity: implications for the effectiveness of health care delivery teams'. *Social Science and Medicine*, 50, 1403–1414.

Duke, D. (1996). 'A normative perspective on organizational leadership'. Paper presented at the Toronto Conference of Values and Educational Leadership, 4 October, Toronto, Canada.

Education Update (1999). 'New goals for teacher evaluation'. *Education Update*, 41(2), 1, 4–5, 8.

Elmore, R. (1979). 'Backward mapping: implementation research and policy decisions'. *Political Science Quarterly*, 94(4), 601–616.

Everard, K. B. and Morris, G. (1996). *Effective School Management* (3rd edn). London: Paul Chapman Publishing.

Feinberg, W. (1998). *Common Schools/Uncommon Identities National Unity and Cultural Difference.* New Haven, CT: Yale University Press.

Fidler, B. (2001). 'A structural critique of school effectiveness and school improvement'. In A. Harris and N. Bennett (eds), *School Effectiveness and School Improvement: Alternative Perspectives* (pp. 47–74). London: Continuum.

Fidler, B. (2002). *Strategic Management for School Development: Leading your School's Improvement Strategy.* London: Sage.

Firestone, W. (1993). 'Alternative arguments for generalising from data as applied to qualitative research'. *Educational Researcher*, 22(4), 16–23.

Fitzgerald, T. (2003). 'Interrogating orthodox voices: gender, ethnicity and educational leadership'. *School Leadership and Management*, 23(4), 431–444.

Foskett, N. and Lumby, J. (2003). *Leading and Managing Education: International Dimensions.* London: Paul Chapman Publishing.

Fraser, B. J., Walberg, H. J., Welch, W. W. and Hattie, J. A. (1987). 'Syntheses of educational productivity research'. *International Journal of Educational Research*, 11(2), 147–247.

Fullan, M. (1991). *The New Meaning of Educational Change.* London: Cassell.

Fullan, M. (1993). *Change Forces: Probing the Depths of Educational Reform.* London: Falmer Press.

Fullan, M. (2001). *Leading in a Culture of Change.* San Francisco, CA: Jossey-Bass.

Gao, L. B. (1998). 'Conceptions of teaching held by school physics teachers in Guangdong, China and their relations to student learning'. Unpublished PhD thesis. University of Hong Kong.

Gardner, H. (1995). *Leading Minds.* New York: Basic Books.

Garvin, D. (1993). 'Building a learning organization'. *Harvard Business Review*, July–August, 78–91.

Giddens, A. (1989). *Sociology.* Cambridge: Polity Press.

Gilsdorf, J. W. (1998). 'Organisational rules on communicating: how employees are – and are not – learning the ropes'. *Journal of Business Communication*, 35, 173–201.

Ginsberg, R. and Gray Davies, T. (2003). 'The emotional side of leadership'. In N. Bennett, M. Crawford and M. Cartwright (eds), *Effective Educational Leadership* (pp. 267–280). London: Paul Chapman Publishing.

Glatter, R. (1994). 'Managing dilemmas in education: the tightrope walk of strategic choice in more autonomous institutions'. Paper presented at the 8th International Intervisitation Program in Educational Administration, 15–27 May, Toronto, Canada and Buffalo, USA.

Glatthorn, A. (1997). *Differentiated Supervision* (2nd edn). Alexandria, VA: ASCD.

Goldring, E. and Rallis, S. (1993). *Principals of Dynamic Schools: Taking Charge of Change.* Newbury Park, CA: Corwin Press.

Gow, L. et al. (1996). 'The learning approaches of Chinese people: a function of socialisation processes and the context of learning?' In M. H. Bond (ed.), *The Handbook of Chinese Psychology* (pp. 109–123). Hong Kong: Oxford University Press.

Grace, G. (1994). *School Leadership: Beyond Educational Management.* London: Falmer Press.

Greenfield, T. and Ribbins, P. (eds) (1993). *Greenfield on Educational Administration: Towards a Humane Science.* London: Routledge.

Grint, K. (2003). 'The arts of leadership'. In N. Bennett, M. Crawford and M. Cartwright (eds), *Effective Educational Leadership* (pp. 89–107). London: Paul Chapman Publishing.

Gronn, P. and Ribbins, P. (1996). 'Leaders in context: postpositivist approaches to understanding educational leadership'. *Educational Administration Quarterly*, 32(3), 452–473.

Hallinger, P. (1995). 'Culture and leadership: developing an international perspective in educational administration'. *UCEA Review*, 36(1), 3–7.

Hallinger, P. (2000). 'Leading educational change in Southeast Asia: the challenge of creating learning systems'. In C. Dimmock and A. Walker (eds), *Future School Administration: Western and Asian Perspectives* (pp. 169–190). Hong Kong: Chinese University Press.

Hallinger, P. and Heck, R. (1996). 'The principal's role in school effectiveness: an assessment of methodological progress, 1980–1995'. *Educational Administration Quarterly*, 32(1), 5–44.

Hallinger, P. and Kantamara, P. (2000a). 'Educational change in Thailand: opening a window into leadership as a cultural process'. *School Leadership and Management*, 20(2), 189–206.

Hallinger, P. and Kantamara, P. (2000b). 'Leading at the confluence of tradition and globalization: the challenge of change in Thai schools'. *Asia Pacific Journal of Education*, 20(2), 46–57.

Hallinger, P. and Leithwood, K. (1996a). 'Culture and educational administration: a case of finding out what you don't know you don't know'. *Journal of Educational Administration*, 34(5), 98–116.

Hallinger, P. and Leithwood, K. (1996b). 'Editorial'. *Journal of Educational Administration*, 34(5), 4–11.

Hallinger, P., Chantarapanya, S. and Kantamara, P. (1999). 'The challenge of educational leadership in Thailand: Jing jai jung, nae born'. In T. Townsend and Y. C. Cheng (eds), *Educational Change and Development in the Asia-Pacific Region: Challenges for Education for the Future* (pp. 207–226). Rotterdam: Swets and Zeitsinger.

Hallinger, P., Leithwood, K. and Murphy, J. (eds) (1993). *Cognitive Perspectives on Educational Administration*. New York: Teachers College Press.

Handy, C. and Aitken, R. (1986). *Understanding Schools as Organisations*. London: Penguin Books.

Hargreaves, D. (1999). 'Helping practitioners explore their school's culture'. In J. Prosser (ed.), *School Culture* (pp. 48–65). London: Paul Chapman Publishing.

Harrison, L. (2000). 'Why culture matters'. In L. Harrison and S. Hungtinton (eds), *Culture Matters: How Values Shape Human Progress* (pp. xiii–xxxiv). New York: Basic Books.

Hart, A. et al. (1997). 'Problem-solving errors of educational leaders'. Paper presented at the annual meeting of the American Educational Research Association, March, Chicago, IL.

Haynes, E. and Licata, J. (1995). 'Creative insubordination of school principals and the legitimacy of the justifiable'. *Journal of Educational Administration*, 33(4), 21–35.

Heck, R. (1996). 'Leadership and culture: conceptual and methodological issues in comparing models across cultural settings'. *Journal of Educational Administration*, 34(5), 74–97.

Heck, R. (1998). 'Conceptual and methodological issues in investigating principal leadership across cultures'. *Peabody Journal of Education*, 73(2), 51–80.

Heck, R. (2002). 'Issues in the investigation of school leadership across cultures'. In A. Walker and C. Dimmock (eds), *School Leadership and Administration: Adopting a Cultural Perspective* (pp. 77–102). New York: RoutledgeFalmer.

Heck, R. and Hallinger, P. (1997). 'Epistemological frames and methods for the study of school leadership'. Paper presented at the annual meeting of the American Educational Research Association, March, Chicago, IL.

Henze, R. C. (2000). 'Leading for diversity: how school leaders achieve racial and ethnic harmony'. Retrieved 8 May 2004, from http//www.cal.org/crede/pubs/ResBrief6.htm.

Henze, R. et al. (2002). *Leading for Diversity: How School Leaders Promote Positive Interethnic Relations*. Thousand Oaks, CA: Corwin Press.

Herbig, P. and Martin, D. (1998). 'Negotiating with Chinese: a cultural perspective'. *Cross Cultural Management*, 5(3), 40–54.

Hess, F. M. (2003). 'A license to lead?' *A New leadership Agenda for America's Schools*. Retrieved from Progressive Policy Institute, accessed online at: http://www.pipionline.org/documents/New_Leadership_0103.pdf.

Hess, R. D. and Azuma, M. (1991). 'Cultural support for schooling: contrasts between Japan and the United States'. *Educational Researcher*, 20(9), 2–8.

HMSO (1988). Education Reform Bill, London: HMSO.

Hodgkinson, C. (1978). *Towards a Philosophy of Administration*. Oxford: Basil Blackwell.

Hofstede, G. H. (1980). *Cultures Consequences: International Differences in Work-related Values*. Beverly Hills, CA: Sage.

Hofstede, G. H. (1991). *Cultures and Organizations: Software of the Mind*. London: McGraw Hill.

Hofstede, G. H. (1994). 'Cultural constraints in management theories'. *International Review of Strategic Management*, 5, 27–48.

Hofstede, G. H. (1995). 'Managerial values: the business of international business is culture'. In T. Jackson (ed.), *Cross-cultural Management* (pp. 150–165). Oxford: Butterworth-Heinemann.

Hofstede, G. H. (1996). 'An American in Paris: the influence of nationality on organizational theories'. *Organization Studies*, 17(3), 525–537.

Hofstede, G. H. and Bond, M. (1984). 'Hofstede's cultural dimensions: an independent validation using Rokeach's value survey'. *Journal of Cross-Cultural Psychology*, 15(4), 417–433.

Holloway, S. D. (1988). 'Concepts of ability and effort in Japan and the US'. *Review of Educational Research*, 58, 327–345.

Holmes, B. (1965). *Problems in Education: A Comparative Approach*. London: Routledge and Kegan Paul.

Hopkins, D. (1993). 'The role of the external consultant'. Keynote address at the National Association of Educational Inspectors, Advisors and Consultants Annual Conference, June, New York.

Huo, Y. P. and Clinow, M. (1995). 'On transplanting human resource practices to China: a culture driven approach'. *International Journal of Manpower*, 16(9), 3–15.

Inglehart, R. (2000). 'Culture and democracy'. In L. Harrison and S. Hungtinton (eds), *Culture Matters: How Values Shape Human Progress* (pp. 80–97). New York: Basic Books.

Jackson, T. and Bak, M. (1998). 'Foreign companies and Chinese workers: employee motivation in the People's Republic of China'. *Journal of Organisational Change Management*, 11(4), 282–300.

Jacobson, S. L. and Battaglia, C. F. (2001). 'Authentic forms of teacher assessment and staff development'. In D. Middlewood and C. Cardno (eds), *Managing Teacher Appraisal and Performance: A Comparative Approach* (pp. 75–89). London: RoutledgeFalmer.

Jin, L. and Cortazzi, M. (1998). 'Dimensions of dialogue, large classes in China', *International Journal of Educational Research*, 29, 739–761.

Johnson, L. S. (2003). 'The diversity imperative: building a culturally responsive school ethos'. *Intercultural Education*, 14(1), 17–30.

Jones, P. (1971). *Comparative Education: Purpose and Method*. St Lucia: University of Queensland Press.

Kanpol, B. and McLaren, P. (eds) (1995). *Critical Multiculturalism – Uncommon Voices in a Common Struggle*. Westport, CT: Bergin and Garvey.

Kember, D. and Gow, L. (1990). 'Cultural specificity of approaches to study'. *British Journal of Educational Psychology*, 60, 356–363.

Kirkbride, P., Tang, S. and Westwood, R. (1991). 'Chinese conflict preferences and negotiating behaviour: cultural and psychological influences'. *Organisational Studies*, 12, 365–386.

Ladson-Billings, G. (1995). 'Making mathematics meaningful in multicultural contexts'. In W. G. Secada, E. Fennema and L. B. Adajian (eds), *New Directions for Equity in Mathematics Education* (pp. 126–142). New York: Cambridge University Press.

Lam, Y. L. J. (2002). 'Defining the effects of transformational leadership on organisational learning: a cross-cultural comparison'. *School Leadership and Management*, 22(4), 439–452.

Lau, C. M., McMahon, G. and Woodman, R. (1996). 'An international comparison of organizational development practice in the USA and Hong Kong'. *Journal of Organizational Change*, 5(2), 4–19.

Lauder, H. (2000). 'The dilemmas of comparative research and policy importation: an extended book review'. *British Journal of Sociology of Education*, 21(3), 465–475.

Lave, J. and Wenger, W. (1991). *Situated Learning: Legitimate Peripheral Participation*. Cambridge: Cambirdge University Press.

Lee, W. O. (1996). 'The cultural context for Chinese learners: conceptions of learning in the Confucian tradition'. In D. Watkins and J. Biggs (eds), *The Chinese Learner: Cultural Psychology and Contextual Influences* (pp. 25–42). Hong Kong: Comparative Education Research Centre.

Leeman, Y. A. M. (2003). 'School leadership for intercultural education'. *Intercultural Education*, 14(1), 30–45.

Leithwood, K. (1995). 'Cognitive perspectives on school leadership'. *Journal of School Leadership*, 5(2), 115–135.

Leithwood, K., Begley, P. and Cousins, J. (1994). *Developing Expert Leadership for Future Schools*. London: Falmer Press.

Leithwood, K., Jantzi, D. and Steinbach, R. (2003). 'Fostering teacher leadership'. In N. Bennett, M. Crawford and M. Cartwright (eds), *Effective Educational Leadership* (pp. 186–200). London: Paul Chapman Publishing.

Lewellen, T. (1992). *Political Anthropology: An Introduction (Second Edition)*. Westport, CT: Bergin and Gavey.

Limb, A. (1994). 'Inspiring a shared vision'. In R. Gorringe (ed.), *Changing the Culture of a College* (pp. 65–92). Blagdon: Combe Lodge Reports.

Lincoln, Y. and Guba, E. (1985). *Naturalistic Inquiry*. Newbury Park, CA: Sage.

Lindsey, S. (2000). 'Culture, mental models, and national prosperity'. In L. Harrison and S. Hungtinton (eds), *Culture Matters: How Values Shape Human Progress* (pp. 268–281). New York: Basic Books.

MacBeath, J. (2003). 'Editorial'. *Cambridge Journal of Education*, 33(3), 323–327.

MacPherson of Cluny, Sir William (1999). The Stephen Lawrence Inquiry, Cm 4262-I, London: The Stationery Office (The MacPherson Report).

Marsick, V. J. and Watkins, K. E. (1999). *Facilitating Learning Organizations*. Aldershot: Gower.

Marton, F., Dall'Alba, G. and Tse, L. K. (1996). 'Memorizing and understanding: the keys to the paradox'. In D. A. Watkins and J. B. Biggs (eds), *The Chinese Learner: Cultural, Psychological and Contextual Influences* (pp. 69–84). Hong Kong: Comparative Education Research Centre, University of Hong Kong.

Maurer, R. (1991). *Managing Conflict: Tactics for School Administrators*. Boston, MA: Allyn and Bacon.

McAdams, R. P. (1993). *Lessons from Abroad: How Other Countries Educate their Children*. Lancaster, PA: Technomic.

McLaren, P. (1994). *Life in Schools: An Introduction to Critical Pedagogy in the Foundations of Education*. White Plains, NY: Longman.

Meek, V. L. (1988). 'Organizational culture: origins and weaknesses'. *Organization Studies*, 9(4), 453–473.

Middlewood, D. and Cardno, C. (eds) (2001). *Managing Teacher Appraisal and Performance: A Comparative Approach*. London: RoutledgeFalmer.

Miles, M. and Huberman, A. (1994). *Qualitative Data Analysis* (2nd edn). Thousand Oaks, CA: Sage.

Mintzberg, H. (1994). *The Rise and Fall of Strategic Planning*. New York: Prentice-Hall.

Mo, K., Conners, R. and McCormick, J. (1998). 'Teacher appraisal in Hong Kong self- managing secondary schools: factors for effective practices'. *Journal of Personnel Evaluation in Education*, 12(1), 19–42.

Moos, L. and Møller, J. (2003). 'Schools and leadership in transition: the case of Scandinavia'. *Cambridge Journal of Education*, 33(3), 353–370.

Morris, P. and Lo, M. L. (2000). 'Shaping the curriculum: contexts and cultures'. *School Leadership and Management*, 20(2), 175–188.

Morrison, K. (2002). *School Leadership and Complexity Theory*. London: RoutledgeFalmer.

Murphy, J. (1994). 'Transformational change and the evolving role of the principal: early empirical evidence'. In J. Murphy and K. Seashore Louis (eds), *Reshaping the Principalship* (pp. 20–55). Thousand Oaks, CA: Sage.

Newton, P. (2001). *The Headteachers' Leadership and Management Programme (Headlamp) Review*. Nottingham: NCSL.

Nieto, S. (1992). *Affirming Diversity: The Sociopolitical Context of Multicultural Education*. New York: Longman.

Norte, E. (1999). 'Structures beneath the skin: how school leaders use their power and authority to create institutional opportunities for developing positive interethnic communities'. *Journal of Negro Education*, 68(4), 466–485.

North Central Regional Educational Laboratory (1995). *Promising Programs and Practices in Multicultural Education*. Retrieved 18 August 2004 from http://www.ncrel.org/sdrs/areas/issues/educatrs/leadrshp/le4pppme.htm.

O'Donoghue, T. and Dimmock, C. (1998). *School Restructuring: International Perspectives*. London: Kogan Page.

O'Donoghue, T., Aspland, T. and Brooker, R. (1993). 'Dilemmas in teachers' conceptions of the nature of their curriculum work: a Queensland case study'. *Curriculum Perspectives*, 13(3), 11–22.

Oduro, G. K. T. and MacBeath, J. (2003). 'Traditions and tensions in leadership: the Ghanaian experience'. *Cambridge Journal of Education*, 33(3), 441–455.

Ogbonna, E. (1993). 'Managing organisational culture: fantasy or reality?' *Human Resource Management Journal*, 3(2), 42–54.

Ohmae, K. (1995). *The End of the Nation State: The Rise of Regional Economies*. New York: Free Press.

Pai, Y. and Adler, S. A. (2000). *Cultural Foundations of Education*. Englewood Cliffs, NJ: Prentice-Hall

Patterson, J. (1992). *Leadership for Tomorrow's Schools*. Alexandria, VA: ASCD.

Pounder, D. (ed.) (1998). *Restructuring Schools for Collaboration*. Albany, NY: University of New York Press.

Prosser, J. (1999). *School Culture*. London: Paul Chapman Publishing.

Pye, L. (2000). '"Asian values": from dynamos to dominoes?' In L. Harrison and S. Hungtington (eds), *Culture Matters: How Values Shape Human Progress* (pp. 244–255). New York: Basic Books.

Quong, T., Walker, A. and Stott, K. (1998). *Values-based Strategic Planning*. Singapore: Simon and Schuster.

Redding, S. G. (1977). 'Some perceptions of psychological needs among managers in Southeast Asia'. In Y. Poortinga (ed.), *Basic Problems in Cross-cultural Psychology* (pp. 338–352). Amsterdam: Swets and Zeitlinger.

Redding, S. G. (1990). *The Spirit of Chinese Capitalism*. Berlin: De Gruyter.

Redding, S. G. (1994). 'Comparative management theory: jungle, zoo or fossil bed?' *Organization Studies*, 15(3), 323–359.

Redding, S. G. and Wong, G. (1986). 'The psychology of Chinese organizational behavior'. In M. Bond (ed.), *The Psychology of the Chinese People* (pp. 267–295). Hong Kong: Oxford University Press.

Reynolds, D. (2000). 'School effectiveness: the international dimension'. In C. Teddlie and D. Reynolds (eds), *The International Handbook of School Effectiveness Research* (pp. 232–256). London: Falmer Press.

Reynolds, D. and Farrell, S. (1996). *World's Apart?: A Review of International Surveys of Educational Achievement Involving England*. OFSTED *(Office for Standards in Education)*. London: Her Majesty's Stationery Office.

Rizvi, F. (1997). 'Beyond the East–West divide: education and the dynamics of Australia–Asia relations'. In J. Blackmore and K. A. Toh (eds), *Educational Research: Building New Partnerships* (pp. 13–26). Singapore: Singapore Educational Research Association.

Ronan, S. (1986). *Comparative and Multinational Management*. New York: Wiley.

Rosenstreich, G. D. (2003). 'Unpacking diversity training'. Paper presented at the European Confederation of Educational Research, 17–20 September, Hamburg University. Retrieved 24 March 2004 from http://www.leeds.ac.uk/educol/documents/00003217.htm.

Rothstein-Fisch, C., Greenfield, P. M. and Trumbull, E. (1999). 'Bridging cultures with classroom strategies'. *Educational Leadership*, 56(7), 64–67.

Rutter, M. et al. (1979). *Fifteen Thousand Hours: Secondary Schools and their Effects on Children*. London: Open Books.

Salili, F. (1996). 'Accepting personal responsibility for learning'. In D. Watkins and J. Biggs (eds), *The Chinese Learner*. Melbourne: Australia Council for Educational Research.

Saphier, J. and King, M. (1985). 'Good seeds grow in strong cultures'. *Educational Leadership*, 42(6), 67–74.

Schein, E. (1985). *Organizational Culture and Leadership*. San Francisco, CA: Jossey-Bass.

School Management Initiative Section (SMI) (1998). *Teacher Appraisal*. September. Hong Kong: Hong Kong Education Department.

Schratz, M. (2003). 'From administering to leading a school: challenges in German-speaking countries'. *Cambridge Journal of Education*, 33(3), 395–416.

Seashore Louis, K. (2003). 'School leaders facing real change: shifting geography, uncertain paths'. *Cambridge Journal of Education*, 33(3), 371–382.

Senge, P. (1993). *The Fifth Discipline*. London: Century Business.

Sergiovanni, T. (1995). *The Principalship: A Reflective Practice Perspective* (3rd edn). Boston, MA: Allyn and Bacon.

Sharp, L. and Gopinathan, S. (2000). 'Leadership in high achieving schools in Singapore: the influence of societal culture'. *Asia-Pacific Journal of Education*, 20(2), 99–109.

Shaw, M. and Welton, J. (1996). 'The application of education management models and theories to the processes of education policy making and management: a case of compound cross-cultural confusion'. Paper presented at the 8th International Conference of the Commonwealth Council for Educational Administration, 19–24 August, Kuala Lumpur, Malaysia.

Shields, C. M. (2002). 'Cross-cultural leadership and communities of difference: thinking about leading in diverse schools'. In K. Leithwood and P. Hallinger (eds), *Second International Handbook of Educational Leadership and Administration* (pp. 206–244). Dordrecht: Kluwer Academic.

Shields, C. M., Laroque, L. J. and Oberg, S. L. (2002). 'A dialogue about race and ethnicity in education: struggling to understand issues in cross-cultural leadership'. *Journal of School Leadership*, 12(2), 116–137.

Shweder, T. (2000). 'Moral maps, "First world" conceits and the new evangelists'. In L. Harrison and S. Hungtinton (eds), *Culture Matters: How Values Shape Human Progress* (pp. 158–177). New York: Basic Books.

Simons, H. (1982). *Conversation Piece: The Practice of Uttering, Muttering, Collecting, Using and Reporting Talk for Social and Educational Research*. London: Grant McIntyre.

Siskin, L. (1994). *Realms of Knowledge: Academic Departments in Secondary Schools*. London: Falmer Press.

Siskin, L. (1997). 'The challenge of leadership in comprehensive high schools: school vision and department divisions'. *Educational Administration Quarterly*, 33, 604–623.

Sleeter, C. and Grant, C. (1987). 'An analysis of multicultural education in the United States'. *Harvard Education Review*, 57(4), 421–444.

Sleeter, C. and Grant, C. (1993). *Making Choices for Multicultural Education: Five Approaches to Race, Class and Gender*. New York: Macmillan.

Smith, M. (1997). 'Are traditional management tools sufficient for diverse teams?' *Team Performance Management*, 3(1), 3–11.

Southworth, G. (1994). 'The learning school'. In P. Ribbins and E. Burridge (eds), *Improving Education: Promoting Quality in Schools* (pp. 52–73). London: Cassell.

Southworth, G. (2000). 'School leadership in English schools at the close of the 20th century: puzzles, problems and cultural insights'. Paper presented at the meeting of the American Educational Research Association Annual Conference, April, New Orleans, LA.

Spear, M., Gould, K. and Lee, B. (2000). *Who Would Be a Teacher? A Review of Factors Motivating and Demotivating Prospective and Practising Teachers*. Slough: NFER.

Stevenson, H. W. and Lee, S. Y. (1996). 'The academic achievement of Chinese students'. In M. H. Bond (ed.), *The Handbook of Chinese Psychology* (pp. 124–142). New York: Oxford University Press.

Stevenson, H. W. and Stigler, J. W. (1992). *The Learning Gap: Why our Schools Are Failing and What We Can Learn from Japanese and Chinese Education.* New York: Simon and Schuster.

Stigler, J. W. and Hiebert, J. (1999). *The Teaching Gap: Best Ideas from the World's Teachers for Improving Education in the Classroom.* New York: Free Press.

Stoll, L. (1999). 'School culture: black hole or fertile garden for school improvement?' In J. Prosser (ed.), *School Culture* (pp. 30–47). London: Paul Chapman Publishing.

Stoll, L. and Fink, D. (1996). *The Power of School Culture in Changing our Schools.* Buckingham: Open University Press.

Suttles, G. (1968). *The Social Order of the Slum.* Chicago, IL: University of Chicago Press.

Tang, C. (1996). 'Collaborative learning: the latent dimension in Chinese students' learning'. In D. A. Watkins and J. Biggs (eds), *The Chinese Learner: Cultural, Psychological and Contextual Influences* (pp. 183–204). Hong Kong: Comparative Education Research Centre, University of Hong Kong.

Taylor, S. and Bogdan, R. (1984). *Introduction to Qualitative Research Methods – the Search for Meaning.* New York: John Wiley.

Telford, H. (1996). *Transforming Schools through Collaborative Leadership.* London: Falmer Press.

The Chinese Culture Connection (1987). 'Chinese values and the search for culture-free dimensions of culture'. *Journal of Cross-Cultural Psychology*, 18, 143–164.

The Economist (1996). 'Cultural explanation: the man in the Baghdad café'. *The Economist*, 9 November, 23–30.

Thrupp, M. (2001). 'Sociological and political concerns about school effectiveness research: time for a new research agenda'. *School Effectiveness and School Improvement*, 12(1), 7–40.

Tierney, W. (1996). 'Leadership and postmodernism: one voice and qualitative method'. *Leadership Studies*, 7(3), 371–383.

Tjosvold, S. and Leung, K. (eds) (1998). *Conflict Management in the Asia Pacific: Assumptions and Approaches in Diverse Cultures.* New York: John Wiley.

Torrington, D. and Tan, C. H. (1994). *Human Resource Management for Southeast Asia.* Singapore: Prentice-Hall.

Triandis, H. and Bhawuk, D. (1997). 'Culture theory and meaning of relatedness'. In P. Earley and M. Erez (eds), *New Perspectives on Industrial/Organisational Psychology.* San Francisco, CA: New Lexington Press.

Triandis, H. and Gelfand, M. J. (1998). 'Converging measurement of horizontal and vertical individualism and collectivism'. *Journal of Personality and Social Psychology*, 74, 118–128.

Trice, H. and Beyer, J. M. (1993). *The Cultures of Work Organizations.* Englewood Cliffs, NJ: Prentice-Hall.

Trompenaars, F. and Hampden-Turner, C. (1997). *Riding the Waves of Culture* (2nd edn). London: Nicholas Brealey.

Turay, A. (1994). 'All homework and no play for HK schoolkids'. *South China Morning Post*, 3 April, 3.

Turner, C. (1990). *Organisational Culture*, Blagdon: Mendip Papers.

Vulliamy, G., Lewin, K. and Stephens, D. (1990). *Doing Educational Research in Developing Countries.* London: Falmer Press.

Walker, A. (1997). 'Shape, impression and blockage: a case of leadership and culture change'. *Educational Studies*, 23(1), 63–86.

Walker, A. (2003). 'Developing cross-cultural perspectives on education and community'. In P. Begley and O. Johansoon (eds), *The Ethical Dimensions of School Leadership* (pp. 145–160). Dordrecht: Kluwer Academic.

Walker, A. (2004). 'Constitution and culture: exploring the deep leadership structures of Hong Kong schools'. *Discourse: Studies in the Cultural Politics of Education*, 25(1), 75–94.

Walker, A. and Dimmock, C. (1998). 'Hong Kong's return to mainland China: education policy in times of uncertainty'. *Journal of Education Policy*, 13(1), 3–25.

Walker, A. and Dimmock, C. (1999a). 'A cross-cultural approach to the study of educational leadership: an emerging framework'. *Journal of School Leadership*, 9(4), 321–348.

Walker, A. and Dimmock, C. (1999b). 'Exploring principals' dilemmas in Hong Kong: increasing cross-cultural understanding of school leadership'. *International Journal of Educational Reform*, 8(1), 15–24.

Walker, A. and Dimmock, C. (2000a). 'Developing educational administration: the impact of societal culture on theory and practice'. In C. Dimmock and A. Walker (eds), *Future School Administration: Western and Asian Perspectives* (pp. 3–24). Hong Kong: Chinese University Press.

Walker, A. and Dimmock, C. (2000b). 'School principals' dilemmas in Hong Kong: sources, perceptions and outcomes'. *Australian Journal of Education*, 44(1), 5–25.

Walker, A. and Dimmock, C. (2000c). 'One size fits all? Teacher appraisal in a Chinese culture'. *Journal of Personnel Evaluation in Education*, 14(2), 155–178.

Walker, A. and Dimmock, C. (2000d). 'Mapping the way ahead: leading educational leadership into the globalized world'. *School Leadership and Management*, 20(2), 227–33.

Walker, A. and Dimmock, C. (eds) (2002a). *School Leadership and Administration: Adopting a Cross-cultural perspective*. New York: RoutledgeFalmer.

Walker, A. and Dimmock, C. (eds) (2002b). *Development of a Cross-cultural Framework and Accompanying Instrumentation for Comparative Analysis in Educational Administration*. Final report to the Hong Kong Research Grants Council for Competitive Earmarked Research Grant CUHK 4327/98H. Chinese University of Hong Kong.

Walker, A. and Quong, K. (1998). 'Valuing difference for dealing with tensions of educational leadership in a global society'. *Peabody Journal of Education*, 73(2), 81–105.

Walker, A. and Walker, J. (1998). 'Challenging the boundaries of sameness: leadership through valuing difference'. *Journal of Educational Administration*, 36(1), 8–28.

Walker, A., Bridges, E. and Chan, B. (1996). 'Wisdom gained, wisdom given: instituting PBL in a Chinese culture'. *Journal of Educational Administration*, 34(5), 12–31. (Reprinted in 2003 in *Curriculum and Assessment for Hong Kong*. Hong Kong: Open University Press.

Walker, A., Poon, A. and Dimmock, C. (1998). 'Accounting for culture in the principalship: a case study of four Hong Kong principals'. Paper presented at the Annual meeting of the American Educational Research Association, April, San Diego.

Wallace, M. and Pocklington, K. (2002). *Managing Complex Educational Change*. London: Routledge Falmer.

Walumba, O. and Lawler, J. (2003). 'Building effective organisations: transforming leadership, collectivist orientation, work-centred attitudes and withdrawal behaviour in three economies'. *International Journal of Human Resource Management*, 14(7), 1083–1101.

Waters, M. (1995). *Globalization*. London: Routledge.

Watkins, D. (2000). 'Learning and teaching: a cross-cultural perspective'. *School Leadership and Management*, 20(2), 161–174.

Watkins, D. A. and Biggs, J. B. (1996). *The Chinese Learner: Cultural, Psychological and Contextual Influences*. Hong Kong: Comparative Education Research Centre, University of Hong Kong.

Watkins, P. (1989). 'Leadership, power and symbols in educational administration'. In J. Smyth (ed.), *Critical Perspectives on Educational Administration* (pp. 9–38). London: Falmer Press.

Watson, W. E., Johnson, L. and Zgourides, G. D. (2002). 'The influence of ethnic diversity on leadership, group processes and performance: an examination of learning teams'. *International Journal of Intercultural Relations*, 26, 1–16.

Webb, G. (1994). *Making the Most of Appraisal*. London: Kogan Page.

Weick, K. E. (1976). 'Educational organizations as loosely-coupled systems'. *Administrative Science Quarterly*, 21, 1–19.

Westwood, R. (ed.) (1992). *Organisational Behaviour: Southeast Asian Perspectives*. Hong Kong: Longman.

Westwood, R. I. and Kirkbride, P. S. (1998). 'International strategies of corporate culture change: emulation, consumption and hybridity'. *Journal of Organisational Change Management*, 11(6), 554–577.

Wilkinson, B. (1996). 'Culture, institutions and business in East Asia'. *Organization Studies*, 17(3), 421–447.

Winter, R. (1982). 'Dilemma analysis: a contribution to methodology for action research'. *Cambridge Journal of Education*, 12(3), 166–173.

Yang, K. S. (1970). 'Authoritarianism and the evaluation of the appropriateness of role behaviour'. *Journal of Social Psychology*, 80, 171–181.

Yu, A-B. (1996). 'Ultimate life concerns, self, and Chinese achievement motivation'. In M. Bond (ed.), *The Handbook of Chinese Psychology* (pp. 227–246). New York: Oxford University Press.

Yuval-Davis, N. (1999). 'Institutional racism, cultural diversity and citizenship: some reflections on reading the Stephen Lawrence Inquiry Report'. *Sociological Research Online*, 4(1). Retrieved 17 March 2004, from http://www.socreonline.org.uk/4/lawrence/yuval-davis.html.

Index

Lightning Source UK Ltd.
Milton Keynes UK
UKOW06f1848100215

246043UK00004B/180/P